To Jared Leonar...
Happy Easter
With lots of love from
Grandma and Grandpa Kostiuk

THE CHILDREN'S BIBLE

in 365 stories

Copyright © 1985 and 1995 Lion Publishing
Text copyright © 1985 and 1995 Mary Batchelor

Published by
Lion Publishing plc
Sandy Lane West, Oxford, England
ISBN 0 7459 3068 9
ISBN 0 7459 3214 2 (export edition)
ISBN 0 7459 3215 0 (red gift edition)
ISBN 0 7459 3216 9 (white gift edition)
ISBN 0 7459 3217 7 (leather gift edition)
Lion Publishing
20 Lincoln Avenue, Elgin, Illinois 60120, USA
ISBN 0 7459 3068 9
ISBN 0 7459 3214 2 (export edition)
ISBN 0 7459 3215 0 (red gift edition)
ISBN 0 7459 3216 9 (white gift edition)
ISBN 0 7459 3217 7 (leather gift edition)
Albatross Books Pty Ltd
PO Box 320, Sutherland, NSW 2232, Australia
ISBN 0 7324 0976 4
ISBN 0 7324 1235 8 (red gift edition)
ISBN 0 7324 1236 6 (white gift edition)
ISBN 0 7324 1403 2 (leather gift edition)

First edition 1985
Second edition 1995
10 9 8 7 6 5 4 3 2 1

Acknowledgments
Bible quotations on pages 263–265
are from the *Good News Bible*, copyright © 1966,
1971 and 1976 American Bible Society, published
by Bible Societies/Collins

A catalogue record for this title is available
from the British Library

Library of Congress Cataloging-in-Publication Data
Batchelor, Mary
    The Children's Bible in 365 stories
    1. Bible stories, English
    I. Title II. Haysom, John III. Bible,
    English. Selections. 1985
    BS551.2B37   1985   220.9'505   85-10246
    ISBN 0 7459 1333 4

Printed and bound in Slovenia

The Children's Bible

in 365 stories

By Mary Batchelor
Illustrated by John Haysom

A LION BOOK

INTRODUCTION

All the stories in this book—one for every day in the year—come from the Bible, which is like a whole library in itself. It contains sixty-six books of adventure, history, poetry, letters and much more, written by many different people over hundreds of years. It is in two main parts—the Old Testament, originally written in Hebrew, the language of the ancient Jews, and the New Testament, written first in Greek, which was understood by everyone in the Roman Empire when Jesus lived on earth.

Not everything in the Bible could possibly have been squeezed into this book, so I have picked out the most exciting stories and the best-loved ones. But I chose with another purpose too. Although the Bible may seem to be a puzzling mixture of different kinds of writing, the separate parts fit together, like pieces in a jig-saw, to make one whole picture. I wanted to make that picture plain.

The Bible shows us what God is like, and what we are really like too. Because God never changes and human nature stays the same, the Bible is always up-to-date. It answers the sort of questions which people are always asking: 'What is God like?' 'Why is there unhappiness and evil and death in our world?' 'What is the purpose of living?' and 'Does it matter how I behave?'

In the Old Testament God spoke through men and women but in the New Testament he visits our world himself, in the person of his Son, Jesus. Jesus showed us exactly what God is like. Best of all, he put right the mess we have made of ourselves and our world by accepting death on our behalf. He won the fight against death and evil and came back to new and never-ending life. The Bible closes with a vision of the future, when Jesus will reign for ever and bring justice and peace to a new and happy world.

John Haysom and I have had a great deal of pleasure and excitement in painting and writing these stories. We hope you will enjoy them so much that before long you will buy a modern translation of the Bible and read the whole story for yourselves.

Mary Batchelor

CONTENTS

THE OLD TESTAMENT

THE NEW TESTAMENT

THE OLD TESTAMENT

The word 'Testament' means an agreement or covenant. The Old Testament tells the story of God's covenant with Abraham and his family, who became God's special people. Men and women had turned away from God and spoiled the perfect world he had made. So God taught his people all about himself. He promised to care for them and they agreed to keep his laws. They often failed, but God stayed true to his covenant.

The Story of Creation

1

God Makes the World

GENESIS 1

Long ago, before time began, our world was dark and desolate. Then God began to create order and beauty.

First he commanded light to break into the darkness. And there was light.

Next he ordered the raging oceans to go back, so that dry land appeared. But the land was empty and silent, except for the lapping of the waves and the sigh of the wind. So God commanded the earth to produce trees and plants. How lovely the first green leaves and bright flowers looked!

Then, high above in the lofty skies that he had made, God commanded the sun to shine in the day and the moon to give a gentler light by night.

He created the stars to twinkle in the velvety darkness.

Still sky and sea were silent and empty. So God made creatures to swim and play in the ocean, from the tiniest fish to the largest whale. He made the birds, to sing sweetly as they flew among the trees. It was a beautiful world and God saw how good it was.

But the land was still empty. So God made the animals. He created small, furry creatures and huge, strong beasts as well. The woods and the forests, the fields and the plains, came alive with the animals that God had made.

God told all the fishes and birds and animals to bear young and to grow in number so that his whole world could be full and busy and content. God looked at all that he had made and said, 'It is very good.'

2
God Makes People

GENESIS 1—2

God looked with gladness at the vast universe and the beautiful world that he had made but he knew that he had still to make the most wonderful part of his creation.

'Now I will make human beings,' God said. 'They will have minds to think and know and love me, and I will put them in charge of this world to keep it in order.'

First God made the man, called Adam. But even with all the animals to care for and play with, Adam was lonely. So God made the woman, Eve, to be his wife, so that they could plan and talk and laugh and love together.

God blessed them both and told them to enjoy everything in the world that he had made. They were to have children to help them in the task that God had given them. But although they were in charge of the world, they must always obey God. He loved them and knew what was best for them. They would be happy as long as they did as he told them.

God gave Adam and Eve a beautiful garden to live in. There were trees laden with ripe fruit for them to eat.

'Pick the fruit and eat it freely,' God told them, 'but do not eat the fruit from that one tree in the middle of the garden. That is the tree of the knowledge of good and evil. If you eat the fruit from that tree, you will die.'

God brought all the animals and birds to Adam, so that he could give them names. Adam and Eve talked to the animals and played with them and they did just as Adam and Eve told them.

Adam and Eve looked after the garden for God. They took good care of all the plants and trees.

Every evening, when it was cool, God came to talk to them. They would walk up and down, sharing all that had happened, until darkness fell to end another perfect day.

Creation Spoiled

📖 **3**
The Tempting Fruit
GENESIS 3

Nothing could spoil the happiness of Adam and Eve in the Garden of Eden. Or so it seemed. But there was one person who was plotting to spoil all that God had made. He was Satan, the enemy of God, who hated all that was good and lovely.

One day, the snake, who was the most cunning of all the creatures in the garden, whispered to Eve.

'Did God *really* say that you must not eat any of the fruit from these lovely trees?'

'Of course not,' Eve replied, 'we can eat all the fruit we want—except for just that one tree over there. God says that we must not eat that fruit, for if we do we shall die.'

'That's not true,' the snake hissed softly. 'God knows that if you eat that fruit you will be as wise and clever as he is. That is why he has told you not to.'

Eve looked with new eyes at the luscious fruit that hung in clusters from the forbidden tree. How lovely it looked! She imagined how good it would taste. Then she thought how wonderful it would be to become as wise as the snake had promised. Then, her mind made up, she quickly picked one of the tempting fruits, bit into it and handed it to Adam to try too.

But instead of feeling clever and wise, they both felt miserable and ashamed. They had disobeyed the wise and loving God who was their Creator and their Friend.

When evening came, they did not hurry out to meet God. They were ashamed because they had disobeyed him. They picked some large leaves to try to cover their bodies, and then hid silently in the bushes.

Every other evening they had eagerly waited for God's loving call. Now they listened in fear for the well-known sound of God's voice. At last they heard him.

'Where are you, Adam?' God called.

With downcast eyes, they crept out to meet the God they no longer wanted to see.

4
Paradise Lost
GENESIS 3

Adam and Eve came slowly out to meet God. He looked long and sadly at the guilty pair.

'Why were you hiding?' he asked them.

'I was afraid to see you, because I am naked,' Adam stammered.

'Who told you that?' God asked. 'Have you eaten the fruit from the tree that gives knowledge of what is good and what is evil?'

'It was not *my* fault,' Adam said. 'Eve persuaded me.'

'It was not *my* fault,' Eve said. 'The snake tricked me into eating it.'

God spoke to each of them in turn. He explained that by disobeying him they had spoiled his lovely world. Now, weeds and thorns would spring up among the crops and flowers. Work would become hard and wearisome.

There was something even sadder to follow. 'You can no longer stay in this garden,' God said. 'We have walked and talked together here, but now you have chosen to do what *you* want, and that means you have chosen to go away from me. Now you must go out into the world and make your own way. And when the end comes, you will die.'

With heavy hearts, Adam and Eve left the beautiful Garden of Eden.

God's messengers, with swords of flame, guarded the gates of the paradise that mankind had lost, so it seemed, forever.

Cain and Abel

📖 **5**
The Two Brothers
GENESIS 4

Two sons were born to Adam and Eve after they had been banished from the Garden of Eden. The boys grew up and Cain, the older one, became a farmer, growing crops. Abel, the younger brother, became a shepherd.

One day, the two young men decided to bring presents to offer to God. Cain brought a sheaf of ripe, golden corn, gleaned from his harvest field. Abel's present was a new-born lamb, chosen from his flock. God looked at the fine offerings they had brought, and then he looked at the two brothers themselves. He saw the kind of people they were. He knew that Abel loved and trusted him, so he accepted Abel and his gift.

But God refused Cain's present. He could not accept Cain because he was cold and proud and self-willed.

Cain was furious. He scowled angrily and turned on his heel to leave God's presence. Before he could go right away, God spoke to him.

'Why are you so angry, Cain?' he asked. 'If you had done right, you would be happy now. I should have accepted your present. But evil is like a wild animal. It is crouching close. waiting to spring at you and overpower you. You must fight against it.'

But Cain did not want to listen to God, or to take any notice of his warning.

Sullen and hot with anger, he strode back to his fields. He hated Abel because he was good and because God was pleased with him.

The First Murder

GENESIS 4

God was pleased with Abel but he
had refused Cain's gift. Cain was
furiously jealous of his brother and
the sight of Abel's happy face only
made him angrier. He determined to
get even with him somehow.

'Let's go for a walk in the fields,' he
called to Abel one day.

'All right,' Abel replied readily.
Perhaps, after all, his brother wanted
to be friends with him again. As they
walked together through the peaceful
countryside, Cain's anger burned
more and more fiercely against the
brother who had done him no wrong.

With sudden hot hatred Cain
turned on the unsuspecting Abel, and
killed him with a violent blow. It was
all over in a moment. Without a
backward look, Cain walked quickly
away.

Then God spoke to Cain.

'Where is your brother?' he asked.

Cain's heart missed a beat, but he
answered casually, 'How should *I*
know? Am I supposed to look after
him all the time?'

'Cain, why have you done this
terrible thing?' God said sadly.

Then Cain realized that God had
seen all that had happened and knew
about all the hatred and jealousy in
his heart.

'Your brother's blood cries out for justice,' God told Cain, 'and this will be your punishment. The earth will no longer grow fine crops for you. You will become a homeless wanderer for the rest of your life.'

'My punishment is too great to bear!' Cain cried out, 'those who find out what I have done will kill me.'

'I will protect you,' God said. 'You will not be killed.'

So Cain went away from his farm and from his home. Worse still, he went away from God. He had been too proud to listen to God's warning. He had chosen to hate Abel and to murder him instead of loving his brother and being happy with him.

The Story of Noah

Noah Starts Building
GENESIS 6

Cain's murder of his brother Abel was only a beginning of wickedness in the world. Although people began to invent all kinds of lovely and useful things, they also found more and more ways to disobey God and hurt one another.

God knew that nothing he could do would bring people back to loving him and being good. They would not even listen to him! Everything that was rotten and bad would have to be swept away. There must be a new beginning.

But God found one man who loved and obeyed him and who did what was right and good to his family and to everyone around. His name was Noah.

One day God told Noah what he planned to do.

'I must put an end to all the wickedness,' God said. 'People have spoiled my world with all their bad and cruel deeds. I am going to send a flood that will destroy everything. But you and your family will be kept safe. You must start building a big boat.

God gave Noah the pattern and the measurements for the huge ark that would be able to survive the flood that he was going to send. It was to be made of strong wood, lined and covered with waterproof tar.

The ark must be big enough to hold Noah, his wife, their three sons and their wives. Noah must also make stalls and pens for two of every animal and bird, so that they too could be saved from the flood water.

Noah did just as God said. It took a long time to collect all the materials and build that enormous boat. Passers-by and those who lived near wondered what Noah was doing and made fun of him. As he hammered away, Noah warned them of the flood that was coming. He tried to persuade them to stop doing wrong and to obey God.

But no one paid any attention to what Noah said.

8
Rain, Rain, Rain!
GENESIS 7

For a long time Noah went on building his boat and trying to persuade people to change their ways and tell God they were sorry for the bad things that they had done.

Then, one day, the hammering stopped. Noah's ark was finished. But there was still plenty of work to be done. Food must be gathered and made ready for all the passengers—human and animal. Then the animals had to be collected. Noah's family worked as hard as he did.

At last the preparations were done. 'It is time to go into the ark,' God said. 'Go in, Noah, with your family and all the animals. The rain will begin in a week's time.'

In that week Noah got everything and everyone stowed on board. At the end of the week, the rain began to fall, as God had said it would. When Noah and his family and all the animals were safely on board, God shut the door of the ark.

The rain fell night and day without stopping. Soon the torrential downpour began to swell the streams and rivers. Water lapped the bottom of the huge ark. As the water rose, the wooden boat creaked and groaned and shifted. Then, gently, the water began to lift the ark. They were afloat!

The huge craft began to drift slowly, buffeted by rain and floods. But Noah had done his work well. The ark was safe and watertight.

Gradually, as the flood waters rose higher, all the well-known landmarks disappeared. Soon, even the tops of the highest hills were covered by the water. There was nothing to see but water all around. People and animals had all disappeared beneath the flood.

For six weeks the rain fell.

But God had not forgotten Noah and his family. At last, as he had promised, the rain stopped.

9
A New Beginning
GENESIS 8

When at long last the rain stopped, Noah heard a strong wind blowing. He was glad to hear it whistling around the ark, for he knew that it would help to dry the ground.

Gradually the water sank lower and the ark, that had floated and drifted helplessly for so many days, grunted and groaned and ground to a halt on the mountains of Ararat. How good it was to be steady and firm on land again! But still they could not venture out of their hiding-place.

Noah waited patiently for six more long weeks, then he released a raven, to see if there was land to settle on. The raven was so glad to be free that he stayed, circling the air, waiting for the tree-tops to reappear.

Then Noah set free a dove, but by night time she had come back home to her master and the familiar ark. Noah gently took her inside, waited another week and sent her off again. This time she flew back with an olive leaf in her beak.

How excited everyone was to see something green and growing once more!

Noah waited patiently for another week, then sent the dove off for a third time. She did not come back.

Now Noah knew for sure that there was enough dry land for them all to leave the ark. He took off the huge covering roof of the ark, letting in a stream of welcome daylight. Then God spoke to Noah. 'Go out of the ark,' he said, 'all of you. The flood is over.'

10
Rainbow in the Sky
GENESIS 9

How happy Noah and his family were to get out of the ark and into the fresh air once again! The animals frolicked and scampered, and the birds flew singing into the clear blue sky. Before they did anything else, Noah and his

family thanked God for his kindness and care for them during the terrible flood. They piled up stones to make an open air altar and offered gifts on it to God.

God had kept them safe and given them a fresh start in a new world.

Then God blessed Noah and his sons, Shem, Ham and Japheth. 'Have many children,' God said. 'Spread out and fill the earth. Care for the world and for all the creatures in it. 'I am going to make you a promise. Never again will I send a flood, or destroy all living things. For as long as the earth lasts, I will send you day and night, heat and cold, summer and winter. I will send a season for sowing and a season for harvest.

'I am going to give you a sign to remind you always of my promise. Whenever you look up and see a rainbow in the sky, think of my promise to you and be sure that I will keep it.'

After the terrible flood, Noah and his family felt a bit frightened whenever it began to rain. But they would look up, as the sun burst through the clouds, and see the rainbow shining in the sky. They remembered then that they were really safe. God would keep his promise.

The Tower of Babel

The Sky's the Limit!
GENESIS 11

Noah and his sons settled down to farm the land and Noah planted vines. They had many children and their children had many children too.

They began to spread out and fill the world as God had instructed Noah. One group of wanderers decided to settle down and make themselves famous.

'Let's stop here in this plain,' they said, 'and build a great city. We shall be famous far and wide, for we shall build the highest tower that anyone has ever seen. We'll reach the sky itself!'

They set to work at once, making bricks from mud and straw and baking them hard in the hot sun. They used tar for mortar to fix the bricks together.

But God was not pleased. It made him sad and angry to see that once again people wanted to please themselves and try to become great and self-important. They were too full of pride and selfishness to follow his wise plans for them.

God knew that there would be no end to the schemes they would make

to go their own foolish way. Soon they would become as bad as the people who had lived before the Flood. So he decided to scatter them in all directions, before they grew even more boastful and ambitious.

They could not understand one another any more, for their languages were different. This was part of God's plan to stop them from plotting together to bring evil and disaster on the world, as mankind had done in the days of Noah.

The proud Tower of Babel stood unfinished for ever, soon to be nothing but a heap of tumbled bricks.

The Story of Abraham

📖 **12**

God Calls Abraham

GENESIS 11—12

Many of Shem's descendants lived in cities on the rich fertile plain of Mesopotamia. In one of the cities, called Ur, lived a man named Abraham.

Ur was a fine city. There were merchants and scribes and comfortable houses for rich and wealthy citizens like Abraham. The people worshipped the moon goddess at the beautiful ziggurat temple.

One day, God spoke to Abraham. He had something very surprising to say.

'Leave Ur,' God said, 'and set out for a country that I will show you. I will make you great and bless you. I will make *you* a blessing to all people everywhere.'

Abraham had to think hard. If he did as God said, he would leave the comfort of city life and have no settled home. He would live in a tent, moving from one source of water to the next.

But Abraham trusted God enough to obey him. He and Sarah, his wife, packed up their possessions and got ready to leave Ur.

At first they stayed at Haran, many miles to the north, until Abraham's old father died. Then Abraham, Sarah and Lot, their nephew, set off on the journey that would last for the resr of Abraham's life.

Abraham and Sarah had no children but there were many servants and herdsmen belonging to Lot as well as to Abraham. There were sheep and goats, and donkeys to carry all the baggage.

Slowly they trekked from one well or spring to the next, setting up their large black goatskin tents. They were making their way to the country of Canaan, as God told Abraham to do.

13
Lot has First Choice
GENESIS 13

Abraham and Lot journeyed slowly on until they reached the land of Canaan. Still Abraham did not settle down for long in one place. He moved from one end of the country to the other, looking for water and grassland.

He did not forget to stop, so that he could take time to praise and thank God for helping and guiding him ever since he left Ur.

God blessed Abraham and made him rich, as he had promised to do. He owned a great many sheep and goats, and so did Lot. They had so many animals between them that every bit of green grass that they found was soon nibbled bare. Then they had to move on to find fresh pasture.

As soon as they reached a new camping place, their servants and shepherds would rush to get first share of the water from the well. There would be shouts and blows as Abraham's herdsmen and Lot's men began to squabble. Both fought to get the best for their master's flocks.

At last Abraham spoke to Lot about it. 'Families should not argue and fight like this,' he said. 'We have too many animals for us to stay together. We shall have to split up and go separate ways.'

Abraham was much older than Lot and he should have had first choice, but instead he said:

'Lot, have a good look east and west and choose which way you would like to go. I'll go the other way.'

Lot looked at the lush green plain of the River Jordan valley. How much better it looked than the dry scrubby hill-country to the west!

'I'll go *that* way,' he pointed.

Sadly, they said goodbye and Lot set off with his family and flocks to the green valley.

When he had left, God spoke to Abraham: 'Look about you,' he said, 'in *every* direction. All the land that you can see I will give to your descendants for ever.' So, with God's promise to cheer him, Abraham set off in the opposite direction to Lot, thanking and praising God.

14
God's Promise

GENESIS 15

Lot chose the green plain of Jordan and left his uncle Abraham to wander the bare, rocky hills, but in spite of choosing the best for himself, Lot was soon in trouble. He settled in Sodom, one of the cities on the plain. War broke out between chiefs of nearby cities and Lot was taken hostage by a chieftain who raided Sodom.

Abraham came quickly to the rescue with a strong band of his own men, and set Lot free. Abraham would not take payment or reward from the chiefs he had helped. But God talked to Abraham once more saying,

'Don't be afraid, Abraham. I will keep you safe and I will give you a great reward.'

Abraham wanted neither riches nor honour. There was only one thing he and Sarah longed for—a child of their own.

'What good will riches do me?' he asked bitterly, 'I have no son to inherit my wealth. Sarah and I are too old now to have children. When I die, one of my slaves will be my heir.'

'Come outside your tent,' God told him, 'and look up at the sky.'

Abraham went out into the cool evening air. The night was bright with stars.

'Can you count those stars?' God asked. 'I promise that you will have as many descendants as there are stars in the sky. I am the God who brought you out of Ur, I will be your God and your children's God for ever. I am going to give you and Sarah a son and I will give you this country for his descendants to live in.'

Although God's promises sounded impossible, as Abraham stood there in the velvety darkness he believed with all his heart that God would keep his word.

God was glad that Abraham trusted him. He accepted Abraham because he put his whole faith in God.

📖 15
Hagar Runs Away
GENESIS 16

God had solemnly promised Abraham that he would have a son, even though he and Sarah were old. But the years went by and no child was born. Every year that passed made it less likely that Sarah would have a baby, for she was getting very old.

Sarah was sad that they had no child but she thought of a way in which she and Abraham could become parents. She decided to copy the custom of the people who lived around, in order to solve their problem. She would let Abraham marry her slave-girl, Hagar. When Hagar had a child, it could count as theirs.

Abraham agreed to her plan and soon Hagar found that she was expecting a child. She began to boast and put on airs. She thought she was more important than her mistress now.

At last Sarah could bear it no longer. 'It's your fault,' she complained to Abraham. 'My slave-girl despises me.'

'Do as you like with her,' Abraham replied.

Sarah treated Hagar so badly and made her so unhappy that she ran away. She wandered for a long time in the dry, hot desert. At last she sat down by a desert spring, tired and thirsty.

Then God, who had seen all that had happened, spoke to Hagar gently.

'Where are you going?' he asked.

'I'm running away from my mistress,' Hagar replied.

'Go back to her,' God said. 'I have heard your tears and cries. I will look after you. You will have a son and call him Ishmael.'

Hagar thought it was wonderful that God should see and help her, when she was just a poor slave-girl whom nobody thought important. She called him 'The God who sees'.

Then, content, she went back to her mistress, Sarah. Not long afterwards her son Ishmael was born.

📖 16
The Special Visitors
GENESIS 18

One day, Abraham was sitting at the opening of his tent while Sarah tried to keep cool inside. The midday sun was beating down. Abraham looked up and was surprised to see three men coming near. People did not usually travel at this hottest time of the day.

Abraham ran to meet them, knowing that they would need shade and water.

'Please stop and rest,' he invited them. 'Sit under this tree while I fetch you water to drink and wash with.' The men sat down gratefully, and Abraham hurried in to Sarah and asked her to get a good meal ready for their unexpected visitors. There was bread to be baked, a calf to be killed and cooked, milk and cream to be fetched. All was hustle and bustle.

At last Abraham served the visitors with a fine outdoor banquet under the tree.

Then the leader of the three strangers asked, 'Where is Sarah?'

'In the tent,' Abraham replied, surprised.

'In nine months' time she will have a son,' the man said. Sarah, who was curious to know more about these visitors, had been standing just inside the tent flap, listening. When she heard what the stranger said, she burst out laughing. It was impossible! She was far too old to have a son.

'Why did Sarah laugh?' the man asked.

'I didn't!' called out Sarah, guiltily.

'But you did,' the man replied. 'Is anything too hard for the Lord? I will certainly do as I have promised.'

When he heard those words, Abraham realized with a shock that none of his visitors were ordinary men. Their leader spoke the words of God himself.

cities,' he said. 'The people who live there do all kinds of cruel and bad things. They are so wicked that the only cure is to destroy them completely.'

The two angels walked on, to visit Sodom for themselves, but God stayed talking to Abraham.

Abraham did not want Sodom to be harmed. He thought of his nephew Lot, living there with his family. So he pleaded with God to change his mind.

'Surely you don't want to kill good people along with the bad people in Sodom,' he asked God. 'You are the Judge of the whole world. Surely you could not do anything so unfair.'

'If there are fifty good people living in Sodom, I will not destroy the city,' God promised.

Abraham thought that there might not be as many as fifty good people

17
On the Way to Sodom
GENESIS 18

When Abraham's special visitors had rested and eaten their meal, they were ready to go on their journey again. Abraham went with them to set them on the way.

After a time they reached a place whcre they could look down on the green plain of Jordan and see the twin cities of Sodom and Gomorrah. Then God began to tell Abraham what he planned to do.

'Sodom and Gomorrah are wicked

there, but he went on asking God to spare the city.

God said that he would not destroy Sodom if there were even ten good people living there.

But God knew that Lot was the only good person in the city. He had already planned to rescue Lot and had sent his angels to visit him for that very purpose.

Lost in thought, Abraham parted from his Special Visitor, and walked back to his tent.

📖 18
Lot's Rescue
GENESIS 19

It was evening by the time the two angels who had visited Abraham arrived at Sodom. Lot was sitting at the gate of the city, where all the business was carried on. He came politely forward to greet these strangers and invited them to stay the night in his house.

When they arrived at his home, Lot set his servants to work preparing a good supper. But before they could go to bed, the citizens of Sodom came banging at the door. They shouted threats and insults at Lot and told him to throw out his visitors so that they could ill-treat them.

Lot refused, and the shouting, surging mob jostled and pushed him. But the angels pulled him safely back inside and shut the door tight.

Then they spoke earnestly to Lot. 'We have seen for ourselves now how cruel and bad these people of Sodom are. That is why God is going to destroy the city. You must get ready at once, with all your family, to escape from here. There is no time to be lost. You will have to run for your lives.'

While Lot's wife and daughters began to collect their things together, the angels kept hurrying them on. Still they dawdled and, when at last dawn began to give a faint grey light, the angels took the family by the hand and rushed them quickly out of the city, setting them on the road to the hills.

Then indeed they began to run for their lives, for already the rising sun over Sodom was blood red. The ground beneath their feet began to move. Burning sulphur rained down on the cities of Sodom and Gomorrah.

Breathless, Lot and his daughters ran for the safety of the hills. But Lot's wife stopped running. She looked longingly back at her home and all the comforts of Sodom. She was caught in a hail of salt, and died where she stood.

The Story of Isaac

19
Isaac is Born
GENESIS 21

Of course God kept his promise to Abraham and Sarah. Just as he had said, and at the time that he had foretold, Sarah gave birth to a baby boy. She was so happy that she laughed for joy.

When the time came to give the baby a name, Abraham called him Isaac, which means 'he laughs'. Perhaps he was given the name because he was such a happy, smiling baby, but it was also a reminder for ever of the joy and happiness that his birth had brought to his aged parents. Sarah must have remembered that other time when she had laughed, because she could not believe God's wonderful promise that she would really have a son of her own.

Baby Isaac soon grew and began to toddle everywhere. One day Sarah looked out of the tent and saw big half-brother Ishmael teasing Isaac and making fun of him. Sarah wanted to take the side of her own special son.

She hurried away to find Abraham and asked him to send Ishmael and his mother, the slave-girl Hagar, packing. Abraham was sad and troubled. Isaac was indeed the promised son. God had given him to them by a miracle. But Ishmael was Abraham's son too. He did not want to harm him.

God comforted and reassured Abraham. 'You may do as Sarah says,' God told him, 'I will take care of Ishmael.'

20
Sent Packing
GENESIS 21

Abraham agreed to Sarah's plan to send Hagar and Ishmael away.

Next morning, he filled a leather bottle with water and packed up some food. Then he gave them to Hagar and told her to take her son and set off to make a life on their own, away from the safety and protection of his tents.

Hagar and Ishmael wandered over the rough, dry countryside, not knowing where to go. The sun burned fiercely down. Soon they had eaten their supply of food. Worse still, there was not one drop of water left in the skin bottle.

Hagar knew that they could not hope to live for long without water, in the burning heat. Already Ishmael was weak and light-headed. They could not go any further.

Hagar helped Ishmael to lie down in a patch of shade beside a bush. Then she walked away. She could not bear to hear his moans, or see his parched, swollen lips. She knew that he would soon die. But God had heard Ishmael's cries. He spoke to Hagar.

'Don't be frightened, Hagar,' God said. 'Go to Ishmael and comfort him. He will not die. I will take care of him and make his children into a great family.'

Then God opened Hagar's eyes. Close by, she caught sight of a well of pure, cold water. Thankfully she filled the skin bottle to the brim, then put the life-giving water to Ishmael's lips.

She knew that God who had seen her and helped her when she had run away from Sarah, was with her still, watching over them both.

Put to the Test

GENESIS 22

Little Isaac grew up quickly. His father and mother loved him dearly. When Abraham looked at him, he must have remembered God's wonderful promise that through Isaac and his children's children the whole world would be blessed.

One day God spoke to Abraham again. 'Take your son, Isaac,' God said, 'your own dear son, and offer him as a sacrifice to me on far-off mount Moriah.'

Abraham could not understand why God should ask him to do such a thing. He loved Isaac with all his heart and would gladly have given his own life to save him. But he had learned that it was always best to obey God. He believed that in some way God *would* still keep his promise about Isaac.

Abraham could not bear to tell Sarah what he had to do. Without a word to anyone else, he woke Isaac very early next morning and they set off for the land of Moriah, with two servants, and a donkey to carry the baggage.

On the third day of their journey, Abraham saw the mountain God had chosen.

He told the servants to stay with the donkey. Then he and Isaac began to plod slowly up the hillside.

Isaac carried a bundle of firewood and Abraham had his sharp knife and some fire in a brazier.

'We have fire and wood, but where is the sacrifice to offer to God?' Isaac asked.

A Wife for Isaac

GENESIS 24

Isaac grew up to manhood and in time his mother Sarah died, at a great age. Abraham too was very old but he was comforted as he remembered that Isaac would inherit God's wonderful promises and become the ancestor of a great nation.

One day he called his chief servant and said to him, 'It is time to find a wife for my son. I do not want him to marry a Canaanite woman from around here. Please promise me that you will journey to the country of my own family and find a bride for him there.'

'That is a long way off,' the servant said. 'Perhaps the girl would not be willing to come so far with me. Why not send Isaac back to Mesopotamia instead?'

'Never!' Abraham insisted. 'God has brought me here and promised to give this land to my descendants. Isaac must live here. But if the girl you choose for his bride refuses to come back with you, then you will be free from your promise to me.'

So the servant set out with ten camels on the long journey back to Mesopotamia. It was late one afternoon when he arrived at the well outside the city where Abraham's family lived. He ordered the camels to kneel down, close by the well. Then he began to pray:

'God of my master, Abraham, please help me to choose the right wife for Isaac. The women will soon be coming to fetch water and I shall ask one of them for a drink. Please let the girl who gets me a drink, and also offers to draw water for the camels, be the bride that you have chosen.'

Abraham felt as if his heart would break, but he quietly answered: 'God will provide that, my son.'

At the top of the hill Abraham began to pile up loose stones to build an altar. Then he laid the wood on it. At last Isaac must have guessed the terrible truth. His father gently lifted him on to the altar and tied up his hands and feet.

Abraham took his gleaming knife and lifted it high to plunge into Isaac.

At that very moment God spoke.

'Stop, Abraham!' he called. 'Do not hurt the boy. I know now that you trust me and love me whatever may happen.'

Abraham's arm dropped to his side. For a moment he could hardly believe it was true. Isaac was saved! A great wave of happiness and thankfulness swept over him.

Trembling, he untied Isaac. Then he looked up and saw a ram, caught by its curly horns in the undergrowth.

He killed it with his knife, then thankfully he burned it on the altar as an offering to God. God had provided a sacrifice in place of Isaac. He did not want human sacrifice, such as the people of Canaan offered to their gods.

23
Rebekah is Found
GENESIS 24

Abraham's servant was still beside
the well, praying that God would help
him to choose Isaac's bride, when he
heard footsteps coming near.

He looked up to see a beautiful girl
walking towards the well, her empty
water-pot on her shoulder. As she
filled the jar the servant hurried
forward.

'Please may I have a drink?' he
asked. She readily lowered the jar and
let him drink. Then her eyes strayed
to the waiting camels.

'Shall I get your camels a drink
too?' she offered, and began to fill her
water-pot again and again until the
drinking-trough was full.

The servant was full of joy. His prayer had been answered.

'What is your name?' he asked.

'Rebekah,' she said. 'I am the granddaughter of Nahor.'

The servant knew that Nahor was Abraham's own brother! How good God had been to lead him to his master's family! He brought out rich jewels and put them on Rebekah.

Rebekah took the servant home and there he told his story to the whole family. Rebekah's father and brother agreed that she should marry Isaac, it was so clearly what God wanted.

Next morning the servant was eager to be off. Nothing that Rebekah's reluctant family could say would persuade him to stay longer.

With many tears and kisses they all said good-bye to Rebekah. How glad she was that her old childhood nurse would go with her on the long journey to meet a husband she had never seen.

When they drew near, Rebekah looked eagerly around. Then she caught sight of someone walking in the fields. At that moment he too looked up and saw the camels.

Quickly Rebekah slipped down from her camel.

'Who is that man?' she asked the servant.

'It is my master, Isaac,' he replied.

The moment Isaac met Rebekah he loved her, and he gladly made her his wife.

The Story of the Birthright

24
Jacob's Bargain
GENESIS 25

For many years after they were married, Isaac and Rebekah had no children. Isaac knew all about God's promise to bless his family and make a great nation from them. So he asked God to send them a child.

Soon Rebekah found that she was expecting not one baby but two. At that time the eldest son inherited all the family rights and privileges. But before the babies were born, God told Rebekah that this time the younger one was to become the head of the family. Through him God's promises to Abraham would come true.

Twin boys were born—first Esau, then Jacob, younger by a few minutes and holding tightly to his brother's heel!

The boys grew. Rebekah loved Jacob best. He liked to stay in the tent while Esau was out in the open air, stalking and hunting the wild deer. Isaac loved Esau best and liked nothing better than the delicious venison stew Esau cooked from the deer he caught.

One day Esau arrived home ravenously hungry. An appetizing smell filled the tent, for Jacob was cooking soup.

'Give me some soup!' Esau shouted. 'I'm starving!'

Jacob thought quickly. Here was the chance he had been waiting for. He would bargain with Esau for the thing he wanted most.

'*I'll* give you some soup,' he agreed, 'if *you* give me the rights that belong to the firstborn son.'

'All right,' Esau said impatiently, 'anything you want. I'm sure I'll die of hunger anyway if I don't get something to eat. So what do I care?'

'Promise me,' Jacob insisted.

'Yes, yes,' Esau repeated, and Jacob handed him the steaming soup. Esau drank it hungrily, then turned and left the tent without another thought. That was how much he cared about God's promise.

25
Jacob's Trick
GENESIS 27

Esau quickly forgot about his lost right to be the head of the family that God was going to bless. But Jacob thought about it often. His mother would have told him about God's message to her before the boys were born.

Isaac was old by now and his eyesight was very poor. He took to his bed because he thought that he would soon die. Then he called Esau.

'You are my first-born son,' he said. 'I must give you my blessing before I die. Go out and hunt deer, to make me the venison stew I love. When I have eaten it, I will bless you.'

Esau took his bow and arrow and set off.

But Rebekah had overheard them. If Jacob was to be the head of the family, *he* should receive the special blessing. Instead of leaving God to work out his own plans for the boys, she thought out a scheme to trick Isaac and snatch the blessing from Esau.

'Go and kill two kids in the flock,' she urged Jacob, 'and I will make a stew so good that your father won't know it isn't Esau's. You shall pretend to be Esau and take it to him, and then we'll see who gets the blessing!'

Jacob was afraid that the trick would be discovered. His father would never mistake him for Esau, even though he could not see. But Rebekah had an answer for everything.

Quickly she cooked the meat, then wrapped the skins from the goats round Jacob's neck and arms so that he would feel as hairy as Esau. Then she dressed him in his brother's clothes, which smelled of the fields and woods, and sent him in to his father, carrying the tasty stew.

26
Esau's Return
GENESIS 27

When Jacob came into his tent, Isaac was surprised that his son should have caught and cooked the deer so quickly.

'Who is it?' he called out, his mouth watering as the good smell of the food reached his nose.

'It's Esau,' Jacob replied nervously. 'Are you *really* Esau?' Isaac asked doubtfully. 'It sounds like Jacob's voice. Come closer.'

Trembling a little, Jacob went near and Isaac felt his arms. The hairy skins and the smell of Esau's clothes seemed to set his mind at rest. He began to eat the food with relish.

When he had finished his meal, he solemnly gave to Jacob the father's blessing for a first-born son. In God's name he promised him success and pronounced that he would be the head of the whole family.

Scarcely had he finished and Jacob scurried from the tent than Esau arrived, cheerfully bringing the venison to Isaac.

When Isaac heard the real Esau's voice, he gave a cry of horror. He blurted out the whole story and they realized that a trick had been played on them both.

Esau cried bitterly with disappointment. Then he grew very angry.

'I'll kill Jacob!' he vowed.

Rebekah heard his shouted threats. She knew she must get Jacob safely out of the way. She suggested to Isaac that Jacob should journey back to the country she had come from and find a wife from among her family.

Isaac agreed, and Jacob, shocked and frightened, left the home he loved, said goodbye to his mother and set out on his long journey.

The Story of Jacob

27
Jacob's Dream
GENESIS 28

Jacob felt ashamed as well as sad as he began the long walk north-eastwards, towards his mother's home town. He had cheated and tricked Esau out of his birthright. Now he had to run away before his brother murdered him.

As night fell, he wrapped his cloak around him for warmth and lay down in the open, pillowing his head on a flat stone.

As he slept, he dreamed. He saw a wide, shining stairway, reaching from the earth to heaven. There were bright angels going up and down, carrying God's messages.

As Jacob watched in wonder, he saw God himself, standing close by him.

'I am the God of Abraham and of your father Isaac,' he said to Jacob, 'and I will be your God too. All this land around you I will give to your descendants. Your children will grow into a mighty nation and I will bless the whole world through them. Don't be frightened. I am with you and will take care of you, wherever you go.'

When Jacob woke up he felt full of wonder. God had been with him and spoken to him. He named the place Bethel, which means 'God's House'. He set up the stone that had been his pillow to mark the place, and prayed to God:

'If you will really take care of me and bring me home again safely, I will serve you faithfully all my life.'

Then, feeling helped and comforted, Jacob went on his journey again until he came to the well near his mother's home town of Haran.

He asked some shepherds waiting there with their flocks if they knew his mother's brother, Laban.

'Yes,' they answered, 'and here comes his daughter, Rachel.'

A beautiful girl was coming to the well with her flock of sheep and goats. Jacob came forward and rolled away the heavy stone that covered the mouth of the well, so that she could draw water.

Then he told Rachel who he was. She gladly took him home to the house of his uncle Laban.

28
The Trickster Tricked
GENESIS 28—29

Laban welcomed his sister's son, Jacob, and made him stay with them and their two daughters, Leah and Rachel. Jacob helped by looking after his uncle's flocks.

'I should be paying you for all your hard work,' Uncle Laban said one day.

'I do not want any wages,' Jacob replied. 'If you let me marry Rachel, I will work seven years for you without pay.'

Jacob loved Rachel so much that seven years of hard work seemed a small price to pay in order to have her as his wife.

When the seven years were ended a great marriage feast was arranged. At nightfall, in the darkness, Laban brought Jacob his bride. But when the next morning dawned, Jacob found that the woman he had married was not Rachel—but Leah. Jacob, who had tricked others, had been tricked himself.

When Jacob complained bitterly to Laban, he told him that it would have been unfair to Leah for her younger sister to be married first.

'If you wait until this week's celebrations are over,' Laban promised, 'you shall marry Rachel as well. But you must work another seven years for me in payment.'

At that time, men often had more than one wife, in spite of the jealousy and quarrels that it caused. So both sisters were married to Jacob.

After a while Jacob also took their two maid-servants to be his wives, as the custom then was. Jacob soon had many sons, but Rachel, the wife he loved so dearly, had no children.

Rachel was bitterly jealous of Leah because of all the sons she had, and Leah was very unhappy because Jacob did not love her.

At long last Rachel had a son and called him Joseph.

After Joseph was born, Jacob planned to leave Laban, but the flocks had grown so large since Jacob had looked after them that Laban persuaded him to stay, offering him wages at last. Jacob asked to have for his own any black lambs and speckled goats in the flock.

Laban readily agreed, for there were not many like that. But when many black and speckled ones were born, Laban was cross and tried to cheat Jacob by changing his agreement. But however often Laban cheated Jacob, God made him successful, and soon he had not only made Laban rich but had become a wealthy owner of flocks and herds himself.

One night God told Jacob to return to his home in Canaan. Next day, while Laban was away, he and his wives, their children and all the animals, got ready to set off on the journey. They would go back to the land God had promised to give to Jacob's descendants in time to come.

29
The Strange Wrestling-match
GENESIS 32

As Jacob came nearer and nearer to Canaan, where his father still lived, he kept thinking about his brother Esau. Would he still be angry because Jacob had cheated him out of the older brother's blessing? Would he still want to kill Jacob?

Jacob remembered God's promise at Bethel to keep him safe and bring him home once more, so he prayed:

'O God, when I left home and came this way before, I had nothing but my walking stick. You have made me rich, and now I am coming back with flocks and herds and a large family.

'I don't deserve all your kindness, but please keep me safe from Esau.'

That evening, Jacob sent his servants, his flocks of animals and all his family ahead of him, across the ford. He wanted to be alone that night to be quiet and think.

During the long hours, a man appeared out of the darkness and began to wrestle with him. Jacob sprang to defend himself and the two struggled and grappled together, hour after hour. Neither would give in.

Suddenly, as dawn began to break, the stranger touched Jacob's hip and put it out of joint. Jacob could not fight any longer. Then Jacob guessed that his wrestling partner was more than an ordinary man.

The stranger turned to go, but Jacob clung to him, asking for his blessing.

'What is your name?' the stranger asked him.

'Jacob,' he replied. 'I am going to give you a new name,' the man said. 'You will be called Israel. That name means one who strives and perseveres. You have persevered in your struggles with God and other people. You have held on to God's promises through thick and thin, and you have won your battle.'

'What is *your* name?' Jacob asked him. But the stranger would not tell him. He blessed Jacob and left him, as the sun rose bright.

Jacob limped away, knowing that once again he had met God.

30
Jacob Meets Esau Again
GENESIS 32—33

Jacob asked God to keep him safe when he met his brother Esau again, but he also made plans of his own to win Esau over.

First he sent a polite message to let Esau know that he was on his way. He guessed that his brother would come to meet him.

Then he went round all his flocks and picked out the very best among the sheep, goats, camels and donkeys. He divided these into groups and put a servant in charge of each little herd.

'Go on ahead,' he told the men, 'and leave a gap between each group of animals. When you meet Esau he is sure to ask whose animals they are. Tell him that they belong to his servant, Jacob, but that they are a present for him.'

'Everyone likes to get presents,' Jacob thought. 'Perhaps Esau may relent towards me.'

When the news arrived that Esau was really coming, Jacob was afraid.

'He has 400 strong fighting men with him,' Jacob was told.

Esau *must* be going to attack him! Quickly Jacob arranged the family in order, putting Rachel at the back. He hoped that she might be safer there.

Then, taking his courage in both hands, Jacob strode ahead to meet Esau. As soon as he saw him he bowed low, but Esau rushed towards him and flung his arms round his neck. They hugged each other happily.

How thankful Jacob was to find that Esau really had forgiven him! 'Let's finish the journey home together,' Esau suggested.

But Jacob could only travel slowly. He had small children and young animals to look after. They could not walk as quickly as Esau's strong young men.

So the brothers said goodbye, friends once again.

Joseph the Boy

Trouble at Home
GENESIS 37

Jacob and his family were safely back in Canaan. But the jealousy and quarrels between his wives and their children went on.

Jacob was glad that he had a large family—all fathers wanted sons to help them in those days—but Rachel was the only wife he loved. He was very sad when she died at the birth of her second son, Benjamin. Little Benjamin was to be the last in Jacob's large family.

Because of his love for Rachel, Jacob treated Joseph, her older son, as if he was really his first-born. This made the other, older brothers very angry.

Jacob gave Joseph a special coat with long sleeves, the kind that only a privileged eldest son could hope to own.

Because Jacob loved Joseph so much, the other sons hated him. They would go off to look after Jacob's flocks, grumbling and muttering.

Jacob sent Joseph to help some of his half-brothers look after the sheep. Joseph was shocked by some of the things he saw them doing, and he told his father all about them when he got home. That made matters worse. The brothers hated Joseph so much that they would not even talk to him. When Joseph tried to speak to them they paid no attention and went on laughing and joking among themselves.

No one in that home was really happy.

32
Dreams!
GENESIS 37

One night, Joseph dreamed a very strange dream.

'Do listen to my dream!' he said to his brothers next morning. 'We were all out in the harvest field, tying up the sheaves of corn. Suddenly, the sheaf that I was tying stood up straight. Then all of your sheaves made a circle around mine and bowed down to it.'

If Joseph thought that his brothers would be pleased and interested in his dream, he was sadly mistaken.

'Who do you think you are?' they asked angrily. 'Do you imagine we are all going to bow and scrape to you?'

Not long after, Joseph had another strange dream. This time he told his father about it. 'I dreamed that the sun and moon and stars were all bowing down to me.'

He counted eleven stars and Joseph had eleven brothers. They soon guessed his meaning!

'High and mighty Joseph thinks we shall all have to treat him as the boss,' they said to themselves.

Even Jacob was a little upset. He thought that the sun and moon in the dream might be a picture of him and his wife.

'Do you really think that you will be more important than your parents?' he asked Joseph. But although he scolded Joseph, Jacob went on thinking about the dream. Could it be God's way of telling him that he had chosen Joseph to be someone very special in the family?

33
Into the Pit!
GENESIS 37

One day, Jacob came looking for Joseph. He wanted to send him on a special errand.

'Your brothers have been away for a long time,' he said. 'I'm anxious about them. Go out and look for them. Make sure that they are safe.'

Joseph set off in the direction his brothers had gone, asking for news of them as he went. At last he tracked them down.

When he was still in the distance, his brothers caught sight of him. They recognized him right away by the special coat that Jacob had given him.

'Look!' called out one of them.
'Here comes that dreamer!'

'We've got him on his own now,'
said another. 'Why don't we kill him
while we have the chance? Then we'll
see what becomes of his wonderful
dreams.'

Reuben, Jacob's eldest son, tried to
stop them.

'We ought not to kill him,' he said.
'Let's just throw him down this
dried-up well. That should teach him
a lesson!'

Joseph was close now, so there was
no time for more talk and plans. He
came towards them eagerly, not
suspecting any harm.

Two of the biggest brothers seized
him, while another ripped off his fine
coat. Then, as Reuben had suggested,
they threw him into the deep pit.
There would be no climbing those
steep slippery sides to escape. A little
breathless, but well satisfied, the
brothers sat down to enjoy their meal.
They paid no attention to Joseph's
desperate cries for help.

On the Road to Egypt

GENESIS 37

While the brothers were eating their meal, they saw a long line of camels coming towards them. Soon they could see that it was a caravan of traders, their camels loaded with spices. They would be going to Egypt to sell their goods.

'Why not sell Joseph to the traders?' Judah suggested. 'It's a much better plan than killing him, and we can earn ourselves a bit of money at the same time.'

They all agreed, except for Reuben, who was not with them.

Everything began to happen quickly. While some of the brothers bargained with the traders, others hauled Joseph up from the pit and marched him across to be inspected for sale. He certainly looked healthy and strong, in spite of the muddy smears and scratches. He should fetch a good price in the slave-market.

'I'll give you twenty silver pieces for him,' the trader offered. The deal was agreed, and Joseph was led away.

Very soon Reuben came back. He had been planning to rescue Joseph secretly and smuggle him home to Jacob. When he found the well empty, he was horrified. Had the other brothers killed Joseph already?

But they soon explained to Reuben what they had done. Next they must decide what to tell their father.

They picked up Joseph's fine coat, which they had ripped off him, and smeared it with goat's blood.

As soon as they reached home, they took the spoiled coat to Jacob.

'We found this,' they said. 'Does it belong to your son?'

When Jacob saw the blood-stained coat, he let out a great cry.

'A wild animal must have killed him,' he exclaimed. 'My own dear son Joseph is dead! I shall never see him again! I shall mourn for him as long as I live!'

All this while, Joseph, securely roped, was being pushed and dragged along the road to Egypt. But God was still with him.

Joseph the Slave

Slave in Charge
GENESIS 37 AND 39

When the Midianite traders arrived in Egypt, they took Joseph to the slave-market, where he was put up for sale. A strong, healthy young slave like him should fetch a good price. A man called Potiphar bought Joseph. He was an important officer of the king, in charge of the palace guard. He soon found he had a bargain.

Joseph worked well. He was able to plan and organize work for himself, as well as obeying orders. He was honest and did not grumble or shirk his duties.

Potiphar soon made Joseph his own special servant and began to leave more and more of the running of the household in Joseph's hands. Potiphar could tell that there was something very special about this young man. It was because God was with Joseph, even though he was far from his home and family.

God helped Joseph to do his work well and made him successful.

36
Thrown into Prison!
GENESIS 39

Joseph must have been as content in
Potiphar's home as a slave can ever
be. He was a loved and trusted
servant in an important man's
household. He knew, too, that God
was still with him.

But Joseph was soon in trouble
again, and through no fault of his
own.

Potiphar's wife had taken a great
liking to this handsome young man

and soon she was trying to persuade him to make love to her, while Potiphar was at work.

Joseph would not listen to her.

'My master trusts me with everything he has,' he told her. 'How could I deceive him by taking his wife? Besides, it would be a sin against God, whom I love and serve.'

Potiphar's wife would not take no for an answer. She followed Joseph around, wheedling and pleading with him. Joseph tried to keep out of her way, but one day she found him on his own. When she put her arms around him Joseph took to his heels and ran.

Potiphar's wife was furious and told her husband lies about Joseph. She pretended that it was Joseph who had done wrong.

Potiphar ordered Joseph to be taken off to prison. His feet were put in chains and an iron collar fixed around his neck. He was no longer the trusted slave.

But God was with Joseph, even in the dark prison. He had not forgotten him, or the great plan he had for Joseph's future.

37
The Meaning of Dreams
GENESIS 40

It was not long before the jailer in charge of the prison found out how helpful Joseph could be. He began to give him all kinds of little jobs to do, looking after other prisoners and arranging the prison routine. Whatever Joseph did was well done.

One day, two very important new prisoners arrived. One was the king's wine-steward and the other his chief baker. Both men were high in the king's service but somehow they had displeased their royal master and had been thrown into prison. There they must wait for the king to pass sentence on them.

The jailer gave Joseph the job of looking after them.

One morning, when he brought them their breakfast, Joseph noticed that they were looking very miserable.

'What is the matter?' he asked kindly.

'We both had dreams last night,' they told him, 'and we don't understand what they mean.'

Like all Egyptians they believed that every dream had a meaning, but in prison there was no one to explain them.

'God can explain dreams,' Joseph said. 'Tell them to me.'

He listened, as first the wine-steward and then the baker recounted his dream.

The steward had dreamed of a grape-vine with three branches, from which he squeezed grapes for the king's wine cup, giving it to the king to drink.

The baker had dreamed that he was carrying three baskets of delicious pastries to the king. But the birds flew down and pecked at them.

God helped Joseph to understand what the dreams meant. 'In three days' time', he told the steward, 'you will be called by the king and given back your job.'

But he had to tell the baker, 'In three days' time you will be put to death on the king's orders.'

Everything happened as Joseph had said.

Three days later it was the king's birthday. He ordered the chief baker to be put to death, but he called the steward back into his royal service.

38
The Prisoner and the King

GENESIS 41

When the grateful wine-steward left prison, Joseph asked for his help.

'Please don't forget me,' he pleaded. 'Tell the king that I have done no wrong and do not deserve to be in prison.'

Joseph must have hoped that his troubles would soon be over. But the moment he was back at court, all thought of Joseph went right out of the steward's mind.

Two long years passed.

Then, one night, the king of Egypt had a dream that none of his special advisers could explain. In a flash, the steward remembered his own dream in prison and the wise, kind help that Joseph had given to him.

'I have been wrong,' he told the king. 'I had forgotten until this moment the young man who explained my dream to me in prison. He told me that I would be taken back into your service, and his words came true. Joseph could help you too.'

Orders were given, and servants rushed to the prison to bring out the astonished Joseph. He was hastily washed, shaved and dressed in clean clothes. Then he was ushered into the king's presence.

'I am told that you can explain dreams,' the king said.

'I cannot do so, your majesty,' Joseph answered, 'but God can.'

'In my dream,' the king went on, 'I saw seven fat cows coming up out of the river to feed on the grass. Seven thin, bony cows stood beside them. The thin cows ate up the fat ones. After that, I had another dream. I saw seven full, ripe ears of grain beside seven thin, withered ears. The thin ears ate up the full ones. What *can* these dreams mean?'

'God is telling you what is going to happen, so that you can be prepared,' Joseph explained. 'The two dreams mean the same thing. There are going to be seven years of good crops, when everyone has plenty. But seven years of bad harvests will follow. Those seven years of shortage will use up all the plenty of the good years. That is the meaning of your dreams.'

Joseph the Ruler

📖 39
The New Prime Minister
GENESIS 41

When the king of Egypt heard Joseph explain his dreams, he was horrified. He knew that in spite of seven years of plentiful harvests, the seven years of shortage that were to follow would bring famine and death. But Joseph had something more to say.

'Your majesty,' he went on, 'may I suggest what you should do? Choose one of your men and put him in charge of all food supplies. He can supervise the storing of grain during the years of bumper crops, so that there will be enough to feed everyone during the years when crops fail. Then the people won't starve.'

The king was pleased with Joseph and his wise advice.

'*You* shall be that man!' he announced. 'You have shown how wise you are, so I shall put you in charge of everything that needs to be done in the whole of Egypt. You shall be my new prime minister.'

On the king's orders, Joseph was given a fine chariot, servants of his own, and rich clothes and jewels.

Joseph had learned to trust God and to do his work well, as a slave and even in prison. He set about his important duties in just the same way.

He travelled the length and breadth of Egypt. In every city he gave orders for huge storage buildings to be put up, to hold grain.

Seven years of wonderful harvests brought huge quantities of grain. Joseph arranged for it to be stored all over the country. Before the seven years were up, the new storehouses were so full that even Joseph had lost count of how much grain they held.

Then came the lean and hungry years, when no crops would grow. Joseph was busier than ever, selling the grain and seeing that it was fairly shared out.

Soon, people living in nearby countries, who were also hit by famine, heard that there was grain to be had in Egypt. They travelled to Joseph, to ask if they too could buy grain to take home to their own lands.

Food in Egypt

GENESIS 42

Back in the land of Canaan, Jacob and his sons were hungry too.

'I hear that they have grain to sell in Egypt,' Jacob told his sons. 'Go there and buy some for us.'

All the brothers set out, except for Benjamin. Jacob could not bear to be parted from him, for he was the only remaining child of Rachel—the wife he had loved so dearly.

As soon as the ten strangers were ushered into the presence of Joseph, he recognized his brothers.

But they had no idea who he was. They never expected their brother to be alive, let alone the governor of all Egypt. Besides, he was dressed like an Egyptian.

'Where do you come from?' Joseph asked, sternly. He spoke in the Egyptian language and a servant translated all that was said.

'From Canaan,' they answered. 'We have come to buy grain.'

'I don't believe a word of it!' Joseph said. 'I think you are a bunch of spies, come to find out what is going on here.'

'We are honest men,' they protested.

'Then tell me all about yourselves,' Joseph insisted.

'There were twelve of us, all brothers,' they began. 'But one brother is dead and the youngest is so dear to his father that he would not let him come with us.'

Joseph felt strange when he heard himself described as dead, but he did not let his feelings show.

'Prove that you are innocent by bringing that youngest brother with you next time you come,' he ordered. 'I am going to keep one of you here as a hostage until you return.'

Simeon was taken away and put into prison. The others were allowed to go back to Canaan, with sacks full of grain.

When they arrived home and opened the sacks they were horrified to find their own bags of money lying on top of the grain. They had been given back all they had paid.

'Now we'll be accused of being thieves, as well as spies,' they cried.

They did not know that Joseph had told his servants to put the money there. He was trying to find out what kind of men those cruel brothers had turned out to be.

41
Benjamin's Journey
GENESIS 43

Little by little their supply of
Egyptian grain ran out and soon
Jacob and his large family were
hungry again.

'You must go back to Egypt to buy
more,' Jacob told his sons.

'Only if we can take Benjamin with
us,' they insisted.

'Never!' Jacob cried. 'Joseph is
dead, Simeon in prison and now you
want to take Benjamin away!'

'We shall *all* be put to death as spies
if we don't,' the brothers reasoned.

Then Judah, the one who had
suggested selling Joseph as a slave so
many years before, spoke up.

'I promise on my life to take care of
Benjamin,' he said to Jacob. 'I will be
responsible for him.'

Sadly and reluctantly Jacob agreed,
and watched them all leave for Egypt.

To their great relief they were
kindly welcomed and shown to
Joseph's house.

When, after so long, Joseph saw his
own brother Benjamin, he could
hardly hold back tears of joy. He
ordered Simeon to be released and
then invited them all to dinner.

When they came in nervously to sit
at the table, they were amazed to find
that they had been placed in exact
order of age. How *could* anyone have
known?

Benjamin was served with extra
large helpings, on Joseph's orders.

The brothers were full of
thankfulness and relief. Their
troubles seemed to be over. Soon they
would *all* be safely on their way home,
with fresh supplies of grain.

The Missing Cup

GENESIS 44

A cheerful and relaxed band of brothers took the return route to Canaan. All was well and Benjamin was safe.

Suddenly, out of the blue, they saw a distant horseman speeding towards them. As he came nearer they recognized, with sinking hearts, a servant of the governor of Egypt.

'How dare you steal my master's best silver cup?' he shouted, as he drew level with them.

'We don't know what you mean,' they protested. 'We have stolen nothing. If any one of us has the cup you can put him to death and keep the rest of us as slaves.'

Roughly, the servant searched their baggage and opened their sacks of grain. The last sack he opened was Benjamin's. There, glinting in the sun, nestled the precious cup.

The brothers were horror-struck. They reloaded their donkeys and silently followed the servant back to Joseph. They little guessed that all that had happened was part of Joseph's plan to find out what kind of people they really were.

When he had heard the servant's report, Joseph pronounced, 'None but the guilty man shall be my slave.'

Then Judah stepped bravely forward. 'If you keep Benjamin, my father will die of grief. Please keep me instead.'

Joseph could hardly believe his ears. His brothers were very different now from the heartless gang who had sold him as a slave and made his father believe he was dead. There were tears in his eyes. He could not keep the truth from them any longer.

'Go out of the room!' he told the servants. Then he spoke to his brothers for the first time in their own language.

'I am Joseph,' he told them, 'your long-lost brother.'

43
Family Reunion
GENESIS 45—46

The brothers were terrified when the truth at last sank in. The great governor of Egypt was none other than the brother they had treated so badly many years before. Now he would make them pay for it.

But, instead, Joseph told them to come close to him. Then he hugged and kissed them all in turn, beginning with Benjamin.

'Don't blame yourselves for what you did,' he said kindly. 'God had a plan when he brought me here. I have been able to save many lives.

'Now you must hurry back to fetch our father and all your families. There are still five more years of famine to come. I will see you settled in Goshen, where the pasture is good for your flocks.'

Then, at last, there was laughter and talking and great excitement.

The inquisitive servants were listening and gossiped to everyone. The good news reached the ears of the king himself.

Soon the brothers set off for home. 'Joseph is still alive!' they called out to Jacob, 'and he is governor of all Egypt.'

Old Jacob would not believe them, until he saw the wonderful presents that Joseph had sent for him.

Then the whole family packed up their tents and all their belongings.

They gathered their flocks and herds together and began the slow journey to Egypt, to settle in the land that Joseph was preparing for them.

44
Trouble in Egypt
EXODUS 1

Jacob and his sons and all their families settled down in Goshen, the part of Egypt where the pasture was best for their flocks. Joseph looked after them through all the lean years of famine that God had foretold.

Many years passed.

Old Jacob died, and so did Joseph and all his brothers. But the people of Israel (that was God's special name for Jacob) went on living in Egypt. Many children were born to them, until they became a vast multitude of people.

The king of Egypt had died too.

Other kings came to the throne. They did not know about Joseph's great deeds. They hated all these foreigners living in their country.

'There are far too many of them,' said the king. 'They may plot against us or join with our enemies when we go to war. Something must be done.'

He decided that if he could make them weak and worn out with work they might have fewer children. And certainly they would have no strength left to be a danger to the Egyptians.

So the king set them to work as slaves, helping to build the grand new cities he had planned. They had to drag the heavy stone slabs into position and make thousands and thousands of bricks.

But the people of Israel still flourished. The more the king ill-treated them, the more they grew in numbers.

'I must do something more,' the cruel and frightened king decided. 'I shall make a new law that every baby boy born to the people of Israel shall be thrown into the River Nile and drowned.'

Now things looked black, indeed, for the Israelites. But God had not forgotten his own people.

The Story of Moses

📖 45

The Baby who Survived

EXODUS 2

A new baby boy! How happy his mother Jochebed and father Amram would have been but for the latest law of the cruel Egyptian king. Every new-born Israelite boy was to be thrown into the River Nile.

Jochebed looked at her beautiful baby.

'He must not be drowned,' she said. 'I shall hide him. I know that God can keep him safe.'

At first all went well. But the tiny baby soon grew into a big, bouncing one and his cries grew louder. As she hushed him asleep, Jochebed prayed and thought and planned. Then she began making a cradle from the river-reeds, just like the fishermen made their boats. When it was finished, she smeared the outside with tar to keep it waterproof.

While the baby slept, she put him gently into the cradle and carried him to the water's edge, taking little sister Miriam with her. She placed the basket among the tall reeds and, leaving Miriam to keep watch, sped quickly home.

Still as a mouse, Miriam crouched in her hiding-place and waited. Soon she heard chatter and laughter. The princess, one of the many daughters of the Egyptian king, was coming to

bathe, attended by her slaves. As Miriam watched, her heart beating fast, the princess stopped.

'Look,' she said, 'there's a basket in the reeds. Fetch it.' Her slave waded in, picked up the basket and handed it to the princess. At that, the baby woke up, gave one look at the unknown face, and burst into tears.

'Poor little thing!' said the princess gently. 'He must be an Israelite baby.'

Her kind look gave Miriam courage. She stepped bravely forward.

'Would you like a nurse for the baby?' she asked.

'Yes,' said the princess, and Miriam hurried home and fetched her mother.

The princess looked keenly at Jochebed. Then she said, 'Take this baby and look after him for me. I will pay you. When he is older he shall come to the palace and be brought up as my son. I shall call him Moses.'

Happily, Jochebed and Miriam carried the gurgling baby home. They need not worry who saw him now. God had kept little Moses safe. For a few more years he was theirs to keep and care for.

Prince of Egypt

EXODUS 2

Jochebed took good care of her baby son. As he grew older she told him about the true God who had saved him from death and would care for him, even in the king's palace. One day God would rescue all his people from their hardship and slavery.

The day came for Moses to go to the palace, to the princess. There he was dressed in fine Egyptian cotton, ate the best food and was waited on by slaves. Soon he began lessons—reading and writing and many things beside, for the Egyptians were wise and learned. But although he grew up to look like an Egyptian he never forgot that he was an Israelite. He remembered and loved the God of his own people, not the many strange gods and goddesses of Egypt.

When he went out in his fine chariot he felt angry and sad to see his own people toiling and sweating in the scorching sun, making the grand buildings the Egyptian king was so proud to own. He longed to rescue them from their cruel masters, who whipped them if they stopped even to draw breath.

One day his chance came. One of the Egyptians beat up an Israelite slave. Moses saw it and was furious. He glanced quickly around. No one was about. So Moses killed the Egyptian bully and buried his body in the soft, sandy soil.

Next day, Moses was horrified to come upon two of his own people fighting one another.

'Stop!' he said. 'You are both Israelites!'

'Who do you think you are?' asked the man who had started the quarrel,

'Are you going to kill me like you did that Egyptian, yesterday?'

The secret was out. Soon the story spread to the palace and the king was very angry. He tried to have Moses put to death.

So Moses left his princely finery and wealth and fled for his life into the deserted countryside of Midian. His own people, whom he longed so much to help, would not have him for their prince and leader.

47
Moses Helps the Shepherd Girls
EXODUS 2

Moses had hoped that he would be able to rescue his people from their unhappiness and slavery, but instead he had to escape from Egypt to save his own life.

Now, in the land of Midian, he sat sadly by a well. Soon, seven girls, all sisters, came towards him. They wanted water to fill the troughs for their father's flocks.

Just then, some shepherds arrived and, pushing the girls roughly aside, began to get water for their own flocks.

Moses sprang up at once and went to help the girls. He drew all the water they needed, and the girls went home delighted.

'You are home early!' their father, Jethro, exclaimed.

'A brave Egyptian rescued us from those bullying shepherds,' they told him.

'Where is he now?' Jethro asked. 'Surely you did not leave him at the well! Go and ask him back to dinner.'

The girls hurried to find Moses and brought him home.

Moses stayed with Jethro. He married Zipporah, one of Jethro's daughters, and looked after his flocks. He would lead them across the desert scrub in search of pasture.

Once a prince in Egypt, Moses had now become a hard-working, humble shepherd.

God Calls Moses

EXODUS 3—4

Many years passed while Moses cared for the flocks of Jethro, his father-in-law.

One day the sheep and goats were cropping the grass on the lower slopes of Mount Sinai. Moses looked up and saw a bush that seemed to be on fire. He watched anxiously, in case the fire should spread through the dry, desert land. But, although the fire glowed bright, the bush stayed unharmed. Curious, Moses went nearer, to look more closely.

Then he heard a voice coming from the heart of the fire. Moses knew at once that it was God's voice.

'Take off your shoes, Moses,' God said. 'For this is holy ground.'

Moses obeyed, then waited quietly. His heart beat fast and he covered his face with his cloak.

'I am the God of Abraham, Isaac and Jacob,' God said. 'I have heard the groans and cries of my people who are slaves in Egypt and I am going to rescue them. *You*, Moses, are going to lead them out of Egypt and into the land that I promised to give to the descendants of Abraham.'

'Not me, God,' Moses begged hastily. 'Please don't send me as their leader. I'm just nobody. I could not do it.'

'But I will be with you,' God promised, 'I will help you and you will succeed. You will lead my people to this very mountain to worship me here.'

Moses still did not want to go back to Egypt. He went on making excuses, but God had an answer for every one. He told Moses that his brother Aaron could go with him and do all the talking for him.

'Take your stick with you,' God ordered. 'You will use it to do wonderful things that will prove to my people and to the king of Egypt that I am the one true God, more powerful than the king and the gods he worships.'

Reluctantly, Moses obeyed God. He took his wife and two sons and, stick in hand, set off for the land of Egypt.

Moses and the King of Egypt

49
The King Says 'No'

EXODUS 5

Moses and his family set off on the road to Egypt. Before they arrived, he met his brother Aaron, just as God had promised. Moses told Aaron all that God had told him.

First they called a meeting of the Israelite leaders.

'The God who called Abraham, Isaac and Jacob, knows all about your unhappiness and is going to rescue you,' Aaron said. 'He promised to give the descendants of Israel a land of their own. Now he is going to lead you to that land.'

A great cheer went up. The people were excited and happy. At last their troubles were over.

Next, Moses and Aaron asked for an audience with the king of Egypt.

'The Lord, the God of Israel, says that you must let his people go free from this country,' Aaron told him.

'Who is this God?' the king asked rudely, 'I don't know him and I certainly shall not do as he says.'

He turned to his servants.

'Get those lazy, idle slaves back to work!'

Then he gave new orders to the Egyptian foremen who were in charge of the workers.

'Up to now you have provided them with the straw they need to make their mud bricks strong. Now they must go into the fields and cut their own straw. And see to it that they make as many bricks as they did before.'

It was an impossible task. But when there were too few bricks the foremen whipped the Israelites and treated them worse than ever.

The people of Israel were bitter and angry. God was supposed to be rescuing them, but things were harder, not easier. Their leaders went to Moses and Aaron and told them what they thought of them.

Moses was in despair. He told God just how worried and disappointed he was.

'Wait,' God said. 'I *will* keep my promise. But, because the king will not obey me, he will have many hard lessons to learn. My own people will also begin to understand how great and powerful I am.'

50
Frogs, Flies and Hail
EXODUS 7—10

God had promised Moses that he
would do many terrifying things to
make the king, and the people of
Israel too, understand that he was
able to rescue his people.

Moses and Aaron went back to the
king and warned him that if he did not
obey God and set free his people, all
kinds of misfortunes would come to
Egypt.

But the king simply laughed and
refused to pay any attention.

God kept his promise and nine
terrible disasters struck Egypt—all at
God's command. After each one,
Moses went to the king and gave him
the chance to change his mind and
obey God. But every time the king
hardened his heart.

First, Moses raised his stick, on
God's orders, and the life-giving
water of the River Nile, which
supplied all Egypt, changed to thick,
red, oozing liquid.

Then frogs came jumping out of
the foul waters and hopped
everywhere, into the houses, the beds
and the ovens.

At first the court magicians copied
Moses, showing what wonderful
tricks they could perform. But they
could do nothing to cleanse the Nile
water, or get rid of the frogs.

The king was sorry for himself. He
promised Moses that he would let the
people go if their God would only
take away the frogs. Moses prayed to
God and the frogs died. But the
moment the trouble was over, the
king changed his mind again and said
'No!' to Moses and to God.

Then God sent stinging, whining gnats and fat buzzing flies. Each time, the king promised Moses that if God took away the plague he would let the people go. Each time, Moses listened to the king and, each time, the king changed his mind once the disaster was over and refused to let the Israelites go.

Cows, horses and donkeys died from disease and the people themselves broke out in painful, red, swelling boils. But still the king said, 'No!'

A storm broke and huge hailstones rained down like bullets. But still the king said, 'No!'

A plague of hungry locusts came like a black cloud and devoured all the crops.

After that, the land was plunged for three days into black, inky darkness.

In Goshen, the people of Israel were kept safe from these troubles. God had proved that he was stronger and greater than all the gods of Egypt and their clever magicians.

But still the king said, 'No!'

51
The Last Punishment
EXODUS 11

After each disaster that befell the country and people of Egypt, Moses and Aaron went to see the king. They begged him to change his mind and listen to God. But he refused to obey, and so save his people from yet more trouble.

After God had sent the ninth sign—total darkness for three long days—the king flew into a rage.

'Get out of my sight!' he shouted at Moses. 'I never want to set eyes on you again.

'You won't,' Moses told him. 'But because you will not change your mind God must do one more terrible thing. After that you *will* let his people go.

'God says, "At midnight I shall go through the whole land of Egypt and the first-born son in every family will die—from the palace to the poorest hovel. There will be great crying and mourning in all Egypt."'

But the obstinate king still paid no attention to Moses, or to God's warning.

God told Moses that the Israelite people were to be kept safe from this last and worst disaster, just as they had been from the others.

But this time they must follow God's instructions, which Moses gave to them. If every family did as God said, the eldest son would be safe when the angel of death went through the land.

The Passover

EXODUS 12

Moses called all the Israelite leaders together once again.

'Listen carefully,' he told them, 'for tonight God's angel of death will pass through Egypt, killing the eldest in every family in the land. If you and your families are to be kept safe, this is what God says you must do:

'Tell every father to choose a good, healthy young lamb or goat from his flock. He is to kill it and daub some of the animal's blood over the door of his house and on the door-posts. The mother in every family is to cook the meat for a special dinner. When it gets dark, the whole family must stay indoors.

'The blood on the doors will be the sign to God that you are his obedient people and he will not let his angel of death harm your families.

'When your children ask what all this means, explain to them that this is God's Passover feast—the time when God will pass over your dwellings to protect you, when all the first-born in Egypt die.'

From that day to this, the people of Israel have kept the Passover every year, remembering God's safe-keeping on that never-to-be-forgotten night.

Escape from Egypt

📖 53
Goodbye!
EXODUS 12

The night when God's last, terrible disaster fell on Egypt, every Israelite stayed safely indoors. The mothers prepared a delicious dinner of roast lamb, as God had told them. But when they all sat down to enjoy it, they kept on their outdoor clothes. For Moses had warned them to be ready to leave Egypt as soon as the order was given.

At midnight a terrible cry went up from all the homes in Egypt. When the Israelites heard the wailing they knew that God had done as he said. In every Egyptian home the first-born son was dead. God's own people had been kept safe because they had obeyed and trusted him.

At once the king sent for Moses and Aaron.

'Get out!' he thundered. 'Don't stay in my country another day. Take your women and children, animals and all. Only leave us in peace!'

At once Moses sent the order buzzing around the land of Goshen. It was time to be off.

The fathers urged the mothers to hurry. The dough they had left to rise was not ready, so they wrapped it in pieces of cloth and carried it with them, along with their pots and pans.

Whole families came pouring out of their homes, making their way to the appointed meeting-place. The sheep and goats they drove were bleating in alarm and making it difficult to hurry.

The Egyptians came out of their houses too, and begged the Israelites to hasten away. They were so anxious to see them go that they loaded them with presents of gold and silver, necklaces and bracelets and all kinds of fine materials. They wanted them out of the way before more trouble should strike the land.

With hardly a backward glance, the whole, huge crowd set out, with Moses in the lead. At last God's promise had come true. It was 'Goodbye Egypt' for ever.

God Leads the Way

EXODUS 13:17–22

The people of Israel set off from Egypt with great excitement. At last they were free from the Egyptians who had made them work so hard and treated them so harshly.

Now, with Moses to lead them, they were going to the country God had promised to give them when he had called Abraham to follow him, all those hundreds of years before.

But how were they to find the way to the Promised Land of Canaan? All around them was desert. There were no clear paths to follow and no signposts to show the way.

God told Moses that they were not to take the shortest route to Canaan, because there were frontier guards posted along it. God did not want his people to have to face a battle so soon after they had begun their journey.

He planned to take them by a longer route, and he was going to show them the way.

God went ahead of them. There was a column of cloud in front of them in the day time and a column of fire at night to show them that he was there. When the cloud or the fire moved, the people followed where it led. When it stopped still, the Israelites knew that it was time to put up their tents and stay where they were for a while, until the column of fire or cloud began to move again.

By day or by night, the people could travel on their way, because God was with them, guiding them all the time.

'Slaves, Come Back!'

EXODUS 14

Meanwhile, in his palace in Egypt, the king was having second thoughts. Why *had* he let those Israelite slaves escape? He forgot all about the terrible disaster that had made him send them packing. Now he wondered how he would get his building done without their hard work. He must fetch them all back.

He gave orders for his soldiers to get their horses and chariots ready and to set out in search of the Israelites. They would ride fast through the desert and soon track down the huge, straggling crowd with their children and animals, plodding slowly along. Then they could round them all up and bring them back to Egypt.

The Israelites were busy setting up their camp near the Sea of Reeds. In front of them lay the waters of the lake and all around them stretched the bare, uninviting desert.

Suddenly the bustle of the camp was interrupted by shouts of alarm. Someone had spotted a dust-cloud on the distant horizon and soon the watchers were able to see the shape of the dreaded war-chariots of Egypt, coming nearer by the minute.

A great wave of fear and panic swept through the camp. The people swarmed around Moses and wailed: 'Why didn't you leave us in Egypt, instead of bringing us into this horrible desert to be killed? It's all your fault!'

'Don't be frightened,' Moses said. 'Keep calm and be quiet. God can save us from the Egyptians.'

But the Egyptians were coming steadily nearer. The only way of escape was straight ahead. And ahead lay the waters of the Sea of Reeds. They were trapped!

Then God spoke to Moses:

'Tell the people not to panic but to start marching forward. I am going to rescue my people and show the Egyptians that I am God. All you must do is to hold up your stick over the water. Then wait to see what will happen.'

Crossing the Red Sea

EXODUS 14—15

Moses did just as God had told him. He lifted his stick high over the Sea of Reeds. A strong east wind began to blow. It whipped up the waters of the lake into a bank on either side, leaving a clear pathway through the sea.

At the same time, God's guiding cloud moved from in front of the Israelites to behind them, so that it blocked them from the view of the oncoming Egyptians. As night fell, the cloud's fiery glow gave light to guide the Israelites across the lake.

Quickly the people gathered together their children and flocks and began to file across the path through the sea. All night they marched steadily across.

By this time the Egyptian horses and chariots were almost on their heels. They began to crash recklessly after the lost slaves. But the wheels of their chariots soon clogged and stuck in the mud at the bottom of the lake. The drivers urged on their horses, but in vain. The wheels only skidded and spun.

As morning dawned, the last of the Israelites had safely reached the other side of the sea.

'Hold your stick out over the sea again,' God told Moses. As he did so, the water came flowing back. All of the Egyptian forces were lost.

'You will never see them again,' Moses promised the people.

There was a great shout of happiness and relief. God had saved them!

Moses burst out singing: 'I will sing to the Lord, because he has won a glorious victory; he has thrown the horses and their riders into the sea. The Lord is my strong defender; he is the one who has saved me.'

Then Miriam, Moses' sister, took up her tambourine and played and sang too:

'Sing to the Lord, because he has won a glorious victory; he has thrown the horses and their riders into the sea.'

Everyone joined in, singing and dancing in praise to God, who had saved them from the Egyptians for ever.

57
Food in the Desert
EXODUS 16

All the excitement of escaping from Egypt was over. The Israelites had seen the last of their slave-drivers. Now they had to get used to a different way of life. Slowly they began to make their way to Canaan, the land that God had promised them.

But it was not long before they began to hate the hardship of the desert journey. They soon forgot the toil and the beatings they had suffered in Egypt and came grumbling to Moses.

'Why did you bring us here?' they complained. 'In Egypt we had all the food we wanted. Now we're starving! It's all *your* fault!'

Moses did not know how to answer them, but God said to him, '*I* will give the people food,' and he told Moses how it would happen.

Moses and Aaron went back to the people with God's message.

'When you grumbled at me,' Moses said, 'you were really grumbling at God. *He* is the one who brought you out of Egypt and he is the one who will give you food. Tonight and tomorrow morning you will find out how he is going to do it.'

That very night huge flocks of quails flew low over the black goatskin tents. Some, tired out by their long flight, rested on the ground, where they were quickly caught and turned into a tasty supper.

Next morning something even more amazing happened. The Israelites looked out of their tents and saw, as the dew melted, something white and flaky left all over the ground. They tasted it and it was sweet, like honey biscuits. They did not know what it was, so they called it manna, which means 'what-is-it?'

Every day, except on the Sabbath, it was there waiting for them to collect. They could eat it raw or use it cooked. God told them to collect just enough for each day's meals, except on the sixth day, when they were to collect enough to last for two days. This meant that no one need work on God's special day, the Sabbath.

58
Water in the Desert
EXODUS 15:22–27; 17:1–7

Water—water—that was all anyone could think about. It's bad to be hungry when you are tramping, hot and tired, through dry, parched country, but it's far worse to be thirsty.

For three days the people of Israel had trudged on without finding fresh water, so they were overjoyed at last to catch sight of a quiet pool. Those in

front rushed to get a drink but at once the eagerness on their faces changed to expressions of sour disgust. The water tasted horrible!

'*Do* something, Moses,' they begged, and Moses asked God to help. God showed him a piece of wood lying nearby and Moses threw it into the water. The bitter taste vanished and they were all able to drink.

The Israelites were thankful to camp, soon after, at Elim, a lovely green oasis, where palm trees shaded twelve clear, sparkling springs and everyone could quench his thirst.

But all too soon it was time to take down their tents and be on their way.

At their next camping-place there was no water at all. An angry crowd came to find Moses.

'Give us water,' they threatened, 'Why did you bring us here to die of thirst?'

Moses was worried and a little afraid. The people were angry and some of them even picked up large stones ready to throw at him.

'What can I do with these people?' Moses asked God.

'Take your stick,' God said, 'and go with the leaders of the people to a rock that I will show you. Hit that rock with your stick.'

Moses did just as God said. When he struck the rock with his stick, fresh clear water spurted out, gushing freely for all to drink and quench their thirst.

How Moses wished that the Israelites would learn the lesson that God could look after them!

'Hands Up, Moses!'

EXODUS 17:8–16

The Israelites were not the only people needing to find food and water. The Amalekites, who lived in that part of the desert, wanted to keep the oases to themselves and were determined to stop these newcomers from sharing their water supplies. They crept around the Israelite camp and began to attack them.

Moses knew that he must act quickly to drive off these enemies. He chose Joshua, a brave young man, to lead out some fighting men against the Amalekites the very next day.

'I will stand on that hill over there,' Moses reassured them, 'holding the stick that God told me to carry.'

The Israelites set off and Moses climbed the hill as he had promised, with Aaron his brother and Hur, another leader, beside him. Then Moses held up his arms, to urge the Israelites into battle and to pray for God's help.

The Israelites were not used to fighting. It gave them fresh courage to see Moses, holding up the stick with which he had done so many wonderful things.

Moses' arms began to ache and he had to let them fall to his sides every now and then. But, whenever he did so, the Israelites faltered and began to lose the fight. As soon as he lifted up his arms again they grew strong and drove the Amalekites back.

Hour after hour passed and Moses' arms grew more and more tired. But Aaron and Hur had a good idea. They fetched a comfortably-shaped stone for Moses to sit on. Then, one either side, they propped up Moses' arms until sunset. So the Israelites were able to drive off the Amalekites and stop them from attacking the camp again.

Moses thanked God by building an altar there. He knew that it was God who was caring for his people and had given them the help they needed.

Sharing Out the Work

EXODUS 18

The people of Israel continued their journey until they arrived at the mountain where God had first called to Moses from the burning bush.

God had promised Moses then that he would help him to lead the people to this very place, and he had kept his promise.

But Moses was feeling very tired. He was the one who had to do the planning and thinking for all the people. Often they made his work harder by complaining and grumbling, in spite of God's goodness and help. As well as his other work, Moses had to settle all the quarrels and arguments, and teach the people what was right. He was kept busy deciding cases all day long.

One day an unexpected visitor arrived at the camp. It was Jethro, Moses' father-in-law. Moses was delighted to see him. Jethro had heard about some of the wonderful things that God had done for his people, and Moses eagerly told him the rest.

'Praise the Lord!' Jethro exclaimed.

Moses said nothing about all his own hard work, but next day Jethro watched while he dealt with a long line of Israelites bringing him their problems and differences.

'Why are you dealing with this great queue of people all day long?' he asked Moses that night.

'I must,' Moses answered. 'I have to act as judge and teach them God's laws.'

'At this rate you will soon be worn out,' Jethro told him, 'and the people will get tired of waiting so long for their turn to speak to you. You need help. Take my advice and choose some helpers. They must be men you can trust, who obey God. Let them share the work of settling everyone's quarrels. They need bring only the extra difficult cases to you.'

Although Moses was a great leader, he was humble enough to take Jethro's good advice. He chose trustworthy men to help him in the task of guiding and teaching the Israelite people.

God's Laws

📖 61

God's Mountain

EXODUS 19

The people of Israel set up camp at the foot of Mount Sinai, where God had first called Moses to be their leader. Moses climbed the mountain to be alone and quiet, so that God could speak to him.

'Tell the Israelites,' God said, 'that I have looked after them just like a mother bird looking after her chicks. I will go on caring for them, but they, for their part, must obey me.

'I am going to speak to you, Moses, in front of them all, to show them that you really are my chosen leader. They will see only a cloud, but they will hear my voice.'

Moses hurried down to the camp to give everyone God's message. The Israelites had certainly learned that God was taking care of them, but now they had to realize that God is holy too. Holy means separate or apart. God is not a human being with faults and failings. He is utterly good, with nothing bad in him. His people, too, must love and obey him by doing what is right.

Moses told the people to get ready for God to speak to them. They must wash themselves and everything they wore. That would remind them how pure and clean they needed to be in the presence of God.

Moses marked out a boundary line all around the bottom of the mountain. No one, not even an animal, must cross that line and come too close to God's mountain.

On the third morning, a deep rumble of thunder brought them all to the doors of their tents. Moses led them to the foot of the mountain. The top was wrapped in cloud but, as they watched, the cloud changed to fiery smoke, and the thunder crashed more loudly. Then the air was shattered by the loud, long blast of a trumpet.

The people trembled and shook with fear.

Moses spoke to God, and a roll of thunder came in reply.

'Don't make us stay here!' the frightened people begged. 'God is too great and terrible for us to listen to. *You* speak to us instead and tell us all that God is saying!'

So Moses and Aaron set off alone up the mountain to hear what God had to say.

62
The Ten Commandments —Loving God

EXODUS 20

When God talked to Moses on Mount Sinai he gave him many laws for the people to keep. Because God is our Maker he knows best what will make us happy. If the Israelites obeyed his laws they would live happily together.

Some of the laws God gave to Moses were especially important for people living at that time, but many of them are important for all people everywhere. The best-known of these are the Ten Commandments.

The first five tell us the right way to treat God.

God says, '*Do not worship other gods.*' That is the first commandment.

In those days people had many gods and goddesses, as they did in Egypt. Today people may give all their love and loyalty to money or success. God taught that he alone is God and Maker of all. He alone is fit to be worshipped.

God says, '*Do not make idols to worship.*' That is the second commandment.

The Israelites might well have thought it a good idea to make an image to represent God—of something beautiful and life-giving, perhaps, like the sun; or something strong, like a bull. But God knew that when people make an image they soon begin to worship the image itself. They forget that God is much greater than anything they can make or imagine.

God says, '*Do not take God's name in vain.*' That is the third commandment.

God's name stands for God himself. No one must use it as a swear-word, or promise in God's name to do something and then go back on their word. They must show reverence for God by treating his name with respect.

God says, '*Keep the Sabbath day holy.*' That is the fourth commandment.

Holy means separate or apart. The seventh day, the 'Sabbath', must be set aside especially for God. It was intended to be a day for learning about him and worshipping him. It was also to be a happy holiday, when even the animals had a rest from work.

God says, '*Respect your parents.*' That is the fifth commandment.

God made families and put parents in charge of their children. Duty to God includes showing care and respect for parents.

Jesus summed up all these commandments in the single command to love God with all our heart. We love God when we obey him.

63
The Ten Commandments —Loving Others

EXODUS 20

The first five of the Ten Commandments are about loving and obeying God; the last five are about loving others. To love others means to treat them as we would like them to treat us, and do nothing that would harm them.

God says, '*Do not murder*.' That is the sixth commandment.

It is wrong to kill—out of anger, spite or cruelty, or in order to get money.

God says, '*Do not commit adultery*.' That is the seventh commandment.

God's plan was that a husband and wife should belong to each other for as long as they lived. To commit adultery is to make love to someone else's husband or wife. God says that this is wrong.

God says, '*Do not steal*.' That is the eighth commandment.

No one has the right to take anything that belongs to someone else.

God says, '*Do not tell lies about others*.' That is the ninth commandment. No one must tell lies about someone when he is on trial in a court of law. It is also wrong to tell lies about people behind their backs.

God says, '*Do not covet*.' That is the tenth commandment. To covet means to want something that belongs to someone else so badly that you are really jealous of them. An Israelite might look at someone's house, or donkey, or wife and think how much nicer they were than his own. God said that he was not to be jealous or try to take them for himself.

When God had finished speaking, he told Moses that he would give him two stone tablets with his laws engraved on them. Then the people would know that these were God's own laws.

64
God Cares
EXODUS 21—23

As well as giving Moses the Ten
Commandments, God gave many
smaller rules that would help the
people to live in health and peace
together. God wanted them to be fair
and kind to one another.

God showed his people by his laws
that he cares about their safety, and
wants to protect them.

In Moses' day, quarrels quickly
broke out and often lasted a long time.
If one member of a family was hurt,
his relatives would pay back the
injury. Their revenge often led to
more raids and killings.

God taught his people not to have
long-lasting feuds. If anyone was
harmed, the man who did it must be
fairly punished and there the matter
must end. This law of fair
punishment said that it should be 'an
eye for an eye and a tooth for a
tooth'—and no more. This was not a
cruel or vengeful law: God was
setting a strict limit and softening
ancient customs of savage vengeance.

God showed his people by his laws
that he cares about those who are not
strong enough to fight for their rights.

He gave special laws so that the
badly off, the foreigners and those
unable to earn their living would be
taken care of. And he spoke often of
his special care for orphans and those
with no one to provide for them.

Farmers were to leave a little grain
in the fields and some fruit on the
trees to provide the poor with food. If
a poor man who was unable to pay his
bills had his cloak taken from him in
payment, God said that it must be
given back to him at nights, so that he
could keep warm while he slept.

God showed his people by his laws
that he cares for animals too.

If a donkey fell down under its
load, God's law said that a passer-by
must help it up again, even if it
belonged to his worst enemy. If
anyone found a mother bird sitting on
her nest, God's law said that he was to
let her go free and not harm her.

God's laws taught the people what
God is like. They helped people to
understand that God is just and good
and that he cares about every detail of
life. Even the least important people
matter to him and ordinary everyday
happenings are his concern. God
wanted his people to be like him.

God and his People

The Agreement

EXODUS 24

Many hundreds of years before Moses' time, God had called Abraham and made an agreement or 'covenant' with him. God promised Abraham that he and Sarah would have many descendants and that through them God would bless the whole world. Now those descendants had grown into the nation of Israel.

God told Moses that he wanted to make a covenant with the whole people of Israel. God's side of the covenant would be to take care of them and bring them safely to the land he had promised them. They would be his special people. Moses told everyone this good news of God's promise. Then he told them about *their* side of the covenant.

'You must promise to obey all God's laws and commands to you,' he told them.

'We will, we will,' they eagerly agreed.

Moses read out all God's laws to them, so that they would understand just what they were promising to do. But the people were quite sure that they would be able to please and obey God.

Moses built an altar of twelve large stones at the foot of the mountain. Each stone stood for one of the twelve tribes, or clans, descended from the sons of Israel (Jacob's new name).

Then Moses took the blood of some of the animals killed for sacrifice and sprinkled it on the people to help them to understand that a solemn covenant had been made. It was a way of signing the agreement.

There was no doubt at all that God would keep to his side of the covenant. But would the people of Israel keep to theirs?

66
God's Special Tent
EXODUS 25—31

All the time that the Israelites were on their journey to Canaan, they lived in tents. They could not put up a building in which to worship God. God told Moses that, instead, he was to make a special Tent that would be kept for God. God gave Moses full instructions for making this Tent and promised to give special skill to the workmen who carried out the plans.

The outside of the Tent was to be made of plain goat-hair with a covering of sheepskins, but inside there would be beautiful embroidered curtains and gold and silver furnishings. On a gold-decorated altar, fragrant incense would burn. The whole structure was made to take apart, and the bigger objects had carrying-poles, so that when the Israelites moved camp, God's Tent could go with them.

The most important part of the Tent was hidden away, shut off by thick curtains. The one special piece of furniture inside this Most Holy Place was a chest about the size of a desk. It was to be made of wood, covered with gold, and the lid was of pure gold. Two gold figures stood on the lid of the chest, their wings outspread to cover the chest, as God would 'cover' the people's sins and wrongdoings.

Moses wondered how he would get all the rich materials he needed to make God's Tent. God told him that the people would gladly give them. And so they did.

When Moses told them about the Tent they were so enthusiastic that they brought all that Moses wanted: fine linen and wool, rings and necklaces. All the precious things that the Egyptians had pressed on them when they left Egypt they brought freely and generously to Moses as their gifts to God.

In the end, Moses had to tell them to stop bringing their presents. He had all that he needed in order to make God's Tent—and more beside.

The Calf Made of Gold

EXODUS 32

When Moses disappeared up the mountain to speak to God, the Israelites gazed after him in wonder. The cloud on the mountain-top glowed and dazzled them with its brightness. But the days passed and Moses did not come back.

They grew bored with watching and waiting.

'We want to be on our way again,' they told Aaron. 'We've no idea what has become of Moses. *You* make a god for us who will lead us instead.'

'Take off your gold ear-rings and bring them to me,' Aaron said.

The people gladly stripped off their ornaments and Aaron melted them all down. Then, from the gold, he made a bull-calf.

'Here is our god!' shouted the people in delight.

'Tomorrow we'll have a festival in honour of God,' Aaron promised and they agreed enthusiastically.

Next day they began to celebrate. They set up the image of the calf and danced around it. They feasted and drank, and soon the festival turned into a wild drinking-party.

God knew what was going on. 'Go back down the mountain, Moses,' he said, 'the people have broken my law already.' God was angry and sad that they should so soon break their solemn promises to him.

Moses hurried down, carrying the two stone tablets on which God's law was engraved. Joshua, his right-hand man, was with him.

'It sounds as though there is a battle going on,' Joshua said, puzzled by all the noise.

'That is not fighting, it's singing,' Moses replied grimly.

When Moses got nearer and saw the people dancing and cavorting around the image of the bull-calf, he was furious. He hurled down the stone tablets of the law which God had given him, smashing them into fragments. Then he charged into the camp and seized the golden image.

'Why did you let them do it?' he demanded of Aaron.

'Don't be angry with me,' Aaron pleaded. 'It's all the fault of these wicked and obstinate people.'

Moses ground the calf to powder, mixed the gold dust with water and made the Israelites drink it.

Next day, when the people were subdued and thoroughly ashamed, Moses said, 'You have committed a terrible sin. But I will go up the mountain again and ask God to forgive you.'

Putting Things Right

EXODUS 33–34

Moses begged God to forgive the people for making the gold calf and worshipping it. He offered to take the blame for it himself, but God said that whoever has done wrong must be the one to take the blame. The people would be punished.

God knew that however sorry they might be now, the Israelites would go on disobeying him and doing wrong many times. So he gave Moses instructions about what they were to do to put things right.

Outside God's special Tent there was to be an altar where sacrifices of animals would be burned.

Anyone who did something wrong and broke God's law must bring an animal for the priest to offer to God. It might be a sheep or a young bull. It was as if the animal was taking the punishment that the guilty person deserved. God looked right into the person's heart. When he was really sorry, God forgave him. The animal's death could not take away sin, but God's loving forgiveness put him right again.

People would bring animal sacrifices, as well as gifts of grain, at other times too. They were a way of saying 'thank you' to God.

After the people of Israel had completely broken their covenant with God by asking Aaron to make the image of the bull-calf for them to worship, Moses was afraid that God would not want to look after them any more.

'If you won't come with us, we don't want to go any further on our journey,' he told God.

'I will still be with you,' God promised, 'And now the time has come to set off from this mountain and go on with your journey.'

The people must have been very relieved when Moses came back to them and told them that God was still willing to keep his side of the covenant.

'You must make a fresh start now,' Moses explained. 'You must promise all over again to keep God's laws.'

They willingly agreed. Then, thankfully, they packed up their things and folded their tents, ready to set off at last from Mount Sinai.

On the Borders of Canaan

📖 **69**

The Promised Land in Sight

NUMBERS 13; DEUTERONOMY 1

Whenever the people of Israel packed up their tents to begin another stage of their journey, everything was carefully planned. God had told Moses how to arrange it all.

Moses had two special silver trumpets made, to send signals to the whole camp. If the people heard both trumpets everyone hurried to God's Tent to listen to Moses' instructions. A single blast on one trumpet was a call to the leaders of the people. The trumpets also gave the signal for the tribes to start moving.

Chosen men from Levi's tribe carried God's Tent and all that belonged to it, with six tribes ahead of them and six following. When they set up camp, the people pitched their tents in the same order, keeping in their family groups, with God's Tent in the middle.

At long last they arrived at the oasis of Kadesh Barnea, within sight of the Promised Land. How excited they all were! This was journey's end.

'The land that God has promised to us lies right ahead,' Moses said. 'Get ready to go in and take it.'

'We should send some scouts ahead first,' someone suggested, 'to spy out the land.' Moses agreed and chose twelve men, one from each of the twelve tribes. Then he gave them instructions.

'Go into Canaan and look around everywhere,' he said. 'See what the countryside is like, what crops will grow and bring us back samples of what you find. See too what the people who live there are like and how strong they seem.'

The chosen men set off and the people settled down to wait for their return.

'We Can't Do It!'
NUMBERS 13—14

For six whole weeks the Israelite spies explored the land of Canaan. The people eagerly waited for their return and crowded to meet them when they came back, anxious to hear what news they would bring.

'It is a wonderful country,' the spies began. 'Just look at this fruit we found!' They held up ripe figs and luscious pomegranates and pointed to a huge bunch of mouth-watering grapes that two of them were carrying, tied to a pole.

Then their voices grew sad. 'That land can never be ours,' they went on. 'The cities are so strongly fortified and the people are like giants. We looked like grasshoppers beside them.'

At this bad news the people began to cry and complained bitterly to Moses: 'We should never have left Egypt! God must hate us to bring us all this way to die in the desert—for we'll never live in Canaan!'

Then Caleb, one of the spies who had been silent up to then, spoke up.

'Of course God can give us the land he has promised to us. Let's get ready to go in!'

Joshua, who had also been one of the twelve, joined in, telling everyone to trust God to help them. But the other ten shook their heads and kept repeating, 'We'll never do it—let's give up!'

The people listened to the ten spies and paid no attention to Caleb and Joshua. All night long they wailed and moaned at Moses. 'We shall all be killed. It would be better to go back to Egypt!'

When Caleb and Joshua tried to persuade them to trust God they picked up stones to throw at them.

All at once the dazzling light of God's cloud blazed out above God's Tent.

In the sudden hush God spoke to Moses.

'These people will not believe that I can give them the land I promised them. They will not obey me and go into it. Therefore they will wander in this desert for another forty years. But their children *shall* go into the land and my two faithful servants, Caleb and Joshua, will go in with them.

'Tomorrow you must turn back, away from the borders of Canaan, back into the dry, dusty desert.'

71
Moses Loses his Temper

NUMBERS 20

After they had left the borders of Canaan the Israelites wandered from one oasis to another.

At one camping-place there was no water. They quite forgot that God had always given them the water they needed. As usual, they came grumbling and complaining to Moses.

'Why did you bring us into this dreadful desert?' they demanded, 'Why didn't you leave us in Egypt? We had figs and grapes and pomegranates there—and now we don't even have water to drink!'

Moses and Aaron knew that it was the people's own fault that they were not in Canaan by now, enjoying the fruit there. But they went to the door of God's Tent and waited for God's message.

'Take your stick, Moses,' God said, 'and call all the people together. Then speak to that rock over there, in front of them all, and I will bring water out of it for them.'

Moses picked up his stick and told the people to follow him. But, inside, he was feeling very angry. For years he had put up with the Israelites' grumbles and all the rude things they had said about him and about God. He felt he could stand it no longer.

'Listen to me, you rebels!' he shouted. 'Do I have to bring water out of this rock for you?' He did not do as God had said. Instead, in his anger, he hit the rock twice with all his might.

A great spurt of water gushed out and began streaming down the side of the rock. Everyone rushed to fill their water jars and collect all they needed.

But God was not pleased with Moses. He had disobeyed God and decided to do things his way. When it was too late, Moses deeply regretted his wilfulness.

72
The Bronze Snake
NUMBERS 21

The years slowly passed and still the people wandered in the desert, as God had said, without coming into the Promised Land. Sometimes it seemed that they were learning to trust God but still they grumbled— especially about the food.

'Why did you bring us into this desert, Moses?' they cried, 'We are sick of this manna God sends!'

God had been kind and given them all they needed many times. Now he tried to teach them the lesson in a different way.

The camp was overrun with snakes. First one person, then another, screamed out as he found a darting, venomous snake slithering into his tent, or lying among the sticks he was collecting for his fire.

Everywhere the snakes writhed, flicking out their poisoned fangs. Many of the Israelites were bitten and became feverish and ill with the fiery poison.

Some of the people hurried to Moses.

'We know we have been wrong to grumble,' they said, 'but please ask God to take away these terrible snakes.'

Moses prayed and God told him what to do.

'Make a snake out of bronze,' God said. 'Then fix it to a pole and set it up high, so that everyone in the camp is able to see it. Anyone who has a snake bite must look up at the bronze snake and he will be made better.'

Moses did as God said and everyone who obeyed God's instructions and looked up at the bronze snake got better, as God had promised. Of course there was nothing magic about the snake. It was trusting and obeying God that made them well again.

73
Balaam and his Donkey
NUMBERS 22—24

The Israelites moved nearer to Canaan again and set up camp not far from the border. Balak, chieftain king of the Moabite people, had heard that the Israelites were moving towards their Promised Land and he was determined to stop them. Instead of mustering soldiers to fight them he sent messengers to summon Balaam, a famous wise man.

'Tell him about this huge nation,' King Balak ordered them, 'and ask him to come and pronounce a terrible curse on them.'

The messengers arrived at Balaam's house and gave him the message. They also showed him a huge bag of gold which would be his if he obeyed the king.

That night God told Balaam that he must not be persuaded to go and curse the people God had promised to bless.

But when King Balak sent more messengers, with even more gold, Balaam said 'Yes'.

He set out, his good-natured donkey clip-clopping patiently beneath him. Suddenly the donkey stood stock still. Balaam beat her impatiently. His head was too full of gold for him to see what his donkey had seen.

God's angel was standing in front of them, barring the path.

The donkey crept forward, then squeezed up close to the wall, to get out of the angel's way. Balaam's foot was crushed and with a cry of pain and anger he gave his poor donkey another good beating.

A third time the angel stood in the path. This time the frightened animal lay right down.

Then Balaam flew into a rage. He beat the donkey over and over again.

Suddenly, to his amazement, he heard his own quiet, patient little donkey speak.

'Why are you beating me?' she asked, 'Have I ever disobeyed you before?'

Then Balaam's own eyes were opened and he saw the angel for himself. The angel was stern.

'You should not have beaten your donkey. She has saved your life by stopping when I told her. Now go on with your journey if you must, but say only what I tell you to say.'

When Balaam reached King Balak he made careful preparations to put a curse on Israel. But Balaam could say only what God told him to say. He could not curse God's people—only call down blessings. In spite of all King Balak's promises of money, Balaam could not bring trouble on God's own people.

Moses Says Goodbye

DEUTERONOMY

By the time the Israelites had wandered for forty years in the desert, Moses was a very old man. But he was still healthy and strong, with eyes like a hawk. How he would have loved to lead the people into Canaan!

But God had said to him:

'Moses, you are not going into the Promised Land. You disobeyed me and lost your temper when you hit the rock. I wanted to teach people that I am a patient and loving God but you spoiled the lesson by doing it all in your own way.'

Moses was bitterly disappointed but he knew that God meant what he said, so he did not argue. But in his heart he blamed the people for making him angry.

'You will see the land, even though you cannot go into it,' God went on. 'Climb to the top of the high peak of Mount Pisgah. There you will have a view of the whole land that the people of Israel will have for their own. While you are looking at the Promised Land your life will come to its end.

Then Moses was glad that instead of growing weak and ill, God would take him from life while he was enjoying the wonderful sight of the land he had longed to enter.

Before he went up Mount Pisgah, Moses talked for a long time to the Israelites. He reminded them all over again of God's goodness and of how important it was for them to obey God's laws. He made up a beautiful poem about all that God had done for them.

Then, as God had instructed, he spoke to his faithful follower, Joshua, and told him that he was to be the next leader of Israel.

At last Moses climbed the mountain. He looked long and steadily at the Promised Land, stretching below. And there he died. No one knows where he was buried. God took care of that.

Never again would there be any leader as great as Moses. He did many wonderful things to rescue the Israelites from Egypt and bring them safe to the Promised Land. God treated him just like a friend, talking to him face to face. But Moses never became conceited. All he wanted was to teach the people to obey God and learn how great he is.

The Story of Joshua

75
The New Leader
JOSHUA 1

After Moses had climbed the mountain, never to return, God spoke to Joshua.

'My servant Moses is dead,' he told him. 'You must get ready now to lead the people into the Promised Land of Canaan. I will give you the whole country from the desert in the south to the Lebanon mountains in the north, from the River Euphrates in the east to the Mediterranean Sea in the west.'

Joshua felt very unsure and afraid. He had been Moses' trusted helper for the whole of the long journey from Egypt, but he did not feel that he could ever be the leader. He was not great like Moses, whom he had loved and admired so much. But God cheered and encouraged Joshua.

'Joshua,' God said, 'be strong and very brave! Don't be frightened! I promise to be with you, just as I was with Moses. All you have to do is to pluck up courage and trust in me. I promise that I will be with you all the way. I will make you strong and you will never fail.

'There are two important things that you must do if you are to succeed. You must be determined to go in and win. Don't even think about failing. Be strong and full of confidence.

'The other thing you must do is to keep my law. Study it day and night and teach my people to obey it too. Then all will go well.'

Now that God had promised to help him and be with him, Joshua felt able to take on his new job.

He called all the leaders together and gave them their orders. 'Tell the people to get ready to move in three days' time,' he said. 'We are going to cross the River Jordan and go into the land of Canaan.'

Everyone was very excited. They were quite willing to do as their new leader said.

76
Secret Mission
JOSHUA 2

Two big obstacles stood between the Israelites and the land that God was giving to them. One was the fast-flowing Jordan river; the other was the strong-walled city of Jericho, which stood solid and firm, just inside Canaan's border.

First of all, Joshua sent out spies, as Moses had done so many years before. He chose two men and told them to explore the land and especially Jericho, which blocked their way into the rest of Canaan.

But the king of Jericho, who had been watching this vast multitude of Israelites coming closer and closer to his city, had spies of his own. His secret service soon brought him news that two Israelites had been seen prowling around the walls. Someone had seen them that very evening, creeping silently into the house of Rahab, a woman whose house was built into the thick wall of the city.

The king ordered his men to go straight to Rahab's house to question her. But Rahab was too quick-witted for the king. She guessed that someone might come knocking at her door and she hastily took the two Israelite spies up onto her flat roof. Stalks of flax had been laid out there to dry in the sun, before being made into linen thread. She parted the long stalks, told the men to lie down, then covered them over with the flax.

They lay very still. No one would have guessed that anyone was there.

Rahab had not been a moment too soon. An urgent knocking told her that the king's men had arrived.

'Bring out the men who have come to your house!' they ordered Rahab.

'They are spies!'

'It is true that some men were here,' Rahab answered, 'but they left at sunset before the city gates were closed for the night. You had better go after them at once if you want to catch them. I've no idea which way they went.'

The puzzled servants hurried off and the city gates clanged behind them. Quickly Rahab returned to the roof, to talk to the two Israelites before they settled to sleep for the night.

77
The Red Cord
JOSHUA 2

The two Israelite spies sat up warily from their bed of flax on Rahab's roof. They had some questions to ask her. Why had a citizen of Jericho risked her life to protect two foreign enemies?

Rahab explained: 'I want to save you because I am certain that your God is going to give you this country. I have heard all about the wonderful things he has done for you on your long journey. I am sure that he will give you victory and I trust him too.

'Now, I want you to promise me solemnly that when you come to fight against our city, you will treat me as kindly as I have treated you. Please keep me and my father and mother and all my family safe!'

The two spies gladly promised in God's name that the army would take good care of Rahab and her family when Israel attacked Jericho. But she must tell no one about their visit.

Rahab took them to the window of her house.

'I will let you down from here by a rope,' she explained, 'and you will be safe outside the walls. Escape to the hills and lie low there for three days until the search is called off. Then you can go safely back to your camp.'

The two spies gratefully agreed. Then they told Rahab what *she* must do when the time came for Israel to attack Jericho.

'Tie this length of red cord in the window,' they said. 'When our soldiers see it they will give protection to this house and everyone in it. So get your whole family here with you.

Quickly and quietly Rahab fastened the rope to the window and the spies slithered down.

Then they took to their heels and were off, to the hills, safe from the king's search-party.

📖 78
Across the River Jordan
JOSHUA 3

When the two spies arrived back at the Israelite camp, they were cheerful and excited.

'We are sure that God is going to give us the whole country, just as he promised,' they told Joshua.

But before the people could get into Canaan, they had to cross the River Jordan. That was easier said than done. The men and the young people might have managed to wade over but there were large flocks of sheep and goats, as well as mothers with babies and toddlers to be helped across. Besides, the river was in full flood. This meant that the low-lying jungle-like land on each side of the banks was deep under water and the river itself was a rushing, swollen torrent.

But Joshua trusted and obeyed God's orders, as if there were no raging river in the way.

'The priests are going to carry the covenant chest and step into the river first,' he told the people. 'Then you must all follow.' The gold-covered chest was the most precious piece of furniture in God's Tent.

As soon as the priests waded into the river, the water began to move more sluggishly. Then it stopped flowing altogether. The priests, with their precious load, walked to the middle of the river, then stood there, while all the huge company of Israel walked safely across. When everyone was over, the priests stepped carefully ashore on the far side, and the waters of the Jordan began to flow again, covering their footprints.

Joshua had told one man from each of the twelve tribes to pick up a stone from the river-bed and carry it to the other side. Then Joshua collected all twelve stones and built them up into a mound.

'When your children ask you in years to come what this heap of stones is for,' he told them all, 'you will be able to tell them the wonderful story of how God brought us all safely over the River Jordan and into the Promised Land.'

The Promised Land

Strange Orders
JOSHUA 5—6

The beautiful city of Jericho stood at the entrance to the Promised Land. The city was well watered with springs. Trees flowered in the streets and tall palm trees gave welcome shade.

Joshua knew that if Canaan was to be theirs, Israel must first capture the city of Jericho. As he was thinking and planning how he would make the attack, he suddenly noticed a stranger standing in front of him. What was more, the man was armed with a sword. Joshua sprang to attention and called out:

'Are you one of our soldiers, or are you on the side of the enemy?'

'Neither,' the man answered. 'I have come to take charge of the Lord's army.'

Then Joshua bowed low, because he knew that the stranger was God's Special Messenger. He had come to remind Joshua that he was not the one in charge. God would tell him how to take Jericho. He had only to do as he was told.

The more Joshua listened to what God had to say, the more he wondered at the strange orders that God gave him. But he was wise enough to set about obeying them.

The first people Joshua sent for were not brave young soldiers, but priests.

'Seven of you,' Joshua said, 'are to take your trumpets and march at the front of the procession. Those who follow will carry the covenant chest from God's Tent. That will be a sign that God himself is with us.'

Next Joshua called for the soldiers.

'You are to march behind the priests,' he explained, 'and follow where they lead.'

Nothing was said about swords and spears, bows or arrows, or any weapons needed to attack a city. When everyone was lined up, Joshua gave his next instructions, just as God had given them to him.

'Start marching around the city walls,' he said. 'You priests, keep on blowing your trumpets as you go, but you soldiers, keep quiet. When you have marched once around the walls, come back to the camp. That will be all for today.'

The Walls Fall Down

JOSHUA 6

The horrified king of Jericho had seen the huge crowd of Israelites that had crossed the Jordan and camped near to his city. He ordered the city gates to be shut and barred. Then he waited.

When he heard the first shrill blast of the priests' trumpets, he thought the attack had begun. But the line of priests with their precious gold chest gleaming in the sun, was followed by a silent column of soldiers. Then, one journey around the walls completed, they were gone.

The next day, Joshua gave exactly the same orders to the priests and soldiers.

For six whole days in a row they marched once around the city, then went quietly back to camp. The citizens of Jericho watched and wondered, feeling more and more afraid.

On the seventh day, Joshua had new orders for the Israelites.

'Today you are to march seven times around the city,' Joshua said. 'When you begin the seventh lap, the priests will blow their trumpets, and the soldiers are to shout out loud, for God will give us the city.'

Once, twice, three times around— four, five, six. Then, at the seventh time, above the blare of the trumpets sounded the mighty cry of the Israelites, shouting as if their lungs would burst.

At that very moment, the walls of Jericho trembled and shook—and crashed to the ground.

With whoops of excitement and triumph the soldiers marched straight up into the city and captured it. Some of the soldiers went at once to find Rahab and to rescue her and her family.

She was saved because she trusted in God. And Jericho was captured because Joshua, too, trusted God and did not rely on his own cleverness or strength.

Stale Bread

JOSHUA 9

God planned to give the whole of Canaan to the people of Israel. Hundreds of years before, he had promised Abraham to give it to his and Sarah's descendants. He also told Abraham why it would be so long before he kept his promise. The many different nations living in Canaan were cruel and wicked. But God would not drive them out while there was any chance that they would change their ways. He had waited a long time. Now he was sending the Israelites to take the land from them. While they were in the desert, God told Moses that Israel was not to make friendly agreements with any of the people in Canaan. He knew that if they joined with them they would soon copy their bad ways.

But the people of Gibeon, who lived only a short distance from Jericho, saw Israel's success and wanted to make a treaty with them. They knew that Joshua would say 'no' if he knew they lived in Canaan, so they thought up a clever trick.

They dressed in ragged clothes and worn-out sandals and put stale bread in their donkeys' packs. Then they journeyed to Israel's camp.

'We want to make a peace agreement with you,' they said. 'Where do you come from?' Joshua asked.

'From far away,' they pretended. 'Just look at our clothes and sandals— quite worn out. Our bread was hot from the oven when we left home, and look at these stale crusts now!'

Joshua and the leaders did not wait to ask God's advice. They made a peace treaty at once with the Gibeonites and promised to help them whenever they were in need.

Three days later, they discovered the trick. Now they would not be free to capture the cities of the Gibeonites or drive them out as God had told them to do. But the Gibeonites were very pleased with their bargain. Now they would have the Israelites to help them against their enemies.

📖 82
'Sun, Stand Still!'
JOSHUA 10

It was not long before the Gibeonites, who had tricked Israel into a treaty of friendship, found themselves in trouble. Five kings, who lived near, surrounded the city of Gibeon with their armies. The men of Gibeon sent an urgent message to Joshua.

'You are our friends. Come quickly to help us!'

Joshua and the people did not want to help Gibeon. But they had made a solemn promise to do so and they must keep it. God was sorry that Israel had made that treaty but he was pleased that they were keeping their word.

'I will help you to win,' God promised Joshua, 'even though there are so many armies at Gibeon.'

God kept his promise. All night long the Israelites marched to reach Gibeon. Then they made a surprise attack on the unprepared armies. The enemy soldiers began to run pell-mell down the hills from Gibeon. A terrible hailstorm made it harder for them to escape and helped the Israelites as they chased after them. But Joshua could see that darkness would come before they had time to finish the battle.

'Sun, stand still over Gibeon,' Joshua sang out. 'Moon, stop over Aijalon.'

What happened next no one can explain, but night did not fall until Joshua and his men had won a complete victory against those five kings and their armies.

83
Sharing Out the Land
JOSHUA 13—22

At long last the people of Israel were able to rest from battles. Campaigns in the north and south had driven back their enemies and now the time had come to settle down to live in Canaan.

God chose Joshua, with a priest and some leaders to help him, to be in charge of sharing out the country among the twelve tribes. All the people of Israel were descended from Israel (Jacob) and his twelve sons, who gave their names to the tribes.

Reuben and Simeon, Levi, Judah, Issachar, Zebulon, Benjamin, Dan, Naphtali, Gad and Asher, each gave his name to a tribe. Joseph's name is missing, but instead there are the names of his two sons, Ephraim and Manasseh. That is because it was Israel's special wish that Joseph, Rachel's much-loved son, should have two tribes named after him.

Levi's name is missing from the list too. His tribe did not come to Joshua asking for a share of the land because God had chosen the Levites for a special purpose. They were to be God's priests.

If they had been given land to farm they would not have had time to serve God and teach the people about him. So God said that everyone was to give a share of his own supplies to the Levites, so that they had enough to live on.

Some parts of Canaan are rich and fertile; others are stony and poor. Joshua had a hard task sharing out the land fairly, so that all the tribes would be satisfied.

When it had all been divided out, every tribe took their share of the country as a special gift from God. They would treasure the land and keep it in their family for ever, if they could.

In the Time of the Judges

84
Trouble

JUDGES 1—2

For as long as he lived, Joshua reminded the Israelites to keep God's law and taught them the right things to do.

Even after he died the people went on obeying God. There were many still alive who reminded them about God's greatness and kindness when he brought them across the River Jordan and gave them victory against their enemies. But now, for the first time, the Israelites had no leader. Everyone did as he liked.

Children grew up who did not remember Joshua. They wanted to be friends with the people of Canaan and marry into their families. Then they began to copy their baal worship. The religion of the baals was very cruel. Children and even tiny babies were sometimes thrown on the fire as a sacrifice because the Canaanites thought that the baals would be pleased and give them good crops. God was sad and angry that his people should copy such horrible customs when they worshipped him.

The Israelites had not properly carried out God's plan to drive out the other people living in their land. Now the Canaanites grew stronger than Israel and fought against them. They often made the Israelites pay them heavy taxes.

Whenever the Israelites were in trouble they remembered God again and called out to him for help. And because he loved them God heard their prayers and sent them leaders who set them free from their enemies. These leaders advised and guided the people wisely too. They were called judges.

Ehud the Left-handed

JUDGES 3

King Eglon of Moab was a very fat man. He feasted too well on the grain and fruit and wine that arrived at his palace as taxes from those he had conquered. For eighteen long years Israel suffered under Eglon's cruel power, and the people were very poor and unhappy.

In their despair they asked God to help them. God chose Ehud to be their leader. Ehud belonged to the tribe of Benjamin, and like many in the family, he was left-handed.

The next time that Israel had to take taxes to King Eglon, Ehud himself set off for Moab. He was followed by a long line of servants, obediently laden with the produce they had collected to pay the king.

Ehud was determined to help Israel break free from the power of the Moabites. If he could find a way to kill King Eglon, the army of Moab would be without a leader and Israel might win the victory.

So Ehud took with him his own special dagger with its double-edged blade. Because he was left-handed he hid it on the right side of his flowing robes. Any suspicious Moabite would search only on the left side, where most people kept their weapon, ready to draw.

Ehud and his servants presented their taxes to the king, then left for the journey home. But when they had gone part-way, Ehud doubled back to the palace on his own.

'Your majesty, I have a secret message for you!' he announced.

Eglon ordered all the servants out and took Ehud to his summer room on the palace roof, where breezes cooled the hot air.

Eglon waited, rich and important, for Ehud's message. Ehud swiftly drew out his dagger with his left hand and killed the king.

Quickly and noiselessly he left the room, locking the richly-carved doors behind him. Then he sped back to the hills to call Israel's fighting men to battle.

At King Eglon's palace his servants hesitated outside the barred doors of his room. At last they found courage to burst in on their royal master—and found him dead.

By now Ehud was ready and waiting for the Moabite army. He won a great victory and set the people of Israel free once more.

📖 86
Deborah and Barak
JUDGES 4—5

After the death of left-handed Ehud the Israelites once again forgot about God and his laws.

Trouble soon came from King Jabin in the north of the country. His army was equipped with nine hundred iron chariots and led by General Sisera. Israel's lightly armed soldiers stood no chance against these swift, strong chariots and for twenty years King Jabin treated Israel with great cruelty and violence.

The leader of Israel at this time was a woman called Deborah. She used to sit under one particular palm-tree, so that everyone knew where to come for help or advice.

One day Deborah sent for a man called Barak.

'Barak,' she began, 'God has said that you are to get an army together to fight against Sisera. In spite of his chariots, God will help you win.'

Barak was terrified at the thought of facing Sisera's army. 'I'm not going unless you go with me,' he answered.

'Very well,' Deborah agreed, 'but women will win this battle, not men.'

Barak invited the Israelite tribes living near to send volunteers to fight. Then he lined up his men on the top of a hill where Sisera's chariots would find it difficult to move easily. Sisera, with all his chariots, waited in the valley below.

Then Deborah gave the command to Barak:

'March forward! Today God will give you a victory against Sisera!'

With great courage the Israelite soldiers streamed down the hill to what seemed certain death at the hands of Sisera's waiting men.

At that moment the rain began to fall. Barak and his men moved easily through the heavy downpour but Sisera's heavy chariots soon began to skid and stick in the low valley land now churned to mud.

Instead of chasing and overtaking the Israelites, Sisera's men were trapped in their chariots at the mercy of the faster-moving Israelite soldiers. Barak won a mighty triumph that day, thanks to Deborah's help. Another woman was going to make his victory against Sisera complete.

Hammer and Tent Peg

JUDGES 4

Before the final battle, Sisera, commander of Jabin's army, slipped quietly down from his chariot and escaped, unnoticed, on foot. He may have hoped to get more men together to launch a second attack on Israel.

He was on his way to his home city of Hazor when he came upon the tent of Jael. Jael's husband belonged to a wandering tribe that was friendly to King Jabin.

Jael saw Sisera coming, utterly exhausted from the battle. 'Come in,' she invited. 'Don't be afraid.' Sisera was thankful to be drawn inside the tent and hidden behind the curtain. He was hot and mud-stained, thirsty, and so tired that he could scarcely stand.

'Please give me something to drink,' he begged.

Jael found some fresh goat's milk and gave it to him.

'Stand at the door of the tent and keep watch,' Sisera told her. 'If anyone comes asking for me, say that no one is here!'

Jael gently agreed and soothingly settled Sisera to rest behind the curtain of her tent. In a few moments she heard the sound of steady, deep breathing. Worn out by the trouble and toil of battle, Sisera had fallen into a deep sleep.

Then Jael moved swiftly. The gentle smile on her face changed to a look of grim determination. *She* was no friend of cruel King Jabin!

Nearby lay the hammer that she used for driving in the tent-pegs when they pitched their tents. Quickly she searched for a sharp wooden peg, then silently glided across to the sleeping soldier.

She lifted the hammer and with one hard blow drove the tent peg through Sisera's forehead. He died at once.

It was some hours later that she saw Barak coming in search of his enemy. She called him into her tent.

'Here is the man you are looking for,' she said. Barak's task was done. God's people were safe at last.

The Story of Gideon

The Unwilling Hero

JUDGES 6

The people of Israel soon forgot God and the way he had helped them in trouble. But before long they were frightened out of their wits by a new kind of foe. These enemies, the Midianites, did not attack the people—they plundered the land.

They would wait until harvest was ready, then swoop down on the sountryside and carry off grain and ripe grapes and olives. They stole the donkeys and the sheep and cattle too. The Midianites were joined by fierce desert tribes, riding on swift camels.

The Israelites cowered in caves and hiding-places in the hills until the terrible raids were over. When they crept out, the fields were stripped bare and there was no food to take them through the winter months ahead.

Next harvest-time, they knew, the same thing would happen all over again.

After seven years the Israelites were in despair. When they could do nothing else, they called to God to help them.

Young Gideon, of the tribe of Manasseh, was just as afraid of the Midianite raiders as everyone else in Israel. But he had thought of a way to keep some of the harvest.

He hid in a hollowed-out rock, where grapes were usually pressed. There, well out of sight, he beat out the little bit of wheat they had managed to reap.

Suddenly, as he looked up from his work, he saw a stranger.

'God is with you, brave and mighty man,' his Visitor said. Then, to Gideon's amazement, he went on:

'I am sending you, with all your strength, to rescue Israel from the Midianites.'

Gideon was horrified. *He* was no hero!

'How can *I* rescue Israel?' he objected.

'With my help,' the Stranger answered. 'I will be with you and you will crush the enemy hordes as easily as if they were just one man.'

Gideon Makes Sure

JUDGES 6

Before his Visitor could tell him any more, Gideon begged:

'Please wait while I fetch you some food.' He wanted proof that the Stranger's message really was from God.

'I will stay until you come back,' the Stranger promised.

Gideon hurried home—to return carefully carrying a basket of meat and freshly-baked bread, and a jug of broth.

His Visitor said, 'Put the meat and bread on this rock, then pour the broth over them.

Gideon did as he was told. The Stranger put out his staff and touched the food. At once a flame flared from the rock and burned up the food.

Now Gideon knew for certain that this was God's Special Messenger, bringing him God's words. Then the Visitor disappeared.

Before Gideon was willing to become Israel's leader he wanted to be even more certain that God had called him.

'If you have chosen me to rescue Israel, please give me a sign,' he prayed to God. 'Tonight I will put out a fleece of wool in the place where we thresh wheat. If the wool is wet with dew tomorrow morning, but the ground is dry, I shall know that you have called me.'

Next morning, Gideon's fleece was so wet that he wrung out a whole bowlful of dew from it. Yet the ground on which it lay was dry. Still Gideon was not sure. Perhaps it had been chance.

'Please don't be angry, God,' he prayed. 'Show me once more that you

will use me to lead Israel. This time, please let the ground around my fleece be wet and the wool dry.'

God was not angry. He understood Gideon's worries and fears.

Next morning, sure enough, the fleece was fluffy and dry but the ground was drenched with dew. Now Gideon was certain that God was calling him to set Israel free from the Midianites.

Baal and cutting down the sacred trees, dedicated to the goddess, that grow beside it. Then build a good, strong altar to me in its place.'

Gideon made up his mind to obey God. He wanted to bring the Israelites back to the true worship of God, as well as rescuing them from their enemies. But he was afraid. He knew that the people of the town would be very angry. They would be sure that something terrible would happen to them if the baal altar was destroyed. They believed that the baals were strong and powerful in the land.

So Gideon decided to do what God had told him at night time, when no one would see. He took ten of his servants to help him and in the darkness they worked as quickly and quietly as they could. First they smashed the altar to Baal and chopped down the trees around it. Then they built a firm strong altar to God on the same spot. Before dawn broke, they crept silently home.

But a secret known to ten men is not a secret for very long. Soon everyone knew what had happened and who was to blame. That very morning the townsfolk came knocking at Joash's door.

'Bring out your son, Gideon!' they shouted. 'We're going to kill him for what he has done!'

Whatever Joash may have thought before, he spoke up bravely now for Gideon and for God.

'Are you taking Baal's side?' he asked, 'if he's really a god he can stand up for himself! He's the one whose altar has been smashed. Let him punish my son—if he can!'

Gideon's courage and trust in God were catching! Soon he would show all the people of Israel what God could do.

90
Secret Mission
JUDGES 6

Gideon was surprised at the first thing God told him to do. It had nothing to do with raising an army to fight against Midian—it was something even more important.

The people who lived in Gideon's town had copied the Canaanites in their worship of the baals. Gideon's own father, who was called Joash, had an altar for Baal built on his own land.

'Gideon,' God said, 'you must begin by pulling down that altar to

Gideon Chooses his Army

JUDGES 7

Gideon, and the soldiers who had volunteered to fight in his army, set up camp beside a cool, mountain spring. In the valley a few miles north sprawled the huge camp of the Midianites. Gideon's army seemed far too small to venture against such a vast army.

But God said, 'Your army is too big, Gideon. I am going to teach all Israel that *I* am giving them victory. The battle will not be won by numbers. Tell any soldiers who are frightened to go home now.'

Gideon called the men together and said, 'If any of you feel scared of the battle, go now. No one will blame you.'

Gideon knew that frightened soldiers are a hindrance, not a help, in war.

There was a moment's silence, then one man after another slipped quietly away.

When Gideon counted the men who were left, he found that his army had shrunk to one-third of its size. For every man who stayed, two had gone home.

'The army is still too big, Gideon,' God said. 'Tell the men to go for a drink from the spring, and watch them.'

The men gladly obeyed Gideon's order and made their way to the clear, mountain spring. They had no cups or jugs and, as Gideon watched, he saw that they drank in two different ways. Most of them got down on hands and knees and put their faces close to the water to lap it up. The rest knelt, cupped their hands together and scooped up the water.

'Pick out the men who scooped up the water,' God told Gideon, 'and send the rest home.'

Gideon did exactly as God said. When he counted the little band of soldiers left to him there were only three hundred men.

'With these three hundred I will give you victory against the Midianites,' God promised Gideon.

92
A Whisper in the Night
JUDGES 7

That night God said to Gideon, 'Now is the time to attack the Midianite camp. I promise to give you victory.'

Gideon had trusted and obeyed God up to now, but his heart sank at the thought of attacking the vast enemy camp with so few men.

'If you feel afraid, Gideon,' God went on, you can go down with your servant, Purah, and listen to what the Midianites are saying. What you hear will give you all the courage you need.'

Gideon set off stealthily towards the enemy camp, scrambling down into the valley with his trusted servant at his side. Now that they were close, the enemy looked even more frightening than at a distance. Black tents, full of Midianite soldiers and their allies, lay dense on the ground. On the outskirts of the camp, guards were patrolling and, all around, the dreaded camels lay tethered.

Gideon and Purah crept close to where two sentries were talking.

'I've had a strange dream,' one said. 'I dreamed that a little barley loaf came rolling down the hill, bouncing into our camp. When it hit one of our tents, the tent fell flat.'

'I know what that dream means,' his friend replied. 'That little loaf stands for Gideon, the leader of Israel's army. He is going to attack us—and *win*!'

Gideon did not wait to hear more. He knelt down and thanked God for giving him such comfort and encouragement. He need not be afraid of the Midianites. *They* were afraid of him!

Then, with Purah following, he went as fast as he could back to his own camp and roused his men from sleep.

'Get up!' he shouted, 'this very night God is going to give us victory!'

Trumpets and Lamps

JUDGES 7

When the three hundred men were wide awake and lined up for orders, Gideon split them into three groups of a hundred each. Then he handed out to each man an earthenware jar, a torch of oiled wood and a trumpet made of ram's horn. There were enough to go around because the soldiers who had gone home had left their equipment behind. Then they all listened carefully as Gideon explained to them what they were to do. They trusted their leader completely.

'Put your lighted torch inside your jar,' he said. The jar would hide the tell-tale light and also protect the flame from being blown out.

'When we reach the Midianite camp,' Gideon went on, 'spread around the outside of the camp. Watch what I and my group do and copy us. When we blow our trumpets, you do the same. Then let out a mighty shout.'

Gideon's men arrived at the camp just at the time when the guard was being changed. Most of the Midianites were sound asleep and the rest were busy coming on or off duty. No one heard or saw the three hundred arrive.

Then, as Gideon gave the signal, his hundred men blew a rousing blast on their trumpets. At once, the other two groups blew theirs, all around the camp.

'A sword for the Lord and for Gideon!' they shouted.

At that very moment, Gideon and his men shattered their earthenware jars and the full light of their torches streamed out in the darkness. Immediately the rest of his men did the same. There was the sound of smashing pots, then a blaze of light ringed the whole camp.

The Midianites woke up, terrified. When they heard the blast of the trumpets and the triumphant war cries and saw the flare of torches all around them, they thought an army of thousands had come against them. The startled camels took fright and began to stampede.

Half-awake, the Midianites began to hit out at anyone within reach, attacking their own friends and allies None of Gideon's men needed to strike a blow. While they stood firm all around the camp, the Midianites ran shouting from the camp, as fast as their legs would carry them.

God had given a mighty victory to Gideon and his three hundred men.

The Story of Jephthah

📖 94
Jephthah's Promise
JUDGES 11

Before long, the people of Israel forgot about God and began once again to worship the baals of the land, just as they had before Gideon became their judge. Once more they were attacked and ill-treated by their Canaanite neighbours, this time by the Ammonites.

The city of Gilead had an especially bad time. How the people longed for a leader who would rescue them from the enemy!

Their thoughts turned to Jephthah. He was a brave soldier who had grown up in Gilead, one of a large family, with many half-brothers. When he was a man, his brothers had turned him out.

'Your mother was not married to our father,' they reminded him unkindly, 'so you are not going to share in the family fortune.'

Jephthah left home and lived a wild and wandering life. Now he was chief of a band of young, fighting men.

The people of Gilead sent Jephthah a message.

'Come back, Jephthah,' they said. 'We want you to lead us in battle against the Ammonites.'

'You hated me so much that you turned me out,' Jephthah replied. 'Why do you expect me to come hurrying back, now that you are in trouble? If I do come, I shall want to return as leader in Gilead once the fighting is over.'

The people of Gilead gladly agreed to his terms.

At first Jephthah tried to persuade the Ammonites to make peace, but when he saw that they were set on war, he gathered his army together. Then he did something very foolish and wrong. To try to persuade God to be on his side, he made a rash promise.

'If you give me victory, God,' he vowed, 'I will give you as a sacrifice whatever I first see when I return to my home.'

Jephthah led Israel's army against the Ammonites and won a great victory. Tired but triumphant, he began the journey home.

As he drew near to the house he heard the sound of sweet music. His only, much-loved daughter was coming out to meet him, playing her tambourine and dancing for joy.

Jephthah's happiness turned to horror and dismay as he looked at his only child. 'Why did it have to be *you*?' he sobbed. 'How can I keep my vow?'

Jephthah would not break his promise, though he was heartbroken and his daughter full of grief. But God must have been saddest of all. He did not need Jephthath's bribe. He had shown Abraham that he did not want human sacrifice. He only wanted the trust and loving obedience of his people.

95
'Say Shibboleth!'
JUDGES 12

Attack from the Ammonites was over, but soon Jephthah was in trouble with some of his fellow Israelites, members of the tribe of Ephraim.

'Why didn't you let us join your army?' they complained, now that the war was safely over.

'For eighteen long years the Ammonites waged war on Israel,' Jephthah answered. 'You had plenty of chance to fight them.'

'We're going to burn down your house over your head,' the angry Ephraimites retorted.

Hastily Jephthah recalled his army as the Ephraimites crossed the River Jordan to fight him. Jephthah and his men won the battle and the defeated Ephraimites were soon running for their lives towards the river, to cross back to safety.

There was only one ford over the river, so Jephthah set a guard to stop every man who tried to cross. But how were they to tell the difference between the enemy soldiers and their own side? In this sad and unnecessary fight all looked alike, for they were all Israelites.

Someone thought of a way.

Everyone knew that the Ephraimites could not make the sound 'sh'. Instead they would say 's'. So whenever a soldier arrived at the ford the guards would hold him and demand, 'Say "shibboleth".' (The word means 'ear of grain' but no one was concerned about the meaning. They were waiting to see how the word was pronounced.)

If the frightened, panting soldier said '*S*ibboleth' the guards recognized him for an enemy. If he said '*Sh*ibboleth' they gave him a friendly nod and let him pass.

Samson the Strong

A Special Baby
JUDGES 13

After Jephthah's time a powerful new enemy attacked Israel. They were the Philistines, who lived along the sea coast. They were to cause trouble to the Israelites for many years to come.

Manoah and his wife, like many other people in Israel, longed for God to send another great leader to help them. But even more, Manoah and his wife longed for a child of their own. Husbands and wives in those days wanted many sons and daughters, and Manoah had none.

One day, God's Special Messenger appeared to Manoah's wife.

'For many years you have wanted a son,' he said. 'Soon you will have one. Your child will be very special. God is going to make him strong, so that he can begin to rescue Israel from the Philistines. You must bring him up very carefully. From the day he is born he is to be dedicated to God, so you must *never* cut his hair.'

Manoah's wife understood what was meant by this strange instruction. When anyone in Israel wished to give themselves in a special way to serve God they took a Nazirite vow. 'Nazirite' means set apart. A Nazirite showed that he was set apart for God by growing his hair for all to see. When the time of the vow was over, the hair was cut off. God's Messenger told Manoah's wife that her child's hair was *never* to be cut. That meant that he was to be set apart to serve God for the whole of his life.

Manoah and his wife were a little afraid, but very excited too, at the wonderful news. They began to make plans for the new baby's arrival. They would be very careful to obey all the instructions that God had given to them.

A Wedding is Arranged

JUDGES 14

When their little son was born, Manoah and his wife gazed at him with love and awe. They called him Samson. There had never been such a wonderful child, they thought. And in one way they were right.

They soon discovered that Samson was amazingly strong. When he played with other children he beat them at every game of strength. Already his hair was down to his shoulders, for his parents never cut it, as God had instructed.

Like most children, Samson wanted his own way, and he was usually strong enough to see that he got it. Nor did his quiet, elderly parents often say 'No!'

As he grew up, Samson still expected to have everything he wanted. One day he saw a pretty girl and decided to marry her. Manoah was horrified, for the girl was a Philistine.

'Don't marry a Philistine!' he pleaded. But Samson had made up his mind.

Manoah and his wife set off with Samson to visit the girl's father in Timnah, the town where they lived. They must ask for the daughter's hand in marriage.

On the journey, Samson heard a sound of roaring nearby. He quietly went to investigate the noise. Suddenly he found himself face to face with a strong, young lion. Instead of taking to his heels, Samson boldly grabbed the lion and with a sudden burst of strength, killed it with his bare hands. Then, without a word to his parents about what he had done, he rejoined them on the path to Timnah.

The marriage was arranged and the family party returned home.

It was some time later, when he was going to Timnah for his wedding, that Samson remembered how he had killed the lion. He turned off the road to have a look at the spot where it had happened. There lay the carcase of the lion, by now a skeleton picked bare and whitened by the sun.

Looking closer, Samson saw, to his surprise, that a swarm of wild bees had made their nest inside the skeleton. Cautiously he put in his hand and helped himself to some of the delicious, sweet honey. Then, feeling refreshed, he went on his journey.

98
Answer my Riddle
JUDGES 14

When Samson married his Philistine bride the wedding celebrations lasted for a whole week. On the first day of feasting Samson invited the young Philistine men to guess a riddle. He promised them rich rewards if they could give him the right answer by the end of the week. He thought that his bet was a safe one.

This was the riddle:

Out of the eater came something to eat;

Out of the strong came something sweet.

No one but Samson himself knew about the lion and the bees. They could not make head or tail of it.

After three days of puzzling and racking their brains they came to Samson's bride and said:

'You must persuade your husband to tell you the answer to his riddle. We are not going to be beaten by an Israelite. If you don't get the answer for us we shall burn down your house—with you in it!'

Samson's new wife set about coaxing her husband to tell her the answer to the riddle. 'How could you tell my friends a riddle and not let me into the secret?' she complained.

'I've not even told my parents,' Samson objected, 'so why should I tell you?'

Each day she asked and each day Samson said 'No!'

On the last day of the feast she said, 'You can't *really* love me, Samson, or you *would* tell me,' and she began to cry.

Vexed and worn down by her wheedling, Samson gave in. He told her the answer to his riddle. Quickly she ran to tell the impatient Philistines.

That night the young men came smiling to Samson and said, 'What is sweeter than honey, and what is stronger than a lion?'

Samson was furious. He knew very well that they had won the contest only because his wife had told them about the dead lion and the swarm of honey bees. He stormed off, planning revenge.

For many years Samson carried out attacks against the Philistines, single-handed. He never raised or led an army. For many years, too, the Philistines tried in vain to capture the Israelite champion who was too strong to be held by ropes or chains.

99
Samson and Delilah
JUDGES 16

Some years later, Samson fell in love with another woman, called Delilah. The Philistines heard of this and their leaders came secretly to visit her.

'Find out the secret of Samson's great strength,' they told her, 'and we will each reward you with more than a thousand pieces of silver.'

Delilah was very beautiful and she was also very greedy. She wanted the silver and she did not mind if she betrayed Samson to his enemies.

'Tell me, she begged Samson, next time he came to see her, 'what makes you so strong? If anyone wanted to make you weak and helpless, how could he do it?'

'Tie me up with seven new bowstrings and I'd be no stronger than anyone else,' he lied.

Delilah put his words to the test. Unknown to Samson, she hid some Philistines in the next room. Then, as if in play, she tied him up with seven new bowstrings.

Suddenly she shouted, 'The Philistines are coming, Samson!' The Philistines burst in—and with one shrug Samson snapped the bowstrings and turned to face his enemies.

Samson had lied to her the first time, but Delilah did not give up. Each time she saw him she pleaded with Samson to tell her what made him strong.

'Tie me up with brand-new ropes and I will be weak,' he told her. But when Delilah did so she found that he could easily break free.

'You're teasing me,' Delilah complained. 'Tell me truly how you can be made as weak as other men.'

'Weave the locks of my hair into a loom and fasten it with a peg,' he said. When Samson fell asleep, Delilah gently took each lock of his hair and fastened it to her weaving-loom.

Then she shouted, 'The Philistines are coming!'

With a single jerk Samson pulled his hair free. Once more he had kept from Delilah the true reason for his great strength.

100
Defeat of the Champion
JUDGES 16

their city of Gaza. There they blinded him, put him in heavy chains and set him to grind grain in the prison.

Day after day Delilah went on pleading with Samson to tell her the secret of his strength. She had set her heart on the rich reward that the Philistine leaders had promised.

In the end, Samson could stand her nagging no longer.

'All right,' he said, 'I'll tell you all about it.' Delilah listened intently. This time she felt certain he was telling her the truth.

'My hair has never been cut,' Samson explained. 'From the day of my birth I have been especially set apart for God. My long hair is the sign of my Nazirite vow. If my hair should be cut, my vow to God would be broken and the great strength that God has given me would be lost. I would be no stronger than any ordinary man.'

Delilah sent at once for the doubting Philistine rulers. 'This time I promise that I will hand him over to you, weak and helpless,' she said.

The rulers arrived, bringing their silver, and Delilah hid them while she talked pleasantly to Samson.

Then, gently, she lulled him to sleep, his head on her lap. With a glance, she signalled to a Philistine to come and cut off Samson's hair.

She looked at the shorn head, then called out, 'Get up, Samson! The Philistines are here!'

Samson stretched, then stood up, ready to brace himself to fight off his attackers. He did not know that God was no longer with him to make him strong. He had broken his vow and his strength had gone.

The jubilant Philistines grabbed him, tied him up and took him off to

Strong in Death

JUDGES 16

The Philistines were full of glee. They had caught their Israelite enemy, Samson, and made him a helpless prisoner. Never again, they thought, would he cause them trouble. They would have a huge feast to celebrate and give thanks to their god, Dagon.

When the day came, hundreds packed the great pillared hall and crowded onto the flat roof above. They offered a sacrifice to Dagon, and sang:

'Our God has given us victory over our enemy Samson.'

All this time Samson crouched, wretched and despairing, in his filthy prison. He could not see, but he could remember. He remembered all that his mother had told him about his special birth and how God had chosen him to be Israel's champion. He remembered his long hair, the sign of his vow to serve God.

He knew that his great strength had been God's gift to him, to help him rescue Israel from the Philistines. He had been strong in fighting them but weak in wanting his own way and giving in to the women who had tempted and tricked him.

But now his hair was growing again, and Samson's resolve was growing too. He longed to be strong against the Philistines just once more.

The Philistines feasted and danced and sang. When the party was at its height one of the leaders said, 'Fetch Samson! Let him entertain us!'

A lad was sent to lead blind Samson to the hall. As soon as they saw him the Philistines burst out singing their victory hymn. They teased and made

fun of Samson, knowing that he could
not see to get out of their way, or hit
back.

Then Samson bent towards the boy
who had led him in.

'Guide my hands to touch the two
pillars in the middle of the hall,' he
said, 'so that I can lean on them.' The
boy took Samson's hands and placed
them on the pillars. For a moment
Samson stood quietly, feeling the
smooth surface.

'O God,' he prayed, 'please give me
back my strength, just this once more,
so that I can deal one last blow to my
enemies.'

Then, mustering all his strength,
Samson pushed against the two huge
columns.

'Let me die with the Philistines!' he
shouted, above the noise of the feast.

The mighty pillars cracked, slipped
from their capitals and fell crashing to
the ground. Then the roof they had
supported caved in and the whole
magnificent building collapsed in
ruins. The proud Philistines and the
blinded hero of Israel died together.

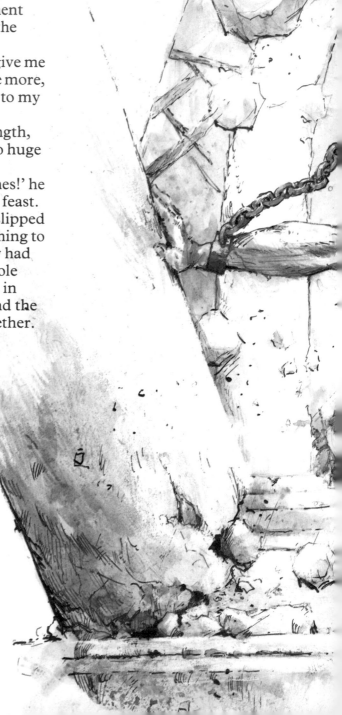

The Story of Ruth

102
Unhappy Times

RUTH 1

In the time when Israel was ruled by the Judges, a man called Elimelech lived in Bethlehem with his wife, Naomi, and their two sons. One year the harvest was so poor that Elimelech could not get enough food for his family. So they decided to leave Israel until the famine was over and go to live in the nearby country of Moab.

While they were there, Elimelech died. By this time the two boys were old enough to look after Naomi and, when they married Moabite girls, they brought them home too.

But not many years later both sons died. Poor Naomi was left in a foreign land, without husband or family. But her daughters-in-law, Orpah and Ruth, were good, kind girls and comforted Naomi as much as they could.

Soon Naomi felt homesick for Bethlehem. She heard that food was plentiful there once again, so she packed up all her belongings into bundles and the three of them set off for Bethlehem.

When they came near to the border with Israel, Naomi stopped.

'You have been very good to me,' she said to Orpah and Ruth, 'but now it's time for you to go back to your own mothers.'

Both girls hugged and kissed Naomi.

'We'll come with you!' they exclaimed.

'No!' Naomi insisted 'I can do nothing to help you or to make you happy, so go back now.'

Orpah kissed Naomi again, then reluctantly started back the way they had come. She went slowly, turning often to wave, for she loved her mother-in-law.

'Now Ruth,' Naomi said, 'you must do the same as Orpah.'

'Please let me come with you!' Ruth begged. 'I want to stay with you wherever you go. I will make your people my own, and take your God for my God. Nothing will make me part from you—except death.'

When Naomi saw that Ruth had set her heart on going with her, she said no more. She was happy and comforted to have Ruth's love and companionship just when she needed it most.

122

103
Ruth Finds Work

RUTH 2

The townswomen of Bethlehem welcomed Naomi back, but they were sorry to see her so poor and unhappy.

In those days women could not earn a living and Naomi had no husband or sons to provide for her. But God had given the Israelites special laws, so that they would help all those in need. Farmers must allow poor and hungry people to come into their harvest fields and pick up any stray stalks of grain that the reapers had dropped or overlooked.

When Naomi and Ruth arrived in Bethlehem they were harvesting the barley.

'Let me go and glean barley,' Ruth suggested. 'If I work hard I can get enough for us both to eat.'

Ruth set out early and chose one field where the reapers were working

busily. She kept close to them all morning, picking up every stray grain stalk she could see.

At midday, Boaz, who owned the land, came to see how the harvest was going.

'Who is that girl gleaning over there?' he asked, pointing to Ruth.

'She is the foreign girl from Moab,' one of his men told him, 'Naomi's daughter-in-law.'

Boaz had heard about Ruth, for news travels fast in a small town. He went across to her.

'Keep near my reapers for the rest of the harvest,' he said. 'I will see that they leave you in peace. When you are thirsty, drink from the water that my men have drawn. Now come and have dinner.'

'Why are you so kind to me?' Ruth asked in surprise.

'I have heard about *your* kindness to Naomi,' Boaz explained. 'May the God whom you have learned to trust keep you safe in his care.'

Without a word to Ruth, Boaz told his reapers to drop some barley stalks on purpose, so that Ruth would have extra to pick up and take home.

Naomi was delighted at Ruth's success.

'However did you get so much?' she asked.

'I went to a field belonging to a man called Boaz,' Ruth told her. 'He was very kind to me.'

'How good God is!' Naomi exclaimed. 'He guided you there. Boaz is a relative of our family. You'll be safe with him.'

104
Happy Endings
RUTH 3—4

While Ruth went gleaning each day, Naomi stayed at home. She thought hard. The harvest would soon be over. How would they manage then?

Soon Naomi had thought of a plan, and one day she said to Ruth:

'The harvest is all gathered in and tonight Boaz will be having his harvest supper. Once it is over and he is all alone, you are to go to him. Ask him to protect and care for us because we are members of his family.'

Although Ruth felt a bit shy, she did exactly as Naomi told her. She knew that in Israel God's law said that the men in the family were to care for widows.

Boaz was delighted that Ruth had chosen to come to *him* for help. He listened carefully to what she had to say, then sent her home with a generous present of grain for Naomi.

Naomi was satisfied.

'He is a good man,' she said. 'He won't rest now until he has made plans to help us.'

Boaz wanted very much to marry Ruth, but there was another, even closer, relative of Elimelech living in Bethlehem. He must be given first chance to help the two widows.

Boaz waited by the town gate until this man came by, then asked if he wanted to look after Naomi and Ruth. It would mean buying back land that had once belonged to Elimelech and marrying Ruth. But the man said 'No.'

Boaz gladly married Ruth himself and took her back to his own farmhouse.

Naomi was as excited as Ruth and Boaz when their first baby was born.

All the women in Bethlehem, who had come to comfort Naomi when she first arrived back, came to see the new little grandson. They told Naomi how happy they were that God had brought her joy and prosperity through Ruth, her loyal and loving daughter-in-law.

The Story of Samuel

A Baby for Hannah
1 SAMUEL 1

When the people of Israel settled in Canaan, the gold covenant chest, the most precious object in God's Tent, was placed in the care of priests at a place called Shiloh. The people used to visit Shiloh to bring presents to God and celebrate together.

Elkanah was an Israelite who brought his family to Shiloh every year. He had two wives, Peninnah, who had children, and Hannah, who had none. Hannah longed desperately for a child of her own.

'Cheer up, Hannah!' Elkanah would say. 'I love you—doesn't that help?'

But Hannah could not cheer up when Peninnah kept teasing and taunting her and showing off her own boys and girls.

Hannah dreaded the annual expedition to Shiloh. These were happy, family times and Peninnah took care to see that Hannah felt miserable and left out.

One year Hannah could bear it no longer. When they sat down for the special family meal, she could only pick at the food. She slipped away from the table and went to the door of the shrine, where the covenant chest was kept. She began to pray, as the tears rolled down her cheeks.

'Please don't forget me, God,' she begged. 'I am so unhappy. I want a child so badly. If you will give me one, I promise that I will give him back to serve you all his life long.'

Someone was watching Hannah. Eli, the old priest, was sitting quietly at the door, wondering whatever was wrong with this woman. Perhaps she had drunk too much wine at the feast. He went to talk to her.

'I am not drunk,' Hannah told Eli, 'only very sad and upset. I have asked God to help me.'

'Then go in peace,' Eli said, 'and may God answer your prayer.'

Hannah went back to Elkanah and Peninnah feeling peaceful and almost happy. She even felt hungry again. All the way home her heart seemed lighter. She had told God her trouble. Now she would wait for his answer.

Small Boy Leaves Home

1 SAMUEL 2

How excited Hannah was when she found that she was going to have a baby! She called her little boy Samuel, which means 'asked of God'. Hannah loved him dearly but she had not forgotten her promise to God.

When the time came for the family visit to Shiloh, she told Elkanah:

'I shall not come this year. When

Samuel is old enough to feed and dress himself, we will go together and take him to Eli. He must stay at the shrine and learn to serve God, as I promised he would.'

When the day came for his parents to take him to Shiloh, Samuel clung tightly to his mother's hand. Hannah's eyes pricked with tears as she loosened the grip of the warm little hand and put it into Eli's large, rough one.

'I promised him to God,' she told Eli, 'please take him and look after him.'

Before they left Shiloh, Hannah prayed again, pouring out praise and thanks to God for giving her Samuel. Then they quickly left for home.

Hannah counted the months to the next visit to Shiloh, when she would see Samuel again. Would he remember her? Had he grown very much?

Once a year Hannah saw Samuel and on every visit she took him a lovely new coat. She always remembered to allow for how much he would have grown since last year.

Eli grew very fond of his little helper and taught him how to be useful at the shrine, as well as teaching him God's law.

'You have been good to give Samuel to God and to me,' he would say to Elkanah and Hannah. 'May God bless you by giving you more children.'

Eli's prayer was answered. In time, Hannah had three more sons and two daughters. She was very busy now, but she did not forget Samuel, the child she had asked God to give her.

'I'm Listening, Lord'

1 SAMUEL 3

The years passed and as Eli grew older his eyes grew weaker. At night he would sleep in his own room, leaving Samuel on guard in the shrine near the gold covenant chest. A light burned all night in the sanctuary and the boy was glad of it.

One night, Samuel woke up at the sound of his own name:

'Samuel!'

He jumped up and hurried to Eli's room.

'Yes, Eli,' he said. 'What can I get for you?'

'I did not call you, my son,' Eli replied. 'Go back to bed.'

Samuel tiptoed back but before he had time to snuggle down he heard the voice again.

'Samuel!'

He was out of bed in a flash and into Eli's room again. But Eli knew nothing of it and ordered him back to bed.

'Samuel!'

A third time the call came. Samuel knew he wasn't dreaming. Once more he went to Eli. This time Eli did not send him away. He had guessed, at last, what must be happening.

'Samuel,' he said, 'I believe it is God calling you. Go back to bed. If the voice calls again, say, "Speak, Lord, your servant is listening".'

Saying the words over to himself, Samuel went back to bed, every muscle strained to listen. Again the voice came clearly:

'Samuel!'

'I'm listening, Lord,' Samuel answered, 'please speak to me.'

When Samuel heard what God had to say, he was sad and shocked. Eli's two sons were not good like their father. They disobeyed God's laws and grabbed for themselves the presents that people brought for God. God told Samuel that he was not going to let Eli's family be his priests any longer.

Early next day Eli came to find Samuel.

'What did God say to you?' he asked.

Samuel went very red and looked down at the ground. He did not want to have to tell Eli the sad news.

'Tell me everything,' Eli insisted.

When Samuel had told him what God had to say about his family, Eli bent his head and nodded quietly.

'God knows what is right and best,' he whispered.

As Samuel grew up, God often spoke to him. God gave him messages to give to all the people of Israel. Everyone began to pay attention to what Samuel had to say.

Disaster

1 SAMUEL 4

Samson's old enemies, the Philistines, grew strong again. They fought against Israel and beat them. The Israelites were in despair until their leaders had an idea.

'Let's carry God's covenant chest into the next battle,' they suggested. 'If we do that, God will have to help us.' They treated the covenant chest as if it was magic and could bring them luck.

When Eli's two sons carried the chest out of the shrine and marched with it at the front of the army, a great shout of joy went up from all the soldiers. The Philistines heard all about it.

'We must fight our hardest this time,' they said.

The Philistines did fight hard, and they won. They killed Eli's sons and carried off the covenant chest in triumph.

Eli waited at Shiloh for news. He was ninety-eight years old and nearly blind. He sat on a seat by the side of the road, listening for footsteps.

One of the Israelite soldiers ran all the way from the battlefield and arrived in Shiloh that same day. Gasping for breath, he ran up and down the street with the terrible news of the defeat. Everyone began to cry out in terror and grief.

'What is happening?' Eli called out in agitation, and the messenger hurried over to him.

'Our army has had a terrible defeat,' he told him. 'Your two sons are dead and the covenant chest has been taken by the Philistines.'

When Eli heard that the precious covenant chest, which he had guarded and cared for so long, was in the hands of their enemies, he fell backwards with shock and grief. Because he was so old and heavy he broke his neck and died.

109
Strange Happenings
1 SAMUEL 6

The Philistines were delighted with their new possession. They thought that by capturing God's covenant chest they had won power over Israel's God. Now they would rule Israel for ever.

They took the gold chest into the temple of their own god, Dagon, and placed it in front of his image.

Early next morning they came to Dagon's temple. They were horrified to see Dagon's image lying flat in front of the covenant chest. They carefully stood the statue upright but next morning it was flat on its face again before the chest. This time both the head and the arms of the statue were broken off and lying in the doorway.

The Philistines were scared. Israel's God must be stronger and greater than Dagon. When an epidemic of illness broke out they felt sure that God was punishing them. They decided to send the chest back, the sooner the better. Then they could feel safe.

They hitched two cows between the shafts of a cart and loaded the covenant chest onto it, along with some valuable presents. They did not put anyone to drive the cart. They decided to let the cows go which way they liked. If they took the road to Israel that would prove that Israel's God had been behind all that had happened.

In spite of their calves, which they had left behind, the cows went straight towards Israel's border, mooing loudly as they went.

Some of the Israelites, busy harvesting in the fields, heard the cows lowing and saw the cart arrive. It jolted to a standstill and they saw its precious load. They jumped for joy. The covenant chest of God was safely back in Israel.

📖 110
'We Want a King'
1 SAMUEL 7—8

Everyone in Israel knew and loved Samuel. They welcomed him as their new judge. Samuel was the last of the judges God gave to the people.

Samuel called the people together.

'If you want to be free from Philistine rule,' he told them, 'you must turn back to obeying God and doing what his law says. You cannot expect God to rescue you while you serve other gods.'

The people listened to Samuel's advice and promised to follow God's ways. Then they grew strong against the Philistines. Samuel also helped and advised anyone in need. He had four different headquarters in Israel. Every year he would visit each place in turn, helping to sort out problems and quarrels. He was a fair and honest judge.

As Samuel grew old, people began to talk about what they would do when he died.

'We need a king,' they said. They invited Samuel to a great meeting where they told him about their plan. Samuel was very sad. It seemed to him that the people were really saying that they did not want him any more. He told God how he felt and God said:

'They are refusing *me* as their leader, Samuel, not *you*. I am their King but they do not want me to rule over them.'

Samuel called the people together to give them an answer. First he gave them a solemn warning. He knew that a king would have complete power in the land. He could do anything he wanted.

'If you have a king,' Samuel told them, 'he will take everything that is yours for himself. He will call up your sons to fight in his army. He will send for your daughters to work in his palace. He will take away your land and demand a share of your crops.'

'But we want a king!' the people insisted. They imagined a brave ruler who would lead their soldiers into battle. They did not think of the bad and weak kings that they might have.

'Let them have what they ask for,' God told Samuel.

'Very well,' Samuel said to the people, 'you shall have your king in due time.'

131

Israel's First King

📖 111
The Lost Donkeys
1 SAMUEL 9

Kish was a wealthy farmer who belonged to the tribe of Benjamin. His son, who helped him, was called Saul. He was a very tall, good-looking young man.

'Saul!' Kish shouted out one morning, 'the donkeys have gone missing! Take one of the men and go and look for them at once!'

Saul and his servant hastily packed up some provisions and set off. They searched in every likely—and unlikely—place, calling the donkeys as they went. Night fell, and they lay down to sleep in the open. Next morning they set off again. Nowhere was there a sign of the runaway donkeys.

On the third morning the servant said glumly, 'There's no food left! We'll have to turn back.'

'My father will be more worried about us than the donkeys by now,' Saul agreed.

'But first let's call at Ramah,' the servant suggested. 'We're close to it and Samuel lives there. He's a wise man of God and he might be able to tell us where the donkeys are.'

In Ramah everything was bustle and excitement. That very day Samuel was giving a feast for everyone in the town. At the top of the hill into Ramah Saul and his servant met Samuel himself.

Before they had a chance to ask, he said, 'Don't worry about the donkeys—they've been found.' Then Samuel looked hard at Saul.

'You are a very special person in Israel,' he told him thoughtfully.

'*Me?*' Saul asked with a laugh. '*I'm* no one important! My father is just an ordinary farmer.'

Samuel smiled and said no more. God had told him that Saul would be coming and had given him some very surprising news about Saul's future.

'Now come to the feast,' Samuel invited, and he led the two men in. The cook brought in two special helpings that he had kept hot for them on Samuel's orders. How the two of them enjoyed that meal!

📖 112
The Astonishing Secret
1 SAMUEL 9—10

That night Saul slept soundly on the bed that Samuel had made for him on the flat roof. The next morning Samuel called up to him and he dressed hastily and went down.

'Time to be off!' Samuel announced. 'I'll come with you to the end of the town.'

When they reached the bottom of the hill Samuel told Saul to send the servant on ahead. He had a secret for Saul's ears alone. Then he turned to Saul and said, 'God has chosen you to be the first king of Israel.'

As Saul stared, speechless, Samuel took a little flask of olive oil and sprinkled a few drops on Saul's head. This was the sign that God had chosen Saul to do something very special for God. Still Saul could not believe Samuel's news.

'Three things will happen to you on your way home,' Samuel told him.

'When they do, it will help you to believe that God is going to keep his promise and that you will be king. First you will meet two men who will tell you the donkeys are safe. Next you will see some men going with gifts to God. They will give you two of their loaves. Lastly you will see a crowd of people singing and dancing and playing music to God. You will be so happy and excited that you will join the procession and dance and sing praises to God too.'

Samuel waved goodbye and Saul rejoined his servant. He was still in a daze. But as they went, everything happened as Samuel had said. Saul began to believe Samuel's amazing promise to him from God.

When they reached home, Saul's uncle came out to meet them.

'Wherever have you been?' he asked.

'Looking for the donkeys,' Saul replied. 'When we couldn't find them, we went to visit Samuel.'

'What did he have to say?' Saul's uncle asked curiously. 'He told us that the donkeys were safely found,' Saul replied. He did not tell his uncle what else Samuel had said. That was to be a secret until Samuel told him what to do next.

113
Saul, the Reluctant King
1 SAMUEL 10—11

Samuel called all the people of Israel together. First they had a special service of worship to God. Then Samuel announced that he was going to tell them who the king was to be. He did not give the name out at once. He wanted them to know that God had chosen this king.

First, out of all the tribes of Israel, he picked the tribe of Benjamin. From Benjamin's tribe he singled out one branch. From that branch he picked out Kish's family.

Everyone waited breathless and silent, as Samuel chose one name from the family of Kish.

'Saul is to be your king!' he proclaimed.

Everyone looked around, wanting to be the first to catch a glimpse of their new king. No one could see him. 'Where is he?' they all began to whisper. Even Samuel could not see him.

'Come on, let's look for him!' someone suggested, and a search began. At last, with a shout of satisfaction, they dragged him out, hot and dusty, from his hiding-place. The thought of standing up in front of all those people had scared Saul so much that he had crouched down out of sight behind a big heap of supplies, at the edge of the crowd.

Now there were shouts and cheers as he was half-dragged and half-carried in triumph to Samuel.

'Here is the man that God has chosen!' Samuel pronounced.

'Three cheers! Long live the king!' the people shouted enthusiastically.

Then Samuel wrote down all the duties of the new king and of all the kings that would follow him. Israel's kings must be different. They were to do what *God* said, not just as they pleased.

The people went home happy and excited and Saul returned to his father's farm for a little longer.

114
A Good Start
1 SAMUEL 11

When Samuel proclaimed Saul as king, not everyone was pleased with the choice. Some Israelites looked down on Saul and despised him.

'Who does he think he is, to become our king?' they asked.

Meanwhile the Ammonites, who lived close to Israel, marched their army against the Israelite city of Jabesh.

'Please don't attack us,' the people of Jabesh pleaded. 'Make a peace treaty instead.'

'We'll sign a treaty on one condition,' the Ammonites replied. 'Before we do so we will blind all your citizens in the right eye.'

The people of Jabesh were horrified. But they knew they were not strong enough to fight off the Ammonite attack.

'Give us seven days,' they begged. 'If no one comes to help us, we agree to your terms.'

Then they hastily sent off messages all through the land of Israel asking for help.

Saul came in from the farm one day to hear a hubbub of anxious voices. The message from Jabesh had reached his town. Saul did not waste one moment but took charge immediately. He sent orders all through Israel for every tribe to send him fighting men.

If they refused, they would be in trouble. All Israel responded and sent soldiers to the appointed meeting-place.

Saul sent a reply to Jabesh, telling the citizens that help would arrive by the next day.

'We will sign your treaty tomorrow,' the people of Jabesh told the Ammonite king. They kept Saul's promise secret.

That night Saul split his army into three companies and they all marched towards Jabesh. At dawn, when the enemy least expected it, they made their surprise attack and won a great victory. Saul's supporters were jubilant. They wanted Samuel to put to death everyone who had not wanted Saul for king.

'No!' Saul said. 'This is a day when God has given us victory. No one is to be put to death.'

'We'll go and proclaim Saul king all over again,' Samuel suggested, for everyone now felt that Saul had proved his fitness to be the ruler of Israel. As for the people of Jabesh— they never forgot Saul's kindness and help, just when they needed it most.

115
Jonathan's Daring Deed
1 SAMUEL 14

Saul became a good soldier-king.
Whenever the Philistines made war,
he led his army into battle.

But the Philistines had one big
advantage. They had blacksmiths
who were clever at making and
repairing weapons. They took good
care to stop any Israelites from
learning these skills. In peace-time
they would sharpen Israelite ploughs
and scythes, for a price, but in war
they refused to sharpen or repair their
enemies' swords. At one time, Saul
and his son Jonathan were the only
two who had good swords to fight
with.

The Israelites were very frightened
because they could not defend
themselves. Saul sat scowling and
hopeless in the Israelite camp, with a
band of only 600 men. Many had
deserted to the Philistines. He did not
notice when Jonathan and his servant
slipped away.

Across the valley, at the top of the hill opposite, two needle-like rocks jutted up sharply towards the sky. The two men gazed up at the jagged outlines. Between those two rocks, they knew, Philistine soldiers were stationed, guarding the narrow mountain pass. For on the other side of the hill lay the camp of the Philistines.

'Let's climb up!' Jonathan suggested. 'It may be that God will help us capture the pass.'

'I'm ready if you are,' his servant answered eagerly.

They ran across the open valley in full view of the Philistine guards. They knew that keen eyes had seen them.

'Hey there!' the Philistine soldiers called out, 'come on up—we can tell you a thing or two!' Then they burst out laughing.

'That's just what we will do! Follow me!' Jonathan told his servant.

They scrambled up the hill as nimbly as mountain goats. They could no longer be seen from the pass above.

Their enemies waited lazily. They were expecting two more deserters, hands above their heads, asking for mercy.

Suddenly, without warning, Jonathan and his man emerged swiftly and silently from behind the rocks. And Jonathan was armed.

Together the two Israelites overcame the Philistine guards and took control of the pass.

The Philistine soldiers in the camp below watched in horror. This, they thought, must be the beginning of a big attack. They took to their heels and fled. Saul and his men saw the panic and their spirits rose. Saul ordered them to give chase and they drove the Philistines right away.

116
Saul Disobeys
1 SAMUEL 13, 15

Saul grew strong and powerful in Israel. He was the one to give all the orders now. But Samuel still told Saul what to do. It was his job to pass on God's orders and to remind Saul of God's laws. But Saul began to want his own way more and more.

One day, Saul prepared his army to fight.

'Wait,' Samuel told him. 'Don't go into battle until I come to you in one week's time.'

Saul waited nearly a week. Still Samuel did not arrive. Saul muttered and fumed and strode up and down looking for him. Then, in exasperation, he began to organize things himself. Samuel arrived just before the seven days were up, to find that Saul had taken over control.

Later on, Saul disobeyed God's instructions again, and again Samuel found him out. Saul made plenty of excuses, but Samuel realized now that Saul was not willing to listen to God's way. He wanted his own way instead.

Samuel knew how much it mattered that the king of Israel should obey God. God was Israel's *real* King. The earthly king must rule on God's behalf, not please himself like the kings of the other nations. He must also set a good example to the people.

'Saul,' Samuel said, 'don't you realize that God wants your obedience more than all the presents you could give him? To disobey God is the worst kind of sin. I have a sad message for you from God. Because you have kept disobeying him, your sons will not rule after you. God will find a king for Israel who will be willing to follow him and obey his laws.'

The Young David

📖 117
Choosing a New King
1 SAMUEL 16

Samuel was sad that Saul had turned out to be a self-willed and disobedient king.

One day God said, 'You must stop being disappointed about Saul and anoint the man I have chosen to be king instead. Go to Bethlehem, where Jesse lives. I have chosen one of his sons to reign after Saul.

'I dare not,' Samuel said. 'If Saul hears about it he will kill me.'

'Saul doesn't need to know,' God reassured him. 'Give a feast in Bethlehem and invite all Jesse's family to come.'

There was great excitement in Bethlehem when Samuel arrived to arrange the feast. Everyone was invited, including Jesse and all his family. When Jesse came forward proudly, to introduce his sons, Samuel looked keenly at Eliab, the eldest. He was handsome and tall—very like Saul when he was young.

'He *must* be God's choicel' Samuel thought. But God's voice inside him said, 'No, Samuel, that is not the man I have chosen. You are looking at the outside, but I look at a person's thoughts and feelings. What a person is like *inside* is what matters most.'

One by one, in order of age, Jesse presented his sons to Samuel—seven handsome, strong young men. As each came forward, Samuel's heart gave a leap but each time God said 'No.'

Samuel was puzzled. There must be some mistake.

'Are these all the sons you have?' he asked Jesse.

'There's just the youngest,' Jesse admitted, 'but he's in the fields with the sheep.'

'We won't begin the feast until he is here too,' Samuel insisted.

Someone went quickly to fetch David. He arrived breathless, still

wearing his rough working clothes.

He looked strong and handsome too. His eyes were bright and his face was tanned and healthy from a life in the open air.

'This is the man I have chosen,' God's voice came to Samuel. 'Anoint him king.'

Samuel took out a little flask of olive oil and sprinkled a few drops on David's head, whispering God's message to him.

Only David knew that one day he would be king of Israel. Many years of hardship would pass before that day came. But from that day on, God was with David in a special way.

118
The Giant's Challenge
1 SAMUEL 17

The Israelites were still waging war against the Philistines. The two armies camped on opposite slopes of the hills, with the valley between them. Jesse's three eldest sons were in Saul's army, and Jesse began to worry about them.

'David!' he called one day. 'Go to the battle front and see if your brothers are all right. Here's some fresh bread for them and take these farm cheeses as a present for their officers. Be careful now and hurry back.'

When David arrived and went to look for his brothers, he found that both sides were lined up ready for battle. Suddenly the noise and chatter died down and everyone was quiet. Then the thunder of a mighty voice broke the stillness.

David looked across the valley. The largest man he had ever seen was striding slowly forward. He was fully armed for battle. In front of him walked another Philistine, dwarfed by the enormous shield that he was carrying for his master.

'Come on, you Israelites!' the huge man thundered. 'Pick a champion to fight me! If he wins, we will serve you. But if *I* win—you will be our slaves!'

'Who does he think he is?' David asked.

'That's Goliath,' the soldiers explained eagerly. 'He comes out night and morning with this terrible challenge. We're all terrified!'

Sure enough, the Israelite soldiers were slinking away to their tents.

David's brothers came across. 'Now then, kid brother,' Eliab began, 'what do you think you are up to? You should be looking after those sheep of yours and minding your own business.'

'I only asked what was happening,' David protested. 'No one has any right to challenge God's people like that. Goliath is not stronger than our God.'

Someone told Saul about the young man who was talking so bravely and David was summoned to the king's tent.

'Your Majesty,' David said to Saul, 'no one need fear this Philistine. I will fight him!'

'*You?*' Saul asked, amazed. 'You're not much more than a lad. Goliath is a professional soldier. What makes you think you could win?'

'God is on our side,' David answered confidently. 'I may be young but I have had good practice as a shepherd. With God's help I have killed both lions and bears when they have attacked my sheep. God will help me now.'

'Very well,' Saul agreed, 'you shall fight Goliath. And may God go with you!'

David the Giant-killer
1 SAMUEL 17

Saul looked David up and down. He must be properly protected. So Saul put his own bronze helmet on David's head and gave him his heavy coat of mail to put on. But when David had strapped on the big sword too, he could hardly move.

'It's no good,' he said breathlessly. 'I'm not a soldier and I can't fight like one. I must use the weapons I know and trust.'

Saul watched uneasily as David ran down to the nearby stream and carefully chose five smooth pebbles from the stones beneath the water.

He put them in his bag and checked his leather sling. Then he went forward to meet the Philistine champion, carrying his shepherd's stick.

Goliath advanced, calling out his challenge. But instead of the usual retreating figures of the terrified Israelites, he saw a man coming to meet him. When he made out David's slight, unarmed figure, he was filled with scorn and anger.

'How dare *you* come to fight *me*?' he roared. 'What's that stick for? Do you think I'm a dog? Get closer and I'll give your dead body to the birds to peck.' Then he began to curse David.

'You fight against me with your sword and spear and your great strength,' David called out boldly, 'but I come in the name of our God. He is stronger than any champion. You have cursed him, but he will give me victory, so that all may know that he is the true God.'

Then David ran towards Goliath. He took one pebble from the bag and fitted it into his sling. With skill he swung it around his head and aimed unerringly.

The stone flew with deadly speed and hit Goliath in the middle of his forehead. Stunned, he fell to the ground, his huge body sprawled senseless. David ran up, seized Goliath's own sword and killed him with it.

Their mighty champion was dead. The Philistines fled in terror from the battlefield.

120
Jealous King Saul
1 SAMUEL 16, 18

Pleasing himself, instead of obeying God, did not make King Saul happy. He knew that God was not with him now, as he had once been. Saul began to have black moods.

One day he sat in his palace, his head sunk on his chest, miserable and silent.

'Music would cheer you up,' one of his courtiers said.

'Find me a musician then,' Saul muttered.

Someone remembered that Jesse's youngest son, David, played the harp well.

'Fetch him,' Saul ordered.

Jesse quickly obeyed the royal command and David arrived at court. Saul was pleased to see him again. Whenever the black cloud hung over Saul, David would play to him and Saul would feel cheerful again.

While he was at court, David learned to be a soldier. Saul was glad to have such a brave and successful officer in his army—until the day he found out that David was becoming more famous and popular than he was himself.

As Saul and David came home in triumph from battle, the women came out to welcome them with dance and song. Saul listened to the words they sang: 'Saul has killed thousands but David tens of thousands!'

'They think this young upstart is a better soldier than I am!' Saul said to himself. 'They'll be wanting to make him king next!' Jealousy began to burn inside him.

That day Saul's mood was blacker than ever before. As David played to soothe him, Saul suddenly picked up his spear and hurled it at him. With lightning speed, David leaped aside and the spear shivered into the wall behind him.

Twice Saul tried to kill David and twice David escaped. David was not afraid of Saul, but Saul grew more and more afraid of David. He saw that God was with David now, just as he had once been with Saul.

Friends for Life

1 SAMUEL 18—19

In spite of Saul's growing hatred, David had one firm friend at court. It was none other than the king's own son, Jonathan.

Jonathan was a brave, good soldier himself, and he warmed at once to the young man who had the courage to fight the champion Goliath in God's name. He felt sure that they would be friends. It never crossed Jonathan's mind to feel jealous of this newcomer, who might spoil his own chances at court.

'Let's make a promise to be friends whatever may happen,' Jonathan said to David. He gave David some of his most precious possessions—his sword and bow and belt—as a sign that their friendship would last through good times and bad.

Saul's jealousy of David began to grow into a kind of madness. He could think of nothing but how to get rid of him.

'I'm going to kill David,' he told Jonathan and the court officials one day. Jonathan hurried away to find David.

'Keep out of the king's way,' he warned him. 'You are in great danger. Stay in hiding until I have talked to my father. I will try to make him change his mind.'

The next day Jonathan found King Saul alone. 'Don't harm David!' he begged him. 'Just think of all that he has done in your service. Remember how he killed Goliath? God gave us victory through David. Many times he has risked his life for you.'

Saul was quiet for a moment, then he said, 'You are right. David does not deserve to die. I promise in God's name that I will not kill him.'

Jonathan felt thankful and relieved. He told David that it was safe for him to come back to court once more.

David in Hiding

📖 122
Escape by Night
1 SAMUEL 19

War broke out again and David led the army that defeated the Philistines. But instead of being grateful, Saul's jealousy of David turned to deadly hatred. Once more he hurled his spear at David while he was playing the harp. The same night Saul sent soldiers to surround David's house and lie in wait until morning.

'Go in and kill him then,' Saul ordered. But David had another ally in Saul's family. Michal, Saul's younger daughter, had fallen in love with the brave young hero of Israel and had married David.

'You must escape before morning,' Michal warned her husband. She helped him climb down from the window. Then she arranged his bed to look as if someone was sleeping in it.

Next morning, Saul's men burst into the house, but Michal would not let them into his room.

'He's not well,' she told them, so the men returned to Saul.

'Fetch him and bring him here— bed and all, if need be!' Saul thundered.

When the soldiers pushed past Michal and went into David's room, they found that the hump in the bed was not a person at all. Michal had tricked them and David had escaped.

By this time David was safely away. He went to find Samuel, the man of God who had told him that one day he was to be king. Would that day ever come?

📖 123
Danger Signal
1 SAMUEL 20

When David left Samuel, he doubled back to find his friend Jonathan.

'What have I done wrong? Why is your father determined to kill me?' he asked bitterly.

'I'm sure he won't really harm you,' Jonathan protested. 'Anyway, my father never does anything without telling me. I'll find out the truth.'

'How will you let me know?' David asked. They were walking in the fields,

144

where no spying eyes would see them.

'Hide near here until I find out my father's feelings,' Jonathan suggested. 'I will come back as soon as I can. I will bring my bow and arrows, to look like target practice. When I get close to this spot I will shoot an arrow and call out to my servant to get it. If I shout out, "The arrow is right by you!" it will mean that all is well. But if I call, "The arrow is further on!" you can be sure that you are in danger and must fly for your life.'

The two friends parted. Jonathan felt sure that he could persuade his father that David was his loyal servant. But when he talked to Saul, the king grew very angry.

'How dare you take sides with David?' he stormed. 'He shall die!'

'Why *should* he die?' Jonathan persisted. 'What has he done wrong?'

Then Saul flew into such a rage that he hurled his spear at Jonathan. Jonathan stormed out of the room in a fury. But as his anger cooled he felt heavy-hearted. He set off for the fields with his servant. Just as they had planned he shot his arrow, then called out clearly, 'The arrow is further on!' The boy scampered off to get it.

Then Jonathan sent the boy home. No one else was in sight, so David could safely come out into the open. The two friends knew that they must part. 'One day God will make you king,' Jonathan said. 'When that day comes, please be loyal to me and my family. May we both be true friends for ever, and may God be with you always.'

David could hardly speak for sadness. But he solemnly promised that he would always be loyal to Jonathan. Then Jonathan went back to the palace.

David did not know where to go. He only knew that he must stay in hiding, away from home and friends.

124
Food and a Sword
1 SAMUEL 21

When David parted from Jonathan, he thought hard about where he could go for safety. He had no food and no weapons but he did not dare to go back to the palace or to his home for supplies. Suddenly he made up his mind. He could safely trust the priests of God. They lived at the shrine at a place called Nob, so David quickly made his way there. When Ahimelech the priest saw David coming, he hurried out to meet him. He was surprised to see him alone.

'Where are your men?' he asked. David was suddenly afraid to tell him the truth.

'I'm meeting up with them later,' he lied. 'I'm on an urgent errand for

the king. I left in such a hurry that I brought no food or weapons. Can you help me?'

'We haven't any bread in the place,' Ahimelech answered, 'only the sacred bread that priests alone are allowed to eat.'

'Please give me that,' David pleaded, 'my need is urgent.'

'Very well,' Ahimelech agreed and got the loaves.

'Have you a sword?' David went on eagerly. Ahimelech smiled.

'We don't keep weapons at God's shrine,' he said gently, 'but we *do* have Goliath's sword here. We keep it in memory of the great victory that God gave the Israelites through you.'

'That's a splendid sword!' David exclaimed. 'Please give it to me.'

Ahimelech unwrapped the great sword and handed it carefully to David.

With food to eat and a weapon to defend himself, David went on his way more cheerfully.

But Ahimelech was not the only person who had seen David. Someone else was watching and listening.

125
The Tell-tale
1 SAMUEL 22

David kept moving for a time, then he set up his headquarters in a large cave. David was a popular hero and all kinds of people began to join him. Some had been ill-treated by their masters. Others owed money. At first they were a grumbling, miserable lot of men, but David soon bound them into a band of brave and loyal followers.

King Saul complained bitterly to his officials because he could not find David.

'You are all plotting against me,' he accused them. 'None of you will tell me where David is hiding.'

Then a chief courtier, called Doeg, stepped forward. 'Your Majesty,' he began smoothly, '*I* can give you some interesting information about David.'

Saul's face brightened.

'I was at the shrine at Nob when David arrived there,' Doeg went on. 'Ahimelech gave him food to eat and a sword to arm himself.'

Saul was furious. 'Send for Ahimelech—and *all* the priests at Nob!' he thundered.

When they were shown into his presence Saul asked, 'Ahimelech, why are you plotting with David against me?'

In vain Ahimelech protested that he knew nothing of plots. He had helped David in all innocence, thinking he was on an urgent errand for the king. Saul would not believe a word of it.

'All these priests shall die!' he shouted.

Only Doeg, an Edomite, was willing to carry out Saul's terrible command.

One priest, called Abiathar, a son of Ahimelech, escaped, and he went straight to David. When he heard what had happened, David was bitterly ashamed.

'It is my fault that all your family are dead,' he confessed. 'I should have guessed that Doeg the Edomite would betray me. Stay with me, Abiathar, and you will be safe. God will take care of us.'

Hide and Seek

1 SAMUEL 24, 26

David and his men moved from one hide-out to another. Someone always gave news of his whereabouts to Saul and the king and his soldiers would chase after them.

While David was lying low in dry desert country, Saul and his men surrounded him. An urgent message arrived in the nick of time warning the king of a Philistine attack. Saul and his men hurried away and David was saved.

David and his men moved to the hills. They were pitted with caves in which they could hide. A spring of fresh water gushed in the ravine below. It was hard for Saul and his fully armed soldiers to move up and down the hillsides as nimbly as David and his few lightly-armed men.

One day David and his men crouched at the back of a deep cave, where they were camping. They could hear Saul's men coming near. Then Saul himself stepped inside the entrance of the cave. The bright sunlight concealed the shapes of the men hidden in the darkness beyond.

'Kill him!' whispered David's followers, but David shook his head. When the king was not looking, David crept noiselessly forward and cut off part of Saul's long robe with his sword. Then he withdrew quickly into the shadows. Saul left the cave, unaware of what had happened. On a sudden impulse David raced after him.

'Your Majesty!' he called after the retreating figure of the king. Saul turned in astonishment and David bowed low.

'You must believe that I do not want to harm you,' David pleaded. 'I could have killed you just now if I had wished. Look!' He held up the piece of Saul's robe.

Saul was bitterly ashamed and tears rolled down his cheeks.

'I have wronged you,' he admitted. 'One day, I know, you will be king. Be kind to my family when that time comes.'

Then Saul went sadly home.

But David knew that in spite of his tears, Saul's feelings towards him had not really changed. The chase would soon begin all over again.

127
Water from Bethlehem's Well

2 SAMUEL 23

The rough crowd of men who first joined David in his cave-home at Adullam had become a brave and united band. Some were especially skilled and courageous but all were intensely loyal to David. They would do anything for the leader who had given them new hope and purpose in life.

One day, David was feeling sad and homesick. He longed for an end to the weary months of wandering and hiding from Saul. He began to think about Bethlehem, the town where his family had lived and he had grown up. He remembered the fields around, where he had spent many happy times looking after his father's sheep. How he used to enjoy a long drink of cold water from the well at the end of a hot day!

'If only I could have a drink from the well of Bethlehem now!' he exclaimed, speaking his thoughts aloud.

Three of David's bravest men heard him. They would get David anything he wanted, if they could.

At that time Bethlehem was occupied by Philistine soldiers. But the three did not stop to worry about the risk they would run. With great courage they set off and together forced their way through the enemy lines. Then, with lightning speed, they filled a waterskin from the well and made a dash back to safety.

When they offered the water to David and he discovered the risks they had taken to make his wish come true, he was full of gratitude and also of shame.

He knew that he could never deserve such love and devotion. It would be wrong for him to drink the water that could have cost them their lives.

'Only God is good enough and great enough to deserve such a precious gift as you have given,' he told them. 'We will offer the water in love to him.'

David the Outlaw

📖 128
Nabal the Fool
1 SAMUEL 25

While David and his men were living like outlaws, hiding from Saul, they kept a friendly eye on any shepherds and their flocks who were nearby. Food was hard to get, so when a wealthy farmer called Nabal gave a feast, David sent messengers to him.

'David sends you his greetings,' they said. 'While your shepherds have been shearing we have taken care of them and your flocks. Now we hear that you are having a feast and we should be glad of any food that you can spare.'

Nabal scowled at the messengers. 'Who does David think he is?' he grumbled. 'I've never heard of him!

I'm not throwing away good food on a runaway slave and his gang of vagabonds.'

When David heard Nabal's reply he was furious.

'Buckle on your swords!' he ordered. 'We shall soon show Nabal who David is!'

One of Nabal's shepherds heard what his master had said and hurried to find Nabal's wife, Abigail.

'Our master has insulted David's men after all their kindness to us,' he told her. 'They looked after us night and day while we were shearing and this is how Nabal repays them. Now David may attack us all!'

Abigail wasted no time. She gathered up loaves of freshly baked bread, piled up roasted meat and dried fruit and filled skins with wine. She loaded everything on to donkeys

and set off, sending the servant ahead to lead the way. She did not say a word to her bad-tempered husband.

When Abigail saw David coming she got off her donkey and bowed low to him.

'Please take no notice of my husband and listen to me,' she begged. ' "Nabal" means "fool" and that is just what he is. Please do not take revenge because of his rudeness but accept these presents and our grateful thanks.'

David was delighted by Abigail's tactful words and by her beauty. He took the food and solemnly promised that no harm would come to Nabal's household.

When Abigail arrived home she found Nabal drunk and quarrelsome. She did not tell him what she had done until next morning, when he was sober.

His anger and shock at what she had to say—with the effects of too much food and wine—brought on a sudden illness. Ten days later he died.

David did not forget Abigail's charm and good sense and later he married her himself.

129
'Tomorrow You Will Die!'
1 SAMUEL 28

When Samuel died, a very old man, both Saul and David were sad. They remembered how he had always brought them God's messages and encouraged them. Saul's last meetings with Samuel had been unhappy, but he still missed him and mourned for him.

Saul's black moods deepened into despair. When the Philistines prepared eagerly for battle once again, he felt weak and helpless. He could not decide what he ought to do

and when he tried to ask God there was no answer. He knew that God had left him to go his own way.

'If only Samuel was near to help!' he thought.

There were people in Canaan called mediums, who would call up the spirits of the dead in return for payment. Earlier in his reign, Saul had banned such people in Israel, because God's law forbade them.

Saul enquired and found out that there was still a medium living at Endor. He would have to pass close to the enemy lines to get there, so he disguised himself and journeyed by night.

The medium was afraid that her visitors were spies, who would report her to the king, and when at last she recognized Saul, she gave a little scream of terror.

'You will not get into trouble,' Saul promised her, 'but you must summon up for me the spirit of Samuel.'

After a while Saul said, 'Tell me what you see.'

'I see an old man appearing,' the woman answered, 'wearing a cloak.'

Saul knew that it was Samuel.

'What am I to do?' Saul called out. 'God has forsaken me.'

'Then I cannot help you,' Samuel replied. 'You chose to disobey God and go your own way and you have brought disaster on yourself. Tomorrow you and your sons will die in battle.'

When he heard these terrible words, Saul collapsed, weak with tiredness, hunger and fear. The woman made him lie down and quickly prepared food for him and his men. Saul ate and rested for a little while, then, with leaden steps, made his way back to the Israelite army camp.

130
David Joins the Enemy
1 SAMUEL 27—29

David, like Saul, was in despair, after weary years of hiding from the king.

'One of these days Saul will kill me,' he complained. 'The only place where I would be safe is among Saul's enemies.' So, for more than a year before Saul's visit to the medium at Endor, David had been living in Philistine country.

One of the Philistine rulers, called Achish, had taken a liking to David. He thought that he and his men would be useful allies and he gave them the fortress town of Ziklag, where they lived with their wives and families.

David went on raiding expeditions for Achish, bringing him all kinds of loot. He let Achish think that these raids were made on Israel but in fact David was raiding the nations around, who were Israel's enemies too.

When the Philistines prepared for battle against Israel, Achish asked David and his men to fight with him as his special bodyguard.

David pretended that he was ready to fight against his own people. He had begun by deceiving Achish, now it was too late to tell the truth.

David and his men left their families at Ziklag and marched to the front lines. When the other Philistine rulers saw David's fighters they were horrified.

'What are those Israelites doing here?' they asked Achish.

'You don't have to worry about David,' Achish reassured them. 'He is completely loyal to me. He will fight well for us.'

'Don't you believe it!' his friends insisted. 'Once the battle begins he will change sides and fight for our enemy. Send him away at once!'

Reluctantly, Achish called David. 'I trust you completely,' he told him, 'but the other leaders will not have you. Please take your men back to Ziklag.'

David pretended to be disappointed but really he was thankful. God had come to his rescue, although he did not deserve it.

131
Everything Lost!

1 SAMUEL 30

David and his men marched for two days, trudging slowly back to Ziklag. As they grew near they saw tell-tale wisps of smoke rising from the city,

and a strong smell of burning came to them on the wind. They broke into a run, afraid of what they might find at their journey's end. When they arrived, no families rushed out to greet them. There was not an animal to be seen. The men gazed at the charred remains of Ziklag and called in vain to their wives and children. There was no answering shout.

Tired and full of grief, they began to cry. When they had worn themselves out with crying, they turned angrily on David, picking up stones to throw at him. The men who had followed him loyally for so long had lost faith in their leader. It seemed as if he had brought them nothing but disaster. They guessed that raiders, who knew they were away at the war, had swooped down on undefended Ziklag, taking everything and leaving the wooden fortress to burn.

David was desperate. Abiathar, who had escaped Saul's terrible murder of the priests of Nob, was still with David.

'Abiathar, please speak to God for me and ask him what I should do,' David implored him.

'Go after the raiders,' Abiathar told him, 'that is God's message to you.'

David felt braver. He encouraged his men to set off to find the raiders, whoever they might be. Once more his men were ready to follow him.

But, when they reached the Besor brook, some of them were too exhausted to wade across and march any further. 'Stay here,' David told them kindly, 'you can look after all the baggage so that the rest of us can travel light and go more quickly.'

So two hundred of his men stayed behind and the rest splashed across the brook and marched eagerly on.

To the Rescue
1 SAMUEL 30

As David and his four hundred men marched on, they came upon a boy lying huddled by the roadside.

'Is he dead?' one asked.

'Just faint—he probably needs food,' another answered.

Together they carried the boy to David and gave him food and water. In no time the boy began to sit up and look more lively.

'I feel better now,' he told them. 'I'd had nothing to eat for three whole days.'

'Where are you from?' David asked gently.

'I'm an Egyptian,' the boy answered, 'but I'm the slave of an Amalekite. My master took me with him when they raided Ziklag. But on the way back I fell ill and he left me here.'

David pricked up his ears. This boy might have just the information they needed.

'Can you show us where the raiders will be?' he asked.

'I'll gladly take you to them,' the boy answered, 'if you promise never to hand me back to my master,' and he gave a frightened shiver.

They set off cheerfully again, following the boy's lead. Their kindness had brought a surprising reward.

At last they came upon the Amalekite raiders, spread out and sprawled on the open ground, eating and drinking. They were so sure that David was far away that they had not even bothered to set a guard.

Quietly David watched and waited. When dawn came and the Amalekites were sleeping off their feast, he and his men attacked the camp.

They rescued everyone and everything that the Amalekites had stolen—and a lot more besides.

How thankful the wives and children were to see the husbands and fathers who had come to take them home! They all set off on the road back to Ziklag.

When they reached the Besor brook, they found their companions waiting for them.

'We'll give them back their wives and children but we won't give them any of the good things we've won,' some of David's men whispered.

'We shall share everything with them,' David insisted. 'God has given us this victory. All we have comes from him. Besides, those who look after the baggage deserve their share, just as much as those who go to fight.'

Everyone was happy now and David felt lighthearted too. Perhaps his troubles would soon be coming to an end.

Together in Death

1 SAMUEL 31; 2 SAMUEL 1

Saul felt sick with fear and despair when he rejoined his army after his visit to the medium at Endor. No wonder that the army of Israel was utterly defeated next day! Many Israelite soldiers were killed and Saul and his sons fled for their lives. The Philistines caught up with them and killed them too.

When the Israelites who lived in the towns nearby heard the terrible news, they left their homes in terror. The triumphant Philistines marched in and took over their cities.

The very next day a messenger arrived at Ziklag and brought David news of the defeat, and of the death of Saul and Jonathan. How sad David was that the best friend he had in all the world was dead! He remembered the good times, before Saul became jealous and mad with anger. Saul and Jonathan must never be forgotten. David wrote a poem of lament to remind people, for ever, of these two great men.

'On the hills of Israel our leaders are dead!
The bravest of our soldiers have fallen!
Saul and Jonathan, so wonderful and dear;
together in life, together in death;
swifter than eagles, stronger than lions.
Jonathan lies dead in the hills.
I grieve for you, my brother Jonathan;
how dear you were to me!
How wonderful was your love for me, better even than the love of women.
The brave soldiers have fallen, their weapons abandoned and useless.'

David the King

134
Long Live King David!
2 SAMUEL 2—5

Now that King Saul was dead, David could safely return to Israel. He asked God what he should do and God told him to go south to the city of Hebron, which belonged to David's own tribe of Judah. There he was gladly welcomed and the people of Judah made him their king.

Meanwhile, Abner, Saul's general, fled for his life to the north of the country, taking with him Ishbosheth, Saul's only remaining son. Abner proclaimed Ishbosheth king of all the northern part of Israel.

For a time there were two kings. David ruled in the south and Ishbosheth in the north.

Joab, David's army leader, and Abner were great rivals. Both wanted the king they served to be king over the whole of Israel. The two of them planned a fight between twelve of David's best men and twelve of Ishbosheth's soldiers to try to settle the matter.

When neither side could beat the other, terrible fighting broke out between the two armies. The struggle went on for a long time but gradually David's men grew stronger and Ishbosheth's men grew weaker. In the end, Abner himself changed sides and joined David.

'I will help you to win over all Israel,' he promised him.

David was glad to have Abner's support but Joab still hated him. Before long Joab found an excuse to kill Abner. Ishbosheth himself was put to death by two of his army officers. David had nothing to do with these murders and was very sad that his reign should begin in such a way.

By now, seven years had passed since Saul's death. At last all the tribes of Israel asked David to be their king. Their leaders came to Hebron and there they proclaimed him king over all Israel.

135
David's City—
the City of God

2 SAMUEL 5

Now that David was king of all Israel, he wanted a new capital city. Jerusalem was just the place. It was a fortress town, set high on the ridge of hills between the north and south of the country. Hills surrounded the city on three sides and on the fourth side were the huge city gates.

But Jerusalem did not belong to Israel. The Israelites had not captured it when they first arrived in Canaan. David decided to take it now, but the Jebusites who lived there looked down from their stronghold and laughed at David's plans.

If David was to be successful, he must take the city by outwitting the Jebusites. He knew that a tunnel ran up through the rocky hill, carrying the water supply right inside the city.

'Will anyone volunteer to climb up the water-shaft?' David asked, and willing men eagerly came forward. The chosen men scrambled up the shaft, emerging inside the city walls. Then they quickly unlocked the gates so that David and his waiting soldiers could flood inside and make a surprise attack on the unsuspecting Jebusites.

They captured Jerusalem, which became known as David's city.

But David wanted it to be God's city too. He decided that God's golden covenant chest, neglected for a long time, should be brought to Jerusalem.

A huge procession of people followed when the priests of God carried the precious chest to its new home. David himself led the way, dancing and singing with joy and thankfulness to God.

When the procession had wound its way up the steep slope into the city, the covenant chest was placed carefully in a special tent. Then David ordered his servants to give out food for everyone to enjoy a huge picnic.

Saul's daughter Michal, the wife who once loved David dearly, looked out of her window at the celebrations. She did not clap or sing. She was disgusted that the king should forget his dignity and dance, without any finery, among ordinary people.

When the day was over she met David.

'You behaved like a fool!' she told him scornfully.

'Don't you understand that *my* greatness doesn't matter?' David replied. 'I wanted to bring praise and glory to God.'

Plans for God's House

2 SAMUEL 7

There was peace and contentment now in Israel. Once David had shown the Philistines that he was strong enough to drive them back into their own land, they did not give any more trouble.

David was settled in his new capital city of Jerusalem. Hiram, king of the nearby country of Tyre, had sent wood from the famous cedar trees of Lebanon, as well as skilled workmen, to make David a beautiful palace.

But David began to be ashamed of his own luxury when he saw God's covenant chest still stored in a tent.

'Here I am,' he said, 'living in comfort in my lovely cedarwood palace, while God's covenant chest is in a makeshift tent. I would like to build a splendid temple for God.'

He told Nathan, the prophet, about his scheme.

'That sounds wonderful!' Nathan said enthusiastically. 'Go ahead with your plans!'

But God spoke to Nathan that night

and in the morning he came to the king with a different message.

'Your Majesty,' he began, 'God has told me that he does not want you to build him a temple. God has never asked for such a building. He has always moved with his people Israel, to be with them wherever they went. But God will allow a son of yours to build him a temple.'

David looked bitterly disappointed, but Nathan went on: 'I have good news for you, too. God is doing something for *you*. He promises that your sons and their sons after them will be kings of Israel for ever. Your kingdom will never end.'

When Nathan had gone, David went to the tent where the covenant chest was kept and poured out his thanks to God.

He thought of Saul, whose sons had never become kings and he felt full of joy that God had chosen his family as kings for all time. He had wanted to do something for God, but God had done something great and wonderful for him instead.

137
David Keeps his Promise
2 SAMUEL 9

David never forgot his great friend, Jonathan, who had been killed by the Philistines. He remembered, too, his solemn promise that he would take care of Jonathan's family once he became king. In those days a new king would put to death his rival's family, but David behaved quite differently.

'Is any member of Saul's family still alive?' he asked his servants. 'I want to be kind to him for Jonathan's sake.'

David's servants sent for Ziba, who had been a servant at Saul's court and David asked him the same question.

'Yes, your Majesty,' Ziba answered, 'Jonathan's son is still alive. He's called Mephibosheth. But you would not want him here at court. He could not serve you because he cannot walk. Both his feet are badly hurt.'

'Bring him here at once!' David ordered.

Mephibosheth was grown up by this time, but he had been a boy of five when his grandfather and his father Jonathan had been killed in battle. When his nurse heard the terrible news she had fled from the palace in terror, carrying the little boy. In her hurry she dropped Mephibosheth, hurting both feet so badly that he never walked again.

When Ziba arrived and Mephibosheth heard that he was summoned to the court he was afraid that David was going to have him put to death. But he had to obey the royal command and go to Jerusalem.

He was helped into the king's presence, and David looked at him closely. He hoped to see a likeness to his dear friend but instead he saw a face full of fear.

'Don't be afraid, Mephibosheth,' David said gently. 'I want to give you back all the land that belonged to your grandfather, Saul. Ziba shall be your servant from now on and farm the land for you. I want *you* to live here at my palace with me and have all your meals at my royal table.'

'I don't deserve your kindness,' Mephibosheth replied in a trembling voice. 'I shall be useless to you.'

But David said, 'For Jonathan's sake you will be dear to me always.'

David's Failures

📖 138
Beautiful Bathsheba
2 SAMUEL 11

It was springtime. Joab, David's general, marched his soldiers off to war, but the king stayed comfortably at home.

Late one afternoon, David woke up from his siesta and climbed up to his summer room on the palace roof. There the gentle breezes would cool him and he could look down over the whole city of Jerusalem.

As he looked, his eye was caught by what was going on in the courtyard of a nearby house. A woman was bathing and she was very beautiful.

David gazed at her, and the more he gazed the more he wished that she belonged to him.

He called for a messenger to find out who she was. The servant scurried off. 'The woman's name is Bathsheba,' he told the king when he got back. 'She is the wife of Uriah, one of your trusted soldiers, who is away at the war with Joab.'

'Fetch her here at once,' David ordered. He did not stop to think about Uriah, who had left the comfort of his home to fight for the king. He did not think about God's law which says, 'do not commit adultery'. (To commit adultery means to steal someone else's husband or wife for yourself.) David thought only about getting what he wanted.

When Bathsheba arrived at the palace, David made love to her. Then Bathsheba went back home.

A few weeks later, Bathsheba sent a message to the king to tell him that she was going to have a child. David knew that the baby would be his, too. That meant that soon everyone would guess that he had stolen Uriah's wife while Uriah was far from home.

He must quickly think of a plan to cover up the wrong he had done, so that Uriah would never know.

139
One Sin Leads to Another
2 SAMUEL 11

'If only Uriah was home with his wife,' David thought, 'no one would guess what I have done.'

So he despatched an urgent message to General Joab, telling him to send Uriah home on leave.

When Uriah arrived, he reported at once to the King. David chatted to him about how the war was going.

Then he said, 'Go back to your wife now and spend some time with her before you return to the war.'

But Uriah did not go home. Next morning David was dismayed to find that, instead, he had spent the night at the palace gate with the king's guards.

'Why didn't you go home to your wife?' David asked him.

'Why should I sleep in comfort when your Majesty's army is sleeping rough?' Uriah replied.

In spite of all that David could do, Uriah spent the next night, too, at the palace gates. David had to admit that his plan to bring Uriah and Bathsheba together had failed. Uriah was too good and loyal a soldier.

'Very well,' David said grimly to himself, 'I shall have to get rid of Uriah.'

He wrote to Joab.

'Put Uriah in the front of the battle, then retreat and leave him to be killed.' He gave Uriah the letter to take to his general.

At once Joab made plans to carry out David's orders.

He placed soldiers where the enemy was strongest and he put Uriah among them.

Uriah was killed, along with many other brave soldiers in David's army.

Then Joab sent a messenger to give news of the battle to David.

'If the king is angry that so many of his best men are dead,' he told the messenger, 'just tell him that Uriah is dead, too.'

When David learned that his plan had succeeded, he was glad. Uriah was dead and could ask no questions. Now he could marry Bathsheba himself.

140
The Little Pet Lamb

2 SAMUEL 12

David and Bathsheba were married and a little son was born to them. If any of the people at court guessed how wrongly David had behaved, they said nothing.

In those days kings did as they pleased and took what they wanted for themselves. But David had to learn that God's king was different. He could not do just as he wanted. He must obey God's laws, just like the ordinary people.

God sent the prophet Nathan to David. (A 'prophet' is a 'spokesman'. Nathan came to speak God's message to the king.)

'There were two men living in the same town,' Nathan began, 'one very rich and the other very poor. The rich man had large flocks of sheep but the poor man had only one little pet lamb. He had brought it up from birth and it followed him everywhere. It used to sit on his lap while he was eating his meals and he would give it a little sip from his own cup. He treated it just as if it was his child.

'One day, the rich man had visitors. Instead of sending his servants to kill one of his own huge flock, he ordered them to take the little pet lamb that the poor man loved, and kill it for his guests' dinner.'

David was horrified at such a heartless, cruel deed.

'That man deserves to die!' he exclaimed.

Quietly Nathan pointed at the King.

'*You* are that man!' he declared. 'God took you as a poor shepherd boy and made you king of all his people. He has given you everything you could want—palace, wives, children. Anything more you wanted, God would have freely given you. Yet you had to take Uriah's one precious possession—his wife. You have disobeyed God's laws and showed no kindness or mercy. Because of that, God says that sadness and trouble will come to *your* family, too.'

'It is true,' David said in a low voice, his head bent. 'I have sinned against God.'

'God forgives you,' Nathan told him. 'You will not die. But the child that belongs to you and Bathsheba *will* die.'

Then Nathan left the palace.

141
Family Troubles
2 SAMUEL 13

David was bitterly upset when Bathsheba's baby boy became sick and died. In time, Bathsheba had another son, called Solomon. David had many other children because he had several wives. As they grew up there was jealousy and rivalry among them. Which son would be the next king? Usually the eldest son succeeded his father, but a king could make his own choice if he wished.

Quarrels quickly flared up in that When Amnon, David's eldest son,

abused his half-sister, Tamar, her full brother, Absalom, was very angry.

David, the king and head of the family, should have punished Amnon himself. But he was soft with his children and did not correct them. So Absalom determined to punish Amnon.

He begged for David's permission to invite Amnon to an outdoor feast in the country. At first David was reluctant to let Amnon go. He half-suspected trouble. But in the end he gave way and all the royal princes went to Absalom's party.

Absalom gave secret orders to his servants beforehand.

'Make Amnon drunk with wine,' he told them, 'then kill him.'

Right in the middle of the merry-making the servants carried out their master's orders.

There was sudden uproar and panic. All David's other sons leapt onto their mules and made for home in terror.

Soon a white-faced servant rushed to David to tell him of a wild tale that had reached the palace. 'Your Majesty!' he announced, '*all* your sons have been murdered by Absalom!'

Someone who had actually been at the feast hurried in to put the story straight, and it was not long before David's sons themselves arrived and told him all that had happened.

David cried bitterly because Amnon, his first-born son, was dead.

Meanwhile Absalom escaped from Israel and went into hiding in nearby Geshur, the place where his mother had been born.

Absalom's Rebellion

📖 142
'Come Home, Absalom!'
2 SAMUEL 14

Two years passed and David longed to see Absalom again. Yet he could not bring himself to overlook the murder of Amnon. Joab, who was David's right-hand man as well as his general, guessed how the king was feeling. He thought of a way to persuade David to recall Absalom to Jerusalem.

Joab sent for a woman who was clever at acting and explained how she could help him change the king's mind.

Any person in Israel who wanted justice done could come to the king and ask him to hear the case. So David was not surprised when a sad, worried-looking woman was ushered into his presence.

'Please help me, your Majesty!' the woman begged. 'My husband is dead but I had two sons to help and look after me. Then there was a terrible quarrel and one son killed the other. Now my relatives are telling me that I must hand over my other son to them, so that they can put him to death for murder. How can I bear to part with him? He is all I have!'

King David felt very sorry for the woman. 'I promise that your son's life will be spared,' he assured her. 'No one will harm him.'

There was a little pause and then the woman went on, more boldly: 'Your Majesty, if that is how you feel, won't you send for *your* son, Absalom, and forgive him? Everyone longs to have him back.'

David guessed what had been going on.

'Tell me, honestly,' he demanded. 'Did Joab put you up to this?'

The woman admitted that she had made up her story on Joab's orders.

Later, David sent for Joab.

'All right,' he agreed, 'you can send for Absalom. He shall not be put to death for murder. But I still refuse to see him.'

Joab sent for Absalom and he returned to Jerusalem, where he lived in his own house.

📖 143
The Plot Thickens
2 SAMUEL 14—15

Absalom was glad to be back in Jerusalem. He had big plans for the future. He knew that he was the best-looking man in the whole land and he was especially proud of his beautiful hair. He had it cut only once a year—and he thought it worth its weight in gold! He could imagine himself dressed in royal robes and with all the powers of a king. But while his father refused to receive him at court he could not hope to be chosen as his successor. He waited two years for David to relent, then sent angrily for Joab.

'What is the good of living in Jerusalem if the king won't see me?' he asked bitterly. 'He might as well put me to death at once, if that's what he thinks I deserve.'

Joab repeated Absalom's words to the king.

'I will see him,' David agreed. Absalom bowed low to the king, but David kissed his son affectionately and the news soon spread that David was friends with Absalom again.

'Who knows,' the people began saying, 'Absalom might be the next king.'

Absalom badly wanted to be king but he was not sure that he wanted to wait until his father died.

He bought a fine chariot and horses and had fifty servants to attend him wherever he went. He looked a very important person.

Next he set about making himself more popular than David. Every morning he stood at the city gate and stopped everyone who came wanting an audience with the king. He talked to them kindly, asking their names and finding out their problems. Then he would say in a friendly way: 'You are clearly in the right and you deserve to have justice done. But the king will be far too busy to bother with you. If only he would appoint me as a judge!'

People began to think what a good king Absalom would make. He was such a friendly person and so fair. How good-looking too!

For four years Absalom set himself to win the love of the people. Then, when he thought the time was ripe, he went to Hebron, once David's capital city, and planned to raise an army. He sent secret messengers to the leaders of all Israel's tribes, saying:

'When you hear the trumpets sound, shout "Absalom is king!"'

144
King David Leaves Jerusalem
2 SAMUEL 15

The very last person to hear about Absalom's plans and plots was King David himself. In the end someone plucked up courage to tell him.

'Your Majesty, all the people are going over to Absalom. He means to proclaim himself king.'

David quickly set about discovering who Absalom's supporters were. To his dismay, he learned that even his most trusted friend and court adviser, Ahithophel, had joined Absalom.

'We will leave Jerusalem at once,' he told his court. 'If we stay, Absalom will arrive with his army and this city will be the scene of terrible bloodshed.'

David led his band of men down from the city, across the Kidron brook and out of Jerusalem. It seemed as though everyone had deserted him, but then his heart was warmed as loyal friends began to join him.

Abiathar the priest was waiting with his colleague, Zadok, who had brought with him God's golden covenant chest.

'Take the covenant chest back to Jerusalem where it rightly belongs,' the king said. 'Who knows? God may bring me safely back, too.' Then he pointed to young Jonathan, Abiathar's son, and to Ahimaaz, the son of Zadok.

'You go back as well,' he told them. 'Act as my spies and bring me news of all that goes on.'

The priests and Levites turned slowly back with their precious burden and David went on his way, tears in his eyes. The sad little procession went as far as the River Jordan, where they rested for a while, tired and dispirited.

At the top of the next hill another friend was waiting. It was Hushai, David's other close adviser at court.

'Hushai,' David said earnestly, 'you can help me most by going back to Jerusalem. Pretend that you are on Absalom's side. Listen carefully to the advice that Ahithophel gives him—it's sure to be good. Then try to persuade Absalom not to follow it but to do just the opposite. Tell Zadok and Abiathar everything that is planned. Their sons will get the news through to me.'

145
Schemes and Spies
2 SAMUEL 17

Absalom arrived with great pomp in Jerusalem, bringing with him Ahithophel, once David's trusted adviser. Absalom was surprised to find David's other adviser, Hushai, waiting for him. He did not guess that Hushai was still loyal to David.

Ahithophel soon suggested a plan of action.

'Let me choose an army and march against David tonight,' he advised. 'He and his men will be tired and down-hearted. I can gain a quick victory.'

Absalom paused a moment.

'I must see what Hushai thinks,' he said.

When Hushai heard Ahithophel's scheme he knew that it was good. David would have no time to prepare for battle if an attack came at once. Somehow he must stop Absalom carrying out the plan.

'This time Ahithophel has given bad advice,' he began. 'You should be the one to lead Israel to victory. The people will flock from one end of the land to the other to fight in your army. Once they are all gathered, you can lead them.'

Absalom liked this plan, even though it would take longer to put into action. He was vain and wanted the glory himself.

'I shall follow Hushai's advice,' he announced grandly.

Hushai told the news to Zadok and Abiathar. A servant girl took messages to their two sons, but a boy who had seen them whispering together reported his suspicions to Absalom. Jonathan and Ahimaaz fled to the home of a couple who were loyal supporters of David. They hid them inside their dried-out water pit and fixed a cover over it. The wife sprinkled grain on top to make it look as though it had not been disturbed. When Absalom's men arrived asking for the spies, David's friends told them that they had crossed the river.

As soon as the search-party left, Jonathan and Ahimaaz scrambled out and ran off to give David Hushai's news.

146
Death in the Woods

2 SAMUEL 17—18

When David heard what the two spies had to say, he lost no time in leading his men across the River Jordan. They marched north-east to the city of Mahanaim.

They were tired and hungry after camping in the desert and were thankful to find supporters of David waiting with supplies for them. There were warm blankets and good food—meat and vegetables, honey, cheese and cream.

After they had eaten and slept well, they were ready to face any foe. David lined up his troops and promised to march with them into battle. But the leaders begged him to stay in the city.

'You are too precious to us, to risk death in battle,' they said. Reluctantly, David agreed. As he watched them go, everyone heard him tell the commanders:

'*Please* be gentle with Absalom! For my sake don't hurt him.'

By this time Absalom had gathered an army and crossed the Jordan, and the battle began. Little by little, David's soldiers gained ground and began to chase Absalom's men away.

A few of David's men, marching through the woods, came upon Absalom himself, riding his mule beneath the trees. As he galloped away he ran into the overhanging branch of a huge oak-tree, and his head caught fast in its boughs. The frightened mule made off, leaving its master stunned by the blow, hanging in mid-air.

One of the men rushed to tell Joab.

'Why didn't you kill him?' Joab asked. 'I would have rewarded you richly.'

'I would not kill Absalom for a fortune,' the soldier replied, 'after what our king said.'

Quickly Joab rode off to find Absalom. He was still hanging from the tree, his beautiful hair tangled and held fast. Without hesitating, Joab and his picked soldiers put him to death.

Then Joab blew a trumpet blast and summoned his army. Now that Absalom was dead, the rebellion against David was over.

'May I run to the king with the news of the victory?' Ahimaaz asked eagerly.

But Joab was afraid that David might be angry with any messenger who brought news of Absalom's death, so he ordered a slave to run to Mahanaim instead.

'I'm going too!' Ahimaaz insisted. So the two swift runners set off.

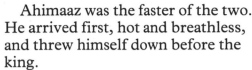147
David Returns in Triumph

2 SAMUEL 18—19

David waited at the city gate, impatient for news of the battle.

'Someone is coming!' the watchman called down, 'and a second runner is not far behind.'

Ahimaaz was the faster of the two. He arrived first, hot and breathless, and threw himself down before the king.

'Praise God!' he panted out, 'you have won the victory!'

All that David could say was, 'What about Absalom? Is he safe?'

'There was a great commotion,' Ahimaaz muttered. 'I don't know all that happened.'

Just then the second runner arrived. 'What is the news of Absalom?' David repeated anxiously.

'He met the end that all the enemies of your Majesty deserve,' the slave replied. David knew that Absalom was dead. He walked slowly away, overcome with sadness. Over and over again he exclaimed:

'O Absalom, my son, my son. I wish that I had died for you, my son, Absalom!'

When the troops arrived in the city, everyone whispered 'Sh!' No one dared celebrate victory when the king was so sad.

At last Joab went to David. 'You are not treating your soldiers fairly,' he told him. 'They will think that you wish *them* dead and *Absalom* alive and well. Come and thank them and rejoice with them!'

David knew that he must put aside his grief and encourage his loyal followers. Before long the people of Israel, who had once sided with Absalom, came to invite David back as king. So David returned in triumph to Jerusalem.

The Golden Age of Solomon

The New King

1 KINGS 1—2

King David was growing old. He was no longer able to ride out with his soldiers, or listen to the complaints brought by his subjects. He stayed in his own room, lying in bed, wrapped in blankets because he felt so cold.

Outside his room, people were talking and planning. Who would be the next king? Now that Absalom was dead, Adonijah was the eldest son. He was good-looking and ambitious too. Abiathar the priest and Joab, David's general, supported him, so Adonijah made up his mind to be crowned at once.

'We'll have a celebration feast,' he announced to his followers, 'and invite everyone to come. Afterwards you will proclaim me king.'

'Don't invite your brother Solomon,' his friends advised, 'or Nathan the prophet, or Zadok the priest.' They knew that Nathan and Zadok supported Solomon's claim to be the next king.

Nathan heard about Adonijah's plot and hurried to see Solomon's mother, Bathsheba.

'Go straight to King David,' he advised her. 'Tell him what is happening and remind him of his promise to you that Solomon should succeed him.'

When Bathsheba was ushered into the king's presence, she bowed low. As she finished telling him about Adonijah's scheme, Nathan arrived with the same story.

David promised Bathsheba that he would keep his promise and make Solomon king.

'Put Solomon on my own royal mule,' he ordered, 'and lead him out through the city. Let Zadok the priest anoint him king. Then blow the trumpet and bring Solomon back in triumph.'

Nathan was quick to obey the king's orders.

Adonijah and his friends were still feasting when they heard the trumpet blast and the cheers of the crowds as the new king rode through the city. They knew that their plot had failed. Solomon was king, at David's own command.

📖 149
Solomon's Dream
1 KINGS 3

Before David died, he gave Solomon much good advice. He reminded him that above all he must obey God's laws.

Once David was dead, Solomon had all the work and worry of ruling the people of Israel single-handed.

One day, he went on a visit to Gibeon, to pray and offer gifts to God. In the night he had a dream. God appeared to him and said:

'What would you like me to give you, Solomon?'

Solomon knew at once what he wanted most. 'Please, God,' he prayed, 'give me wisdom. I am young and have no experience. I don't know how to rule over all the people of Israel unless you help me.'

God was pleased with Solomon's answer. 'You could have asked to be rich, or to live long, or to have your enemies put to death,' God told him. 'Instead, you have asked for wisdom. I will give you wisdom to rule and judge fairly. You will be the wisest man who ever lived. I am also going to give you the things you did not ask me for. You will be rich and respected by everyone. And if you obey me and keep my laws, you will have a long life.'

Solomon woke up and knew that he had been dreaming. But he also knew that God had really been talking to him. He felt comforted that God was going to give him the help he needed to be a good king.

150
Wise Decisions
1 KINGS 3

God answered Solomon's prayer and gave him great wisdom. He composed three thousand wise sayings and wrote a thousand songs. He knew all about animals and birds, fishes and plants and flowers. He became famous far and wide for his wisdom.

God also gave Solomon skill to deal with all the affairs at court.

Many of his subjects came asking for justice and requesting the king to hear their case, just as they once came to David.

One day, two women arrived and were shown into the king's throne-room. As they came in, one tried to snatch a bundle from the arms of the other, but the bundle began to cry and scream! It was a baby!

A courtier took the baby and rocked it, while the two women poured out their story to the king.

'We live together,' the first one began, 'and we both had babies not long ago. My baby was born just two days before hers.

'One night, she smothered her baby by accident and it died. While I was still asleep, she took my baby from beside me and put her dead baby in its place. I woke up to find that the baby beside me was dead. When I looked again, I saw that it wasn't my baby at all, but hers!'

The other woman interrupted angrily. 'The dead baby was yours,' she argued, 'mine is the living baby. Yours died!'

The king let them shout and argue for a moment, then he asked: 'Are you both claiming that this live baby is yours?'

'Yes!' they shouted together.

'Fetch a sword!' the king ordered. A sword was carried in and Solomon said to one of the courtiers:

'Since both these mothers say that the baby is theirs, cut the baby exactly in half and give them half each.'

At once the baby's real mother cried out, 'Don't kill him! I'd rather *she* had him than that!' But the other woman said, 'Go on—do as the king said! It's fair!'

'Stop!' Solomon thundered. 'Don't hurt the baby. I wanted to discover the true mother. The baby belongs to the one who wants to spare his life. Give the baby to her.'

Everyone in Jerusalem heard about the case of the baby and the two mothers. They thought how wise and clever their king must be, if he could think of such a scheme to get at the truth.

151
Solomon's Glory
1 KINGS 4, 7, 9, 10

God kept his promise to make Solomon rich as well as wise. The kingdom of Israel was larger than it would ever be again, for David had driven back Israel's old enemies, the Philistines, and many others. The people were happy and prosperous when Solomon became king.

Solomon began to build himself a magnificent palace. It took him thirteen years to finish. He kept hundreds of workmen busy, cutting fine stone and carving cedar wood ceilings and panelled walls.

There was a grand throne-room, where the king received his subjects and all the admiring visitors who came from other lands.

Six steps led up to the throne where Solomon sat in state. On either side of each step was a carved lion. The throne itself was made of ivory, covered with gold and there was a gold footstool for the king's feet. A carved lion stood beside each arm-rest and a bull's head was carved on the back of the throne. No one had ever seen anything like it before!

When visitors went into the banquet-hall they sat down to eat from plates of pure gold and drank from golden cups. Huge quantities of food were prepared each day for the royal table. The people of Israel had to take turns in providing all the food that was needed at the palace.

Solomon loved horses and built huge stables for them all.

He built a fleet, too, which sailed with the navy of the king of Tyre.

Every three years the ships returned from their long voyage, bringing the king rare and precious treasures. They brought peacocks and apes and monkeys, to preen and play in the palace gardens and gold, silver and ivory, to decorate the palaces that Solomon had built for himself and for his many wives.

Building God's Temple

1 KINGS 5, 7, 8; 1 CHRONICLES 22, 29

When David was king he had wanted to build a temple for God. But God told him that his son, Solomon, would be the one to build it. Instead, David planned and prepared for the great task.

He called for the leaders of Israel and told them:

'The temple that Solomon is going to build must be truly magnificent, because it will be for God. I have given gold, silver, marble and precious stones of my own for the building. Will anyone else give towards it?'

The people gladly brought gifts of every kind.

David gave Solomon instructions about where to build the temple, and plans for making it.

At last the time came to begin.

Solomon wrote to David's old friend, King Hiram of Tyre, and asked for fine cedarwood from the great forests of Lebanon. Hiram was happy to help. His servants cut down trees, tied logs together to make rafts, and floated them down the sea coast, to where Solomon's servants could take them ashore.

Solomon employed hundreds of workmen, as well as skilled builders and craftsmen. They cut and shaped the huge stones for the temple at the quarry, deep underground, so that no noise of hammers should disturb the quiet of the sacred temple site.

For seven years they worked—quarrying, sawing, hammering, carving and casting metals. At last the temple with all its furniture was finished. How beautiful it looked! With solemn ceremony the Levites carried the sacred covenant chest from its tent to the innermost room of the new temple. As they laid it carefully down, a great shout went up from the crowd. The musicians struck up, the trumpets sounded and everyone started singing:

'Praise the Lord, because he is good, and his love is eternal!'

Suddenly the temple was filled with dazzling light, far brighter than the gold with which it gleamed. God's cloud of glory had come to rest upon it.

Solomon was full of wonder and thankfulness to God. He knew that God was too great to live inside any building. But God had shown that he accepted the gift of his people and would be with them, to bless them and hear their prayers.

153
The Visit of the Queen of Sheba

1 KINGS 10

Far away from Israel, at the other end of the ancient trade-routes, a queen ruled in the kingdom of Sheba, now the country of the Yemen.

Visitors brought tales to her court of a great and wealthy king called Solomon, who was famous above all for his great wisdom.

At last the queen made up her mind that she would find out for herself whether this king was as great and wise as she had been told. She would journey to the kingdom of Israel and meet King Solomon herself.

She ordered her servants to load the camels with huge quantities of the rare spices for which her land was famous. She prepared valuable presents to take to the king.

When everything was ready, the long caravan set out, the queen herself at its head. When at last they arrived, she was shown into the king's throne-room. She could scarcely believe her eyes. Such richness and finery! So many servants!

Then the queen of Sheba began to ask Solomon questions—the hardest she could think of. All that she had wondered about and longed to understand, she asked the king. He answered everything she asked. It seemed as though nothing was too difficult for Solomon. It left the queen breathless.

'All that I heard about you is true!' she exclaimed. 'I thought they were far-fetched tales but I find that the visitors to my court did not tell me half about your wealth and wisdom. How happy your servants must be!

How fortunate are all your courtiers, who can listen to you all day!'

The queen gave Solomon the presents she had brought and fragrant spices, more than he had ever had.

Solomon gave her rich presents too, and anything else she could ask for.

Satisfied beyond her wildest dreams, the queen of Sheba set off on the long journey back to her own land.

The Kingdom is Divided

154
Solomon's Sins
1 KINGS 11

Solomon was a great and wlse king and his court was wealthy and magnificent. He built many beautiful palaces as well as the great temple in Jerusalem. Money poured into Solomon's treasury each year. Some came from trading with other countries and some from taxes paid by the peoples around.

But Solomon kept spending much more money than he earned. When he was in debt, he made the people pay heavy taxes. When he needed workmen to build his palaces and repair his city, he sent a court official to force men to come and work for him, and paid them nothing.

So, many people in Israel were poor and unhappy in Solomon's reign.

God was not pleased with Solomon for ill-treating the people because of his own greed, or for doing many other things that God had forbidden. Solomon had a great many wives who came from other lands, and brought with them their own religions. Instead of teaching his wives to know the true God, Solomon built temples for the images of their gods. As he grew older he copied their ways. He was not faithful to God, who had given him all his wisdom and wealth in the first place.

God was sad. He longed to see Solomon following him, as David had done.

'Solomon,' God said, 'I promised to give the kingdom of Israel to you and your descendants, and you promised to obey and serve me truly. You have broken your part of the agreement.

'By rights I should take the kingdom away from you. But because of my promise to David your father, I will leave a small part of the kingdom for your family to rule over for ever.

'But ten out of the twelve tribes of Israel will be taken away from you and given to another man, who will be the king after you are dead.'

155
Astonishing News for Jeroboam
1 KINGS 11

King Solomon was walking around Jerusalem, inspecting the workmen who were repairing the walls, when he noticed one young man who was working especially hard.

'What is your name?' the king asked him.

'Jeroboam,' the young man replied.

The king went to the foreman and said, 'Jeroboam is a good worker. Put him in charge.'

Jeroboam was glad to be promoted. He was eager to do well.

One day he was walking home from work along a quiet country road, when he saw a prophet called Ahijah coming towards him, wearing a brand new cloak.

Without saying a word, Ahijah stopped and began to rip his new cloak into pieces. Jeroboam was shocked. New cloaks cost a lot of money and prophets were usually hard up.

Then Ahijah handed the pieces of

cloth one by one to Jeroboam, until he had given him ten pieces. Only two pieces of the torn cloak were left in the prophet's hand.

'Jeroboam,' Ahijah said, 'this is what God is going to do. He will take away the kingdom from Solomon's family and give it to you.'

Jeroboam looked at the two pieces of cloth still in Ahijah's hand.

'Yes,' Ahijah explained, 'two tribes of Israel will be left for Solomon's sons to inherit.' He pointed to the ten pieces of cloth. 'The other ten tribes will belong to you. Now, Jeroboam, learn from Solomon's mistakes. God is taking the kingdom from his family because he no longer obeys and worships God. See to it that *you* obey and serve God. Then you will prosper and your sons will rule after you.'

Ahijah walked quickly away, leaving the astonished Jeroboam with his mouth open, still clutching the ten torn pieces of cloak.

Could it be true? Even in his wildest dreams he had not imagined he would be king. But if so, why wait till Solomon was dead?

He began to plan and plot to seize the throne but news of his schemes came to Solomon's ears. He decided to put Jeroboam to death, but before he could catch him, Jeroboam fled to Egypt. When Solomon was dead, his chance would come.

156
A Difficult Choice
1 KINGS 12

For forty years Solomon ruled over Israel. When he died, his son Rehoboam became king.

While everyone was busy preparing for the coronation, Jeroboam came hurrying back from Egypt, where he had been living to be safe from Solomon.

The leaders of the northern tribes of Israel welcomed Jeroboam back.

'We want to send representatives to the new king,' they told him, 'Will you go and speak for us?

'We shall ask Rehoboam to be gentler and kinder than his father. We cannot bear any more of those harsh taxes, or the forced work that Solomon demanded.'

'Leave it to me,' Jeroboam assured them. 'I will speak on your behalf.'

Jeroboam and his little group of northerners were shown into the king's presence.

'Your Majesty,' Jeroboam began, 'your father, King Solomon, treated us harshly. He made life miserable for us. He made us pay heavy taxes and forced us to work hard for him without pay.

'If you will promise to treat us kindly and make life easier, we will promise to be your loyal subjects.'

'Give me three days to think about it,' Rehoboam replied. 'Come back then and I will give you my answer.'

The Divided Land

1 KINGS 12

Rehoboam did not know what answer to give to Jeroboam and his followers. First he asked the old men, who had been advisers to his father, King Solomon.

'Shall I be a strict king, and try to stop the people rising against me? Or shall I rule more gently and kindly than my father did?'

The old men answered, 'Be kind to the people. Promise to treat them well and ease their burdens. Then they will serve you loyally.'

Next, Rehoboam asked the young courtiers, who were his own age, the same question. They gave him quite a different answer.

'Tell the people that Solomon's strictness was nothing compared with how you will treat them,' they advised. 'Rule them with a rod of iron. Keep them so firmly under control that they cannot rebel.'

Rehoboam thought this was better advice than the advice of the old men. When Jeroboam and his deputation arrived he warned them:

'My father's strict rule was nothing compared with how I shall treat you.'

Rehoboam's words did not frighten the people into obedience, as he had hoped they would. When Jeroboam gave them Rehoboam's message they shouted:

'Down with Rehoboam! Down with David's family!'

Rehoboam heard about the demonstration and sent an official called Adoniram to punish the people. Everyone knew and hated Adoniram. He was the man who used to round up citizens and force them to work for Solomon.

The angry crowd hurled stones at him and killed him. Then they called for Jeroboam and asked him to be their king.

But Judah and Benjamin, the two tribes in the south of the country, were still loyal to Rehoboam. They had loved David, who belonged to Judah's tribe, and they supported his grandson, too.

Now the country was split in two, with two different kings. Jeroboam ruled ten tribes and his kingdom was called Israel, the name once given to the whole country. Rehoboam's southern kingdom was called Judah.

Troubles in Israel

📖 158
Jeroboam's Failure
1 KINGS 12, 14

Jeroboam was well pleased to be king over almost the whole of Solomon's old kingdom. But Jerusalem, the capital city, where the temple stood, was in Judah, where Rehoboam, Solomon's son, still reigned. All the Israelites went to the temple at least once every year to worship God.

'I must stop my people visiting Jerusalem,' Jeroboam decided, 'or Rehoboam may win them back.'

He ordered two gold images of bull-calves to be made. Then he built two shrines for them, one at each end of his kingdom. He appointed priests who did not belong to the tribe of Levi, which God had chosen for his special service.

When the bull-images were put in the shrines, Jeroboam announced to the people, 'These are your gods, who brought you out of Egypt.'

Each year there was to be a special celebration at both shrines.

The people of Israel quickly turned away from the true worship of God. They copied the wrong and cruel ways of the people who lived in the land before the Israelites, and who worshipped Baal.

One day, Jeroboam's son became ill.

'Visit Ahijah,' Jeroboam told his wife. 'He is the prophet who first told me that I should be king. Go in disguise and ask him if our son will get better.'

Jeroboam's wife changed out of her fine clothes and set off to see Ahijah, taking a present of bread, cakes and a jar of honey.

Ahijah was very old and he could no longer see, but God told him she was coming.

As soon as he heard footsteps, Ahijah called out, 'Come in, Jeroboam's wife—I know who you are, so why pretend to be someone else?'

Then Ahijah told her what God thought about the way that Jeroboam had behaved.

'Tell your husband,' he said, 'that God says: "I took the kingdom from David's family and gave it to you. Yet you have disobeyed me and made my people disobey me too, by making idols and images for them to worship." Now God's punishment will come upon all your family.'

159
Ahab and his Wicked Queen

1 KINGS 14, 15

In time, God's message to Jeroboam through Ahijah came true. When Jeroboam died, one of his sons became king, but he did not rule for long. A rival for the throne murdered him, made himself king, and then cruelly put to death every member of Jeroboam's family. But when the new king died, his son, in turn, was killed by one of his officers, who seized the throne for himself. The palace was full of spies and plots, threats and murders.

One day, an army officer called Omri used his soldiers to help him become king. He was a clever man and became a powerful king, known far and wide for his strong rule.

He built the city of Samaria as the new capital of Israel. But he did not serve God. He carried on with the false worship at the shrines that Jeroboam had begun.

When Omri died, his son Ahab became king. But it was soon clear that the *real* ruler of Israel was Ahab's wife, Queen Jezebel, who had been princess of the nearby country of Sidon. When she came to Israel, she brought with her hundreds of prophets of Baal. Ahab built a fine temple to her Baal in Samaria.

Jezebel was determined to get rid of the worship of Israel's God. She put to death all the prophets of God she could lay her hands on.

It seemed that the people of Israel would soon forget all about God and worship only the baals. They would no longer keep God's good commands or remember the loving care for others which is part of God's law.

But God was still in charge. He had chosen one special man—Elijah—to show the people that he was still the true God, and to try to bring them back to him.

Elijah lived an open-air life and dressed in rough clothes. He did not have the smooth ways and manners of a courtier. But he was a prophet of God who was not afraid to speak God's message to the king himself, and who was determined, with God's help, to stand firm for justice and right.

160
The Long Drought
1 KINGS 17

One day, God's prophet Elijah went boldly to King Ahab and said, 'I tell you, in God's name, there will be no rain in the land for more than two years. None will fall until I give the word. You will learn that my God is the true God. He still has power in Israel.

In such a hot, dry country, rain was very precious. When none fell, the young grain and the green vegetables began to wither and shrivel away. Food soon grew scarce.

Jezebel's Baal was supposed to be the god of rain, but however much they prayed to him, the rain did not come. Ahab and Jezebel were very angry with Elijah. They would have liked to kill him.

'Go and hide from the king by the Cherith brook, on the other side of the Jordan,' God told Elijah. 'I will order ravens to bring you food.'

Elijah did as God said. He stayed well hidden, drinking water from the brook and waiting morning and evening for the strange bird visitors to arrive with his breakfast and dinner. The huge black ravens flew to him with meat and bread in their beaks and claws. Elijah ate the food thankfully.

Still the sun beat down and still no rain fell. The brook began to dry up, until Cherith became an empty stream-bed.

'Elijah,' God said, 'it's time now to leave here and go to Zarephath. There is a widow there who will feed you.'

Elijah tramped north, beyond the country of Israel, into Sidon, the home of the wicked Queen Jezebel.

Just outside the town gate of Zarephath, he saw a woman bending down to pick up sticks for firewood. He knew at once that this was the woman God had told him about.

📖 161
The Food that Never Ran Out

1 KINGS 17

Elijah walked across to the woman who was picking up sticks. She straightened up to look at him.

'Please would you fetch me a drink of water?' Elijah asked.

The drought had reached Sidon and food and water were scarce there, too. But the woman put down her basket and kindly set off to get him a drink.

'Please would you bring me some bread to eat, too?' Elijah called after her. The woman turned back and shook her head sadly.

'I'm sorry,' she said. 'I can't do that. I've been collecting these sticks for a fire so that I can cook the last meal that my son and I shall eat. All I have left in the house is a little bit of flour in my bowl and a tiny drop of oil in my jar—just enough for a small loaf. Once we've eaten that, we shall die of hunger.'

'Don't be frightened,' Elijah said, 'just do as I asked you. Make a little loaf for me first, then use the rest to make one for yourself and your son. God promises that as long as the drought lasts, your bowl will never run out of flour and your jar will never run out of oil.'

The woman believed Elijah and hurried off to do as he had told her.

God's promise came true.

Elijah stayed with the widow and her son, as God had told him to, and each day she found enough flour and oil to make that day's bread. The next day there was enough for a fresh loaf. There was always enough to feed all three of them, as long as the drought lasted.

Elijah Challenges Baal

162
A Contest on the Mountain
1 KINGS 18

Three years passed without a drop of dew or rain and King Ahab grew desperate. One morning, he set off with his chief manager Obadiah. Obadiah still loved and served God and was a true friend to God's prophets.

'We'll cover the whole country,' the king said, 'checking every stream and river. We'll see if there is enough water for our horses and mules. If not, we must slaughter them all. You go one way and I'll go the other.'

Obadiah set off in the opposite direction from the king and began his search. There were many miles to walk.

It was some hours later when he looked up and had the biggest surprise of his life. There in front of him stood Elijah! Obadiah could not believe his eyes.

'I want you to bring King Ahab here,' Elijah said.

'The king has been searching everywhere for you,' Obadiah said. 'If I bring him back and find you've disappeared again, he'll be furious!'

'I'll still be here,' Elijah promised.

When Ahab set eyes on Elijah he spoke rudely. 'It's you, is it?' he asked. 'The one who has brought us all this trouble.'

'*I'm* not the one who's to blame,' Elijah told the king gravely. '*You* have turned away from God and followed Baal.

'Now call the people of Israel to come to the top of Mount Carmel. Bring all the prophets of Baal, too. I am the only prophet of God that Jezebel has left alive. But I will stand up for God against them all.'

163
God Sends Fire
1 KINGS 18

King Ahab called everyone together, as Elijah had said. The people stood waiting, wondering what would happen next.

Elijah stepped forward to speak to them.

'When are you people of Israel going to stop wavering and make up your minds?' he asked. 'Decide who is the true God, and serve him. If Baal is really God, serve him with all your heart. But if *my* God, the God of Israel, is the one true God, then give him all your trust and obedience. You can't try to serve God *and* Baal. Today we shall hold a contest to find out which is the true God.'

Then Elijah turned to the Baal prophets. 'Build an altar to Baal,' he told them. 'Put wood on it and place a sacrifice to Baal on top. But don't set it on fire. Call on Baal to send fire himself, to burn up his sacrifice.'

Baal was the god of rain and storm. *He* should be able to send lightning to set the sacrifice on fire.

The Baal prophets prepared their altar and sacrifice carefully. Then they began to pray for fire to come down and burn it. The people watched in silence.

Nothing happened.

The prophets grew desperate and their prayers became mad yells and screams. They danced wildly around the altar, tearing their hair and imploring Baal to hear them.

Elijah began to tease them. 'Perhaps Baal is busy,' he suggested. 'Or he may have dropped off to sleep. Try to wake him up!'

In spite of all their wild shouts and capers, nothing at all happened. At last they collapsed, exhausted and hopeless.

Then Elijah called the people to come close. First he mended the broken-down altar of God that had once stood on the mountain. He laid wood and meat on it, then dug a trench around it.

'Bring water and pour it over the sacrifice,' he ordered.

Large jars of precious water were brought, and the sacrifice, wood, altar and all were thoroughly soaked.

'Bring more,' Elijah said.

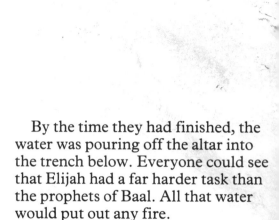

By the time they had finished, the water was pouring off the altar into the trench below. Everyone could see that Elijah had a far harder task than the prophets of Baal. All that water would put out any fire.

Calmly Elijah began to pray. 'O God, you are the God of Abraham, Isaac and Jacob. Prove that you are still the God of Israel by sending fire.'

Immediately the watching crowd saw flames light up the altar. In a moment the sacrifice went up in smoke. Fierce fire burned up the wood and even the stones of the altar. It licked up the water in the trench and scorched the earth around.

The people were amazed. They fell on their faces and shouted, 'God is the true God! He is the only God!'

Elijah ordered them to seize the prophets of Baal and put them to death. Only that way, he believed, could the wicked and cruel worship of Baal be stamped out in the land of Israel.

164
The Clouds Gather
1 KINGS 18

It was a very shaken King Ahab who listened to what Elijah had to say next. 'Go and eat now,' he told the king, 'soon the rain will come.'

The people went quietly to their homes, but Elijah and his servant climbed to the very top of the mountain. Elijah kneeled down, his head bowed low, praying and listening to God. Then he told his servant to go and look towards the sea.

The servant came back. 'There's nothing to be seen,' he reported.

'Look again,' Elijah said.

Six times the servant did as Elijah said. Six times he could see nothing unusual. But the seventh time he came back and told his master, 'I can see a tiny cloud on the horizon. It's no bigger than a man's hand.'

Then Elijah stood up.

'Go and tell Ahab to hurry home if he wants to get there before the rain comes,' he said.

By now Ahab had learned to believe what Elijah said. He gave orders for the chariot to be made ready.

All this time clouds began to gather, thick and fast. The wind began to blow. The whole sky was black and heavy with rain. Ahab set off quickly.

Suddenly Elijah felt full of God's strength. He was triumphant and happy because of all that God had done that day. He hitched up his long robes, tucked them into his leather belt, and began to run.

Ahab's palace at Jezreel was some three hours' chariot drive from Carmel, but Elijah ran ahead of Ahab's galloping horses, all the way to the city gates.

Elijah, God's Messenger

📖 165
Danger!
1 KINGS 19

King Ahab arrived back at his palace in Jezreel and told his wife Jezebel all that had happened. When she heard what Elijah had done to her Baal prophets, she was furious. She stormed and raged, then sent a terrified servant with a message for Elijah.

'Tell that man,' she shouted, 'that by this time tomorrow I shall have done to him exactly what he did to my prophets. May the gods strike me dead, if I don't keep my promise!'

When Elijah heard the angry queen's words, his heart sank. The day before, he had bravely shown all Israel, as well as their faint-hearted king, that God alone was great and powerful. But how could he bring them back to the true God while Jezebel ruled the kingdom?

Without waiting a minute longer, Elijah set out, south, to the land of Judah.

For a whole day he tramped through the brown, desert country, then, hot and exhausted, he sat down in the shade of a solitary tree. He wished he could die.

'What's the use, God?' he asked. 'For all the good I've done, I might as well be dead!'

Worn out, he fell fast asleep.

Suddenly, he felt a touch on his shoulder. He woke up to hear a voice saying, 'Have something to eat!'

To his amazement, Elijah found a loaf of bread and a jar of water, ready beside him on the ground. He fell to, hungrily, then lay down and fell fast asleep again.

A second time the voice woke him.

'Get up and have something to eat, or else the journey will be too much for you.'

By now Elijah was wide awake. He felt better for the sleep and for the new supply of food and water, so wonderfully provided. He knew that God *did* care about him. He had sent his Special Messenger to comfort him and make him strong.

That food kept Elijah going for a long time. He went on with his journey until he came to Mount Sinai. This was the sacred mountain where God had spoken to their great leader, Moses, and had made a covenant with the people of Israel, when he brought them out of Egypt.

The Still, Small Voice

1 KINGS 19

When Elijah reached Mount Sinai, it was getting dark. He crept into a cave in the hill to spend the night there. But in the dark God spoke to him.

'What are you doing here, Elijah?' God asked.

Elijah told God just how he felt.

'I'm the only one left on your side,'

he answered. 'Jezebel has killed all your prophets, and your people have turned away from you to serve Baal.'

When Elijah stopped speaking a sudden, furious wind swept past the opening of the cave. It was as wild and strong as Elijah's own thoughts and feelings. It howled around the hillside, splitting open the rocks with its force.

But God was not in the wind.

The wind was still and Elijah felt the earth beneath his feet stir and tremble. The ground heaved as an earthquake shook the foundations of the mountain.

But God was not in the earthquake.

Then Elijah saw a red glow. The dry shrubs began to blaze, as a desert fire spread swiftly across the hillside, lighting up the night sky.

But God was not in the fire.

After the fire, Elijah heard the small, still whisper of a voice.

God was speaking to him now.

With awe and wonder, Elijah wrapped his cloak over his face and went slowly out of the cave, to stand in the open and listen to God.

'What are you doing here, Elijah?' God asked him again.

Again Elijah poured out his tale of woe.

'Elijah,' God said, 'you are *not* the only person in Israel who loves and serves me. There are seven thousand other people who are loyal to me and refuse to worship Baal.'

Then God told Elijah what to do next. His work for God was not finished yet. God also said, 'Go and anoint Elisha to be prophet after you.'

God realized that Elijah needed a helper and friend. Elisha was the man who would be his companion and carry on his work when Elijah had gone.

belonging to a man called Naboth. He had turned it into a vineyard. He grew rows of grape vines and had hollowed out a trough where he crushed the ripe grapes to make wine.

'If only I had that plot of land to add to mine!' Ahab sighed. 'I could turn it into a lovely vegetable garden.'

A little later he thought, 'Why shouldn't I have it?' and sent for Naboth.

'I want your piece of land to add to mine,' he told him. 'I'm willing to give you another piece of land, or pay you a fair price for it.'

Naboth shook his head quickly. 'Long ago,' he said, 'when Joshua divided the land among the tribes, this land was given to my ancestors. They handed it down to me and I must leave it to my sons. God gave me this land and God forbid that I should sell it to you, however much you might pay me.'

Ahab was angry and disappointed. When the servant announced that dinner was ready he said crossly, 'I don't want any!'

Sulking and silent, he lay on his bed and turned his face to the wall.

Jezebel came looking for him. 'What *is* the matter?' she asked. 'Why are you so miserable?'

Ahab sat up slowly. 'It's all because of Naboth,' he complained. 'I want his vineyard and he won't let me have it.'

Jezebel laughed. 'And you are supposed to be the king?' she said teasingly. 'What's the good of being king if you can't get what you want? Leave it to me! And now cheer up!'

167
Ahab's Kitchen Garden
1 KINGS 21

King Ahab enjoyed living in his summer palace at Jezreel. He loved to walk through the palace gardens, admiring them and planning what he would do next. Next door to the king's garden was a plot of land

The King Gets his Way

1 KINGS 21

Jezebel thought hard. If Naboth would not agree to hand over his land, she must get rid of him and his family. Then Ahab could have what he wanted.

She quickly wrote a letter to the leading citizens in Jezreel. She signed it with the king's name and sealed it with the king's seal.

'Announce a public holiday,' she wrote, 'and call everyone together. See that Naboth is there and put him in a place of importance. Then pay a couple of scoundrels to say that they have heard Naboth calling out curses against God and against the king. Put him on trial for these crimes and, when you have found him guilty, put him to death.'

The city council was afraid of the queen. They quickly obeyed her orders. Before long, a message was delivered at the palace. 'Naboth and his sons are dead,' Jezebel read with satisfaction. She hurried straight to Ahab.

'You can have your precious bit of land,' she told him. 'Naboth is dead.'

Ahab was delighted and took possession of his new land at once.

But God had seen all that had happened, and he sent Elijah to speak to the king.

When Ahab saw Elijah, his face fell.

'My old enemy!' he exclaimed grimly. 'Have you caught up with me?'

'I have,' Elijah answered solemnly. 'I have brought you a message from God. All your life you have done wrong and broken God's law. Now you have done a very wicked thing.

You have brought sudden and violent death to an innocent man. I am warning you now. Death will come suddenly and violently to you and to your wicked wife, Jezebel. Your sons will not reign after you in Israel.'

When Elijah had gone, Ahab felt very ashamed. He knew that Jezebel had done wrong and that he must share the blame. He took off his fine royal robes and put on rough sacking. He did not eat the rich palace food. He went around looking gloomy and sad. He wanted to show how sorry he was for his wrongdoing.

God noticed how Ahab was behaving.

'Ahab really seems sorry for what he has done,' he told Elijah. 'I will put off the time when I will punish him. But his family are not fit to be kings of Israel.'

169
Elijah's Last Journey
2 KINGS 2

Elijah was glad to have Elisha to help him and be his close companion. Elisha thought that Elijah was the most wonderful man that he had ever known. He wished that he could be half as brave and good as his master. Elijah was not afraid of king or people. He stood up for God and for justice and right, even at the risk of his own life.

But now he was growing old and God had told him that his life would soon end. He must hand over his work to Elisha.

As the two of them walked together one day, Elisha knew in his bones that this was the day that he would have to be parted from Elijah. But Elijah was silent, so he said nothing.

When they reached Gilgal, Elijah spoke.

'Stay here,' he ordered Elisha, 'God has told me to go to Bethel.'

'Then I'm coming too,' Elisha answered. 'I'm not going to leave you now.'

When they reached Bethel, a group of prophets came hurrying out to meet them.

194

'Do you know that God is going to take your master away from you today?' they whispered to Elisha, as Elijah strode on.

'I know,' Elisha said, 'but I don't want to talk about it.' And he quickened his steps to catch up with Elijah.

When they reached Bethel, Elijah said, 'Stay here, God has told me to go on to Jericho.'

But again Elisha refused to be parted from his master.

At Jericho another crowd of prophets came out to meet them, and warned Elisha that Elijah would leave him that day.

'Stay here,' Elijah ordered, for the third time. 'God has told me to go to the River Jordan.'

Elisha was determined to stay close to Elijah, so the two walked on together. When they came to the river's edge, they stopped. Then Elijah took off his cloak, folded it and struck the water with it. At once the water divided and left a path through the middle.

Both men crossed to the other side.

The Fiery Chariot

2 KINGS 2

When Elijah and Elisha reached the other side of the river, Elijah began to talk.

'Is there anything you want to ask from me, before I go?' he said.

'I should like to inherit your greatness and power, just as if I were your eldest son,' Elisha answered earnestly.

Elijah paused for a moment. 'That is a difficult thing to ask for,' he admitted, 'but if you see me when I am taken away from you, you shall have your request.'

Slowly they went on walking and talking.

Then, suddenly, Elisha saw a chariot of fire, drawn by horses of fire, plunge towards the earth, cutting him off from his master. He peered intently past the fiery chariot at the figure of Elijah. As he watched, a sudden violent gust of wind took Elijah up—up into the blue sky.

'My father! My father!' Elisha called after him. 'Great prophet of Israel—don't leave me!' He knew that he would never see his much-loved master again.

For a while he stood, rooted to the spot, lost in sadness and wonder. Then he looked down and saw Elijah's cloak, lying on the ground at his feet, where it had fallen from Elijah's shoulders.

Elisha picked it up. Then, with heavy steps, he went back to the River Jordan. He stopped at the brink. He would see if he *had* been given his request. He rolled up the cloak, as Elijah had done, and struck the water with it. The water divided, just as it had done for Elijah.

The prophets from Jericho were still waiting, full of curiosity. When they saw the water part for Elisha, they nodded their heads wisely.

'Elijah's power has been handed on to Elisha,' they agreed.

Israel and Judah

171
The Truthful Prophet
1 KINGS 22

Since the nation of Israel had split into two kingdoms, Israel and Judah, there had often been war between them. But now King Ahab had made peace by marrying his daughter to the son of King Jehoshaphat of Judah.

One day, Jehoshaphat came to Samaria to visit Ahab.

'Will you help me win back Ramoth Gilead from my old enemy, Syria?' Ahab asked him. Ahab had fought many battles against Syria, the country on Israel's northern border.

'I and my army will help you,' Jehoshaphat agreed. But, because he loved and served God, he added, 'Let's first ask God's advice.'

Ahab agreed and called for the court prophets. There were hundreds of them, kept in luxury by the king.

They were always ready to tell Ahab what he wanted to hear.

The two kings sat in state by the city gates and crowds watched as Ahab asked his prophets, 'Shall we go to recapture Ramoth Gilead?'

'Yes!' they shouted encouragingly. 'God will give it to you!'

Jehoshaphat was not taken in by these false flatterers.

'Have you no other prophet who will truly bring you God's message?' he asked.

'There's Micaiah,' Ahab admitted, 'but I hate him! He always prophesies bad things.'

'Don't talk like that,' Jehoshaphat said. 'We want to hear God's word.'

An official went to fetch Micaiah, while the rest of the prophets went on prancing around excitedly. One, called Zedekiah, butted like an angry ram with some wicked-looking horns that he had made out of iron.

'This is how you will win!' he kept shouting.

As the official brought Micaiah to the kings, he advised him, 'Do as the other prophets and tell their majesties that they will win.'

'I swear by God to tell the truth,' Micaiah replied.

'Shall we attack Ramoth Gilead, Micaiah?' Ahab asked.

Micaiah looked at the noisy, excited prophets and answered mockingly, 'Go on—attack!'

'Micaiah—tell the truth!' Ahab ordered.

Micaiah's voice changed. Slowly and sadly he said, 'If you go, the people will be scattered over the hills like sheep without a shepherd. I see the whole army defeated.'

The Death of Ahab

1 KINGS 22

Micaiah's words of doom were followed by a horrified silence. Then a noisy hubbub broke out.

'Didn't I tell you?' Ahab said angrily to Jehoshaphat. 'Micaiah never brings me good news!'

The other prophets shouted indignantly at Micaiah.

'How dare you pretend to know what God has to say!' Zedekiah called out. He dropped the iron horns with a clatter and fetched Micaiah a stinging blow on his face.

'Arrest Micaiah!' Ahab ordered. 'Throw in prison and keep him on bread and water until I return!'

'If you return, then God has not spoken through me,' Micaiah answered gravely.

Next morning, the two kings got ready for battle. Ahab took one precaution.

'I shall go dressed as an ordinary soldier,' he told Jehoshaphat, 'then no one will recognize me. You can wear your royal robes.'

Before the battle, the Syrian general gave the order.

'Kill King Ahab. He is the only one who matters to us.'

As soon as the Syrians saw Jehoshaphat's royal robes, they thought that he was Ahab. When they came nearer, and discovered their mistake, they let him go free.

But one Syrian soldier, shooting at random, hit King Ahab. The arrow pierced his coat of mail, wounding him badly. All day long he stayed, propped up in his chariot, encouraging his troops, but at evening he died. The scattered army of Israel was ordered to go home, defeated. Their king was dead.

173
Singing for Victory
2 CHRONICLES 20

King Jehoshaphat was very frightened. News reached his palace in Jerusalem that three enemy states had joined to attack Judah. Already they had captured one of his towns. Soon they would advance on the capital itself.

The king called everyone to Jerusalem. Families came hurrying to the city, crowding into the temple court where the king was waiting for them.

Next to the king stood the Levites. Their job was to look after the temple, to make music and sing God's praises there.

King Jehoshaphat knew that his army was not strong enough to defeat the enemies. In front of all the people, he asked God to help them. 'God, you rule the whole world,' he prayed. 'We are in great trouble.

Enemies are coming to take away the land that you gave us and we cannot drive them out alone. Please help us.'

Then one of the Levites stepped forward. God had given him an answer.

'Your Majesty, and all the people,' he began, 'God says, "Don't be afraid!" You won't have to fight at all. Set out tomorrow and God will give you victory.'

When they heard this, the king and the people bowed low in thankful praise to God. All the Levites broke out singing:

'Praise God! Thank God!'

Early next morning, Jehoshaphat called his troops together.

'Men of Judah, put your trust in God,' he told them. 'Believe what he has said.'

Then he ordered the temple musicians to march at the head of the army and, as they marched, the Levites sang:

'Praise the Lord! His love is eternal!'

While they were still some way off, panic broke out among the enemy armies. They began to fight furiously against one another.

When the army of Judah arrived, there were only dead bodies to be seen! Jehoshaphat and his men collected up all the spoil left on the battlefield, then marched back in triumph to Jerusalem. They arrived at the temple to a burst of cymbals and trumpets.

Everyone soon knew that God had given them victory. He had rescued them without a single blow being struck.

Stories of Elisha

174
One Problem Solved
2 KINGS 4

Up in the north, in the kingdom of Israel, Elisha was carrying on God's work, now that Elijah had gone. Elisha was very different from his master. Elijah had been strong and stern. People had been a little afraid of him, even while they admired his courage and goodness. Everyone loved Elisha. They could tell him their troubles.

One day, a very worried-looking woman came to see him.

'Sir,' she began, 'my husband has died. He loved and served God and belonged to one of the prophets' schools. Now I'm in real trouble because he owed money. The man he owed says he'll take my two boys as slaves, if I don't settle the debt. But I

haven't any money. Please will you help me?'

Elisha was a poor prophet, too. He could not pay the widow's debt.

'I wonder how I can help you?' he murmured. Then God put a suggestion into Elisha's mind.

'Have you anything at all left in the house?' he asked.

'Just a little jar of olive oil—that's all,' she answered.

'That will do,' Elisha said. 'Call on everyone you know and borrow their empty jars. Collect as many as you can. Take them all home, go indoors with your sons and shut the door. Then start pouring the oil from your little jar into the ones you have borrowed.'

The widow did exactly as Elisha said. When she had collected a good stock of empty jars she began to fill them with oil. The boys took the full jars from her and handed her more empty ones. It seemed as if the supply of oil would never run out.

At last, when she called out, 'Pass me another jar,' the boys replied, 'There aren't any left.'

At that very moment the oil in her own jar ran out. Not a drop was left. She hurried back to Elisha to tell him about the wonderful thing that had happened.

'Go and sell the oil,' Elisha said, 'then pay off your debt. You'll still have enough money to live on.'

📖 175
A Room of his Own
2 KINGS 4

Elisha did not live all the time in one place but went about, teaching and helping the people.

One day, when he visited Shunem,

a rich farmer's wife invited him to dinner.

'Come here for a meal whenever you visit Shunem,' she told him kindly. So Elisha often shared a meal with his new friends.

One day, after he had left, the woman said to her husband: 'The prophet often visits Shunem. Could we build him a room of his own, so that he always has somewhere to stay?'

'Do as you like, my dear,' her husband replied, absent-mindedly.

The woman set to work. She called a builder to add a room onto the flat roof. She ordered the joiner to make a table and chair and a bed to furnish the room. She set an oil lamp on the table.

When Elisha next came she showed him his new room. Elisha was delighted to have somewhere to pray and study, as well as to sleep.

'I wish I could think of some way to repay this woman for all her kindness,' he told Gehazi, his servant. 'But she is rich and needs nothing.'

Gehazi knew from the servants' talk that there was one thing the woman wanted very much indeed.

'She wants a son,' he told his master.

Elisha was sure that if he asked God to give the woman a child, God would hear his prayer.

'Ask her to come here,' he told Gehazi. The servant soon returned with the woman. She stood in the doorway, waiting to hear what the prophet would say.

'By this time next year,' Elisha told her, 'you will be holding your own baby son in your arms.'

The woman could scarcely believe her ears. It seemed too good to be true!

One Dreadful Day

2 KINGS 4

When Elisha's words came true and
her little son was born, the kind
woman of Shunem was overjoyed.
She took great care of her baby.
Nothing was too good for him. Now,
when Elisha came to visit, he would
have to admire the baby's new tooth
or watch his first unsteady steps. As
the boy grew older, his father loved to
have his company, too.

'Come with me to the fields today,'
he said to him one morning. 'You can
help with the harvest.'

His mother watched proudly as her
husband set off, holding their small
son's hand.

For a while the boy ran about
happily among the reapers, collecting
his own small bundle of barley.

Suddenly he cried out to his father,
'My head! My head! It hurts so much!'

His father looked at the flushed
little face in alarm.

'Take him straight home to his
mother!' he ordered a servant.

His mother took the child into the
coolest room in the house and sat with
him on her lap, gently rocking him, as
she had when he was a baby. But at
midday he died.

Without a word to anyone, she
carried the little body upstairs, laid it
gently on Elisha's bed and shut the
door. Then she called her husband.
She did not tell him what had
happened. She just asked him to send
a servant with a donkey, so that she
could visit Elisha.

'Why visit the prophet today?' he
asked.

But still she told him nothing. She
did not want to talk to anyone but
Elisha about what had happened.

'Make the donkey go as fast as he
can,' she said to the servant, and the
two set off.

Alive Again

2 KINGS 4

When the woman was still some way off, Elisha recognized her.

'Look!' he said to Gehazi, his servant, 'There is the woman from Shunem. Hurry out to meet her and find out if anything is wrong.'

Gehazi set off quickly.

'Is all well?' he asked her, breathlessly. The woman said nothing about what had happened but hurried on to find Elisha. Gehazi began to push her aside to stop her from bothering the prophet, but Elisha said, 'Leave her alone—she is very upset. Something has happened but God has not told me what it is.'

As soon as she was with Elisha, the woman poured out her trouble.

'Why did you raise my hopes by asking God to give me a son?' she asked. 'Now he has died. How could you let that happen?'

Elisha turned to Gehazi.

'Take my stick,' he said, 'and go straight to Shunem. Lay my stick on the child. Now hurry! Stop for no one!'

'I'm not leaving you,' the woman told Elisha tearfully.

'We'll go back together,' Elisha said quietly.

Before they had arrived they met Gehazi coming back to meet them. 'It's no good,' he said, handing Elisha back his staff. 'Nothing happened. There's no sign of life in the child.'

When they reached the woman's home, Elisha went straight to his room. There, on his bed, lay the dead child. Elisha closed the door quietly. First he prayed to God. Then he lay gently on the lifeless child, placing his eyes on the boy's eyes, his hands on

the boy's hands and his mouth on the boy's mouth. Gradually a little warmth crept into the cold body.

Elisha got up, paced about the room, then again breathed warmth and air into the dead boy.

Suddenly there was a little sound—'Atishoo!' The boy had sneezed! Then he sneezed again—and again. After that, he opened his eyes wide.

'Get the boy's mother, Gehazi!' Elisha called out.

'Here's your son!' Elisha told her.

His mother picked him up. There were tears in her eyes. The little boy smiled at her. He was alive!

The Girl Prisoner

2 KINGS 5

The Syrians began to attack Israel again by making raids over the border. They would seize anything that they could lay hands on, then make a dash for home. One day they carried off a young girl and handed her over to their general, Naaman.

Naaman was a fine soldier, popular with all his men and highly thought of by the king of Syria. He had won important victories against Israel.

The little Israelite girl looked strong and healthy and Naaman decided to take her home as a present for his wife.

The girl soon settled down to her new way of life. If she was homesick she did not show it. She knew that compared with most slaves, she was lucky. She had a kind mistress and a good home.

One day her mistress began to talk to her sadly.

'Do you know that your master is ill?' she asked her. 'He suffers from a terrible skin disease that cannot be cured. He can only get worse.'

The girl's thoughts flew to home. She remembered Elisha the prophet, who had done so many wonderful things with God's help.

'If only we were in Israel!' she exclaimed. 'My master could go to the prophet—he would cure him!'

Naaman's wife told her husband what her slave had said and Naaman repeated it to the king of Syria.

'I'd do anything in my power to make you well,' the king said. 'I'll write to the king of Israel and send you to him with presents and money for your cure.'

When Naaman arrived in Samaria with his horses and chariots, the king of Israel was horrified. He read the letter:

'This is to introduce my army general Naaman. I want you to cure him of his disease.'

'Who does he think I am?' the king of Israel exclaimed. '*I* can't cure Naaman. But if I refuse, he'll make that an excuse to declare war on me!'

Someone told Elisha what had happened. He sent a message at once to the king.

'Send Naaman to me,' he wrote. 'He will find out that there *is* a prophet of God in Israel.'

Cure for Naaman

2 KINGS 5

Naaman arrived at Elisha's house expecting something wonderful and exciting to happen. The prophet would come out to greet him, then perhaps he would wave his hand over him and say some magic words.

But Elisha did not seem to have noticed the splendid horses and chariots drawn up outside his door. He just sent out his servant with this message:

'Go and wash seven times in the River Jordan and you will be cured.'

Naaman jumped back into his chariot and ordered the horses to drive off at top speed. He was furious.

'Why should I wash in their dirty old river?' he raged. 'We have far cleaner rivers of our own in Syria.'

But one of his servants said gently: 'If he'd asked you to do something hard, you would gladly have tried it. Why not follow his advice when he asks such an easy thing?'

Naaman's anger was quickly gone. He laughed when he realized how full of his own importance he had been.

He climbed down from the chariot and washed seven times in the river. Then he looked down at his body. The skin was as healthy and firm as a child's.

A great flood of joy swept over Naaman.

Back they all went to Elisha. This time the prophet came out to meet his important visitor.

'Your God is the only true God,' Naaman told him. 'I will worship him too.' Then he offered Elisha money and rich presents.

'I will take nothing from you,' Elisha said. 'I am God's servant and he has cured you.'

But Gehazi, Elisha's servant, who was listening, thought that his master was very foolish to refuse such wealth. When Naaman's procession had left, he set off after them. He would get something for himself.

'Excuse me,' he said to Naaman, 'but some poor prophets have just arrived at my master's house. Could he have some money after all, to give to them?'

Naaman gladly handed Gehazi a generous gift.

Gehazi smuggled his treasures home, then went in to see Elisha as if nothing had happened.

'Where have you been?' Elisha asked.

'Nowhere!' Gehazi lied.

'Gehazi,' Elisha said sternly. 'I know everything that you have done. I know all about your greed and your lies. This will be your punishment: You will suffer from the very same disease that Naaman had.'

180
Eyes to See
2 KINGS 6

Once more Syria and Israel were at war. But things kept going wrong for the king of Syria. *Someone* kept telling the king of Israel his most secret plans!

'There must be a spy in the palace,' he grumbled.

'We are all loyal to you,' his officers assured him. 'It is the prophet Elisha who tells his king everything that's going on.

'Then send the army to seize Elisha!' the king ordered.

A strong Syrian force was despatched to Dothan, where Elisha was living.

When Elisha's servant went to fetch water next morning, he was horrified. The whole town was surrounded by enemy soldiers. He ran to Elisha with the bad news.

'Whatever shall we do?' he asked in panic.

'Don't be frightened,' Elisha said. 'There are more fighting on our side than on the side of the enemy.' Then Elisha prayed: 'O God, please open this young man's eyes.'

When the servant looked up again, he saw that the hillside all around was covered with horses and chariots of fire. God's angels were protecting

Elisha and his servant, too.

When the Syrians closed in to attack, Elisha prayed again, 'O God, please close these men's eyes.'

The Syrian soldiers suddenly found that they could not see. Elisha went forward and offered to lead them. He took them straight to the king of Israel!

Only when they were safely inside Samaria did Elisha ask God to give the Syrians back their sight.

The king of Israel was delighted. Now he had his enemy at his mercy.

'Shall I kill them all?' he asked Elisha excitedly.

'Certainly not!' Elisha said. 'Give them a meal and send them home.'

How surprised the terrified soldiers were to be treated to a royal feast by their enemies! They went home with very different feelings towards the people of Israel. There were no more raids against Israel after that.

181
Hunger in the City
2 KINGS 7

Some time later, the king of Syria marched with his whole army against Samaria, the capital city of Israel. They camped outside, letting nothing in or out of the city.

Food soon became scarce inside Samaria. There was nothing left to buy. The very rich people even paid huge sums to get hold of a donkey's head to cook for dinner. The poor people just went hungry.

The king walked around the walls, talking to his people. When he discovered how desperate they were for food, he was beside himself with worry.

'I blame Elisha!' he said. 'I'll kill him!'

Elisha, sitting in his house, knew all that the king was thinking. He waited for the royal visitor to arrive.

'God has brought all this trouble on us,' the king complained to Elisha. 'Why doesn't he *do* something?'

'I promise you,' Elisha told the king, 'by this time tomorrow, God says, the best wheat and barley will be sold in Samaria for one fifth the price that you have been paying for the rubbish on sale today.'

The king's chief officer laughed out loud.

'That couldn't happen if God sent barley raining down from heaven!' he said.

Elisha looked at him hard. 'What God has said *will* happen,' he promised. 'You will see it for yourself. But because you don't believe what God can do, you will not eat any of that food.'

182
Good News!
2 KINGS 7

There were four men outside the gates of Samaria, even worse off than the citizens inside. These Israelites were not allowed into the city because they were suffering from a dreaded disease and had to stay away from towns and people.

'We shall die of hunger,' one said.

'We'd be no better off if we got into the city,' the second remarked.

'Why don't we go across to the Syrians?' the third suggested. 'I know they might kill us outright but, then again, they might give us something to eat.'

'We shouldn't be worse off,' the fourth agreed, 'and we might save our lives.'

It was growing dark when all four set off towards the Syrian camp. They crept along stealthily, on the look out for a friendly Syrian soldier. But they saw no one and heard nothing.

Cautiously they looked inside the first tent they came to. There was not a Syrian to be seen. But there was food and wine in plenty on the table.

They set to, ravenously, eating and drinking to their heart's content. Then, with great sighs of satisfaction, they came slowly out of that tent and looked inside the next one. It was empty, too.

Now that they were no longer hungry, they noticed all the other things that were lying around—silver and gold, and rich embroidered robes. They rubbed their hands with glee. They had never had such luck. The whole camp was deserted and they could help themselves to everything they wanted.

Then one of them paused. 'Wait a bit,' he said. 'We should not be carrying on like this. We've got good news for all our people and we're keeping it to ourselves.'

Quickly they hurried back to Samaria and roused the guards. The king got up from his bed and hurried to see what all the fuss was about. At first he did not believe the four men's story.

'It's a trick!' he said. 'The Syrians want to lure us out, so that they can take the city.'

But he agreed to send a small band of soldiers to investigate. They found everything just as the four had reported. God had rescued Israel. The Syrians, thinking they heard sounds of a great army advancing against them, had fled for their lives.

God's word through Elisha came true. Syrian food supplies were brought in to sell at the city gate.

The king ordered his chief officer to control the crowds that came to buy. But in the mad excitement to get food, someone knocked him to the ground and he died in the crush of people.

Troubles in Judah and Israel

📖 183
Secret Mission
2 KINGS 9

King Ahab of Israel was dead but his wicked queen, Jezebel, still lived. King Joram, their son, was no better than his parents.

God told Elisha that the time had come to end the rule of this wicked family. He sent for a young prophet.

'Take this jar of olive oil,' he said, 'and go to the army camp. Find Jehu, one of the army officers. Get him on his own and anoint him king. Then fly for your life.'

Elisha knew only too well what would happen to the prophet if King Joram found out what he had done.

The young man arrived at the camp and found the officers sitting out in the open, discussing military plans.

'I have a message for you, sir,' he said to Jehu.

When Jehu took him indoors the prophet anointed him with oil and announced, 'God proclaims you king over Israel.'

Then the young man made off as fast as he could and Jehu went back to the other officers, his mind whirling.

'Is everything all right?' they asked. 'What did that crazy chap have to say?'

'Can't you guess?' Jehu asked. He felt as if the secret must be written all over his face.

'We've no idea,' they answered.

'I am to be king,' Jehu told them.

A great cheer went up. The officers spread their cloaks on the top step and made Jehu stand there.

'Jehu is king!' they shouted.

📖 184
The Crazy Driver
2 KINGS 9

Jehu lost no time. He and his followers got into their chariots and set off for Jezreel, driving fast.

King Joram was resting quietly in his summer palace at Jezreel. He had been wounded in battle while fighting against Syria with the help of his nephew, King Ahaziah of Judah.

'Get my chariot ready at once,' Joram ordered. Then he and King Ahaziah of Judah rode out to meet Jehu.

'Are you coming in peace?' King Joram called out, as the chariots drew alongside.

'How can there be peace while you and your mother, Jezebel, rule over Israel?' Jehu replied.

'It's treason, Ahaziah!' Joram shouted.

Swiftly they wheeled their chariots around to return to Jezreel. But Jehu shot an arrow with all his force. It struck Joram in the back and pierced through to his heart, killing him instantly. Then Jehu pursued and killed Ahaziah King of Judah, too.

Quickly news was brought to Jezebel that Jehu had killed her son.

She did her hair carefully, put on eye-shadow and looked for Jehu from an upstairs window of the palace. Jehu's chariot soon came clattering up.

'You murderer!' Jezebel shouted down. 'What are you doing here?'

Jehu did not answer her.

'Is there anyone on my side?' he called up.

A few cautious heads appeared at the window.

'Throw her down!' Jehu ordered, in a loud voice.

Without a word, some of the palace servants took hold of Jezebel and threw her from the window, killing her outright.

Jehu, now king, showed no mercy. He killed every member of Ahab's family and many more people besides. He believed he was God's servant, getting rid of Baal-worship in Israel. But God was not pleased with Jehu's brutal actions. He did not serve God with all his heart.

The guard on top of the watch-tower at the city gate saw Jehu's cavalcade in the distance and reported it to the king.

'Send a messenger to find out if they are friends or enemies,' Joram ordered.

When a messenger on horseback galloped up, Jehu would tell him nothing. But soon the guard on watch called out, 'I know who is coming! Only one man drives as madly as that. It's Jehu!'

185
King in Hiding
2 KINGS 11

Athaliah, Jezebel's daughter, was queen mother in Judah. When she heard that her son, young King Ahaziah, had been killed by Jehu, she did not stop to shed tears but set about gaining power for herself. She gave orders for the whole royal family to be put to death, so that she could reign supreme.

For six terrible years, Athaliah ruled Judah and taught the people to worship Baal.

But one little prince had escaped the queen's cruel order. He was Joash, Ahaziah's baby son. His aunt snatched him to safety and hid him where his grandmother would never look—in the temple building itself. For Aunt Jehosheba was married to Jehoiada, a priest of God in the temple.

The tiny baby grew into a toddler and then a small boy, and still the secret was kept. When he was seven years old, his uncle and aunt decided that the time had come to crown him king.

Jehoiada sent for all the palace and temple guards and swore them to secrecy. Then he showed them the young prince. They were all ready to help make him king. No one loved wicked Athaliah and her Baal priests.

Jehoiada chose the time of day when the guards were changed, so that both shifts would be present to help. He ordered some soldiers to stand at the palace, others at the city gate and an armed band to be at the temple to protect Joash.

All went as planned. When every soldier was at his post, Jehoiada led the boy out and placed the crown on his head. He put a copy of God's law in his hands. Then he proclaimed:

'This is your king!'

The crowd that had gathered clapped their hands and began to shout:

'Long live the king!'

Athaliah heard the noise and hurried to the temple. She took one look at the small boy, standing gravely with the crown on his head and knew she had been betrayed.

'Treason!' she called out.

But no one rushed to defend her. Everyone there was glad that her wicked reign was over.

Until Joash grew up, his uncle Jehoiada helped him to rule well and obey God. The city was happy and peaceful, now that a good king was once more on the throne of Judah.

186
Swindlers and Robbers!
AMOS

When Jehu died, his son and grandson reigned after him. But it was his great-grandson, Jeroboam II, who made Israel strong again. He had a long and successful reign of over forty years. But he did not trust or obey God, and there was much that was wrong in the land.

God sent Amos to remind Israel of his laws and to warn them to change their ways. Amos was a sheep-breeder who lived in the southern kingdom of Judah. When he went to Israel he took with him wool to sell.

Amos stood up in the market-place at Bethel and told the people what God thought of them.

'You traders cheat your customers,' he called out in ringing tones. 'You use false weights, so that they get less than they pay for. Your prices are so high that poor people can't afford to buy and, when they do, you sell them rubbish instead of the good grain on display. If anyone can't pay his bill, you take him as a slave— or else you take his cloak from him and leave him shivering with cold at night. God will not tolerate injustice like that!'

Amos caught sight of a wealthy woman, picking her way between the stalls. She was dressed in a rich, embroidered gown and smothered in expensive perfume.

'You women are to blame, too,' he went on. 'You are the ones who make your husbands cheat and swindle, so that you have money to spend on fine clothes and wine. All you rich people want to do is sit around all day, swilling wine and playing new songs, while your slaves toil, hungry and exhausted. God demands kindness and fair play.

'All you people of Israel, listen! God wants justice in the courts. As it is, no one gets a fair trial unless he can hand the judge a fat bribe. God says, "Let justice flow freely and show fairness and kindness to each other."'

But the people did not want to listen to God's words. When Amos dared to speak against the bull-calf shrine at Bethel and even to criticize the king, one of the priests threatened him.

'Go back to Judah,' he said, 'and do your preaching there.'

'Please Come Back!'
HOSEA

Amos left Israel but, not long after, Hosea, a prophet who belonged to the northern kingdom, brought the people God's message.

Hosea was married to a pretty girl called Gomer and he loved her dearly. Soon they had a baby son, but Gomer did not want to stay at home, looking after the baby. She liked to be off to the town, to have a good time.

When her little daughter was born, Hosea hoped that Gomer would settle down. But things were no better and, when a third child was born, Gomer went out one day, leaving the children, and did not come back.

Hosea was heartbroken. He loved Gomer so much. He felt lonely and miserable without her.

Then God spoke to him. 'Hosea, I know just how you are feeling,' he said. 'I love the people of Israel just as dearly as you love Gomer. They have gone away and stopped loving me, just as Gomer has deserted you.'

Hosea had never thought of God like that. He began to understand how Israel's disobedience hurt God. God went on:

'Don't stop loving Gomer, any more than I have stopped loving Israel. Go and find her and win her back.'

No man in those days would go looking for an unfaithful wife. He would divorce her. But Hosea did not think of his pride. He left someone to care for the children and set off to find Gomer. He found her, a poor wretched slave to some man who had bought her. Her good time had not lasted long.

Hosea gave all the money he had to buy her back and made up the price with the grain from the pantry. He loved Gomer in spite of her silliness and the wrong that she had done to him.

Now Hosea began to preach God's message in a new way.

'God loves you so much,' he told the people. 'It makes him very sad that you run away from him to serve the Baals. God does not want to punish you, or be parted from you.

But if you refuse to listen and return to God, you will bring misery and suffering on the whole nation. Come back to God and tell him you are sorry. He is waiting to love and forgive you.'

188
Isaiah's Vision
ISAIAH 6

At the time when King Jeroboam II was enjoying his long and prosperous reign in Israel, King Uzziah was on the throne of Judah. He, too, had a long and prosperous reign, and for most of his life he loved and obeyed God. When he died, the people wondered what would happen next in Judah.

Young Isaiah was a nobleman who shared these feelings. One day, when he was at the temple, thinking and praying about the future of his country, he had a wonderful vision God. Describing it afterwards, he said:

'I saw God, sitting on his throne, high above all. His royal robe filled the temple. Creatures of flame stood around him, shielding their faces with their wings from the brightness of God's glory. They kept calling to each other, "Holy! Holy! Holy! The Lord Almighty is holy! His glory fills the whole world."

'As the sound of their voices pulsed through the temple, the whole building seemed to shiver and shake. Billowing smoke filled the whole place. I was terrified. God was so great and good, and I felt wretched and ashamed. I called out:

' "What will become of me? I have seen God, the holy one—and I am sinful. I belong to a wicked nation."

'Then one of the fiery creatures flew towards me. He had picked up a live coal with tongs from the altar, and he touched my lips with it.

' "You are made clean," he said, "and your sin is forgiven."

'Then God spoke: "Who can I send?" he asked. "Who will be my messenger?"

'At once I answered, "I'll go—send me!" '

God gave Isaiah his message, but warned him in advance that the people would be hard-hearted. They would not listen to him or tell God they were sorry. But Isaiah was still willing to be God's prophet.

Keep Calm!

ISAIAH 7

King Ahaz of Judah was scared out of his wits and the people were shaking with fear. An enemy was coming.

Way up in the north-west, beyond Israel and Judah, there was a great, new power. The Assyrians were a strong and cruel people—their chief god was the god of war. Their kings hunted lions and conquered nations with the same skill and enjoyment. The king of Assyria had forced both Syria and Israel to swear to be loyal to him, and pay him huge sums of money in order to be left alive in their own lands.

But the kings of Syria and Israel, once enemies, joined together to rebel against their cruel overlord. They planned to march into Judah and force the king to help them fight against Assyria.

Now, a messenger had brought King Ahaz news that the two armies of Syria and Israel were already in his country. Soon they would reach the capital.

Ahaz did not know what to do, or where to turn for help and advice.

God sent Isaiah, his prophet, to reassure the king.

'Go and meet Ahaz by the reservoir,' God said. Ahaz was busy inspecting the city water supply, in case there was a siege.

He looked up when Isaiah came towards him, his face worried and frightened.

'God says, "Keep wide awake, but stay calm,"' Isaiah told him.

'"You have nothing to fear from the kings of Syria and Israel. They are about as dangerous as a couple of damp squibs. They may want to besiege Jerusalem and take the throne from you, but I, God, promise that this will never happen. You do not need to send for any other army to help you. All you have to do is trust me. If you don't keep trusting me, you will not survive."'

Ahaz listened but he did not obey. He was not willing to sit still and wait for God to save him. Instead he did a very foolish thing. He sent a messenger to the fierce king of Assyria, asking him to come to his rescue. He was putting his head right into the lion's mouth.

Critical Times in Judah

190
The Emperor States his Price

2 KINGS 17—18

The northern kingdom of Israel had fallen to the mighty power of Assyria.

The Assyrians were cruel conquerors. They tortured and killed, then marched long strings of half-naked captives far from their

own land. Only the weakest inhabitants were left in Israel. The Assyrians imported captives from other lands to share the country with them.

God was sad that his people had suffered so much because they had refused to pay any attention to the prophets' warnings. He hoped that Judah would learn from Israel's disaster.

But instead of trusting God, foolish King Ahaz invited the emperor of Assyria to help him fight his enemies. The Assyrians rescued Judah but the emperor made Ahaz pay him huge sums of gold and silver, and promise to be loyal to him.

Ahaz died twenty years later and his son Hezekiah became king. He loved and obeyed God and taught the people to keep God's laws.

It was then that the emperor of Assyria decided at last to invade Judah and conquer it, as he had done Israel. He actually seized some of the towns near Judah's border, so Hezekiah sent him an urgent message.

'Please leave us in peace and we will pay what you ask.'

The emperor asked a very high price indeed. Hezekiah had to strip the temple of some of its beautiful treasures, in order to get enough gold and silver.

Now, the king hoped, the emperor and his army would leave Judah in peace.

191
Enemy at the Gate
2 KINGS 18—19

The emperor of Assyria took Hezekiah's gold but, instead of marching away, he sent his chief officer with a large army to Jerusalem.

They spread across the road outside the city, proud and fierce, calling out to the king to surrender.

Hezekiah told the people to do and say nothing. Then he despatched three trusted advisers to talk with the Assyrian envoy.

'If you defy Assyria,' the official began, 'no one can help you—not even your God.'

'Please don't speak in the language that the people understand,' Hezekiah's officers begged. 'We don't want them to hear such talk.'

'They are the very ones who *should* hear,' the messenger replied. He cupped his hands and shouted up to the crowd on the city wall:

'Listen to the mighty emperor of Assyria and *He* can't save you! Don't

trust your God but trust us! We will take you to a lovely land where you'll all be happy.'

No one answered a word. They did as Hezekiah ordered and kept quiet.

When the officials reported to Hezekiah, he went straight to the temple to pray. He sent his three officials to the prophet Isaiah to ask him to pray for God's help, too.

Isaiah sent the king a message.

'God says, don't be frightened of the Assyrians. Do not listen when they say that God can't help you. God will make the emperor return to his own land without harming you.'

When the emperor heard that Hezekiah would not surrender, he sent him a letter.

'Your God says that you won't fall into my power,' he wrote, 'but don't believe it! The gods of other lands did not help them—so why should yours?'

Hezekiah showed the letter to no one but God. He took it with him to the temple.

'Please look at what the emperor is saying,' he prayed. 'Rescue us from him, so that all the world will know that you are God.'

God's answer came through Isaiah.

'The emperor has boasted that he is stronger than God, but he can do nothing unless God allows it. God will protect you. The Assyrians will go home without shooting a single arrow at Jerusalem.'

Before long the Assyrian army had pitched camp ready to lay siege to Jerusalem. But that same night, disaster struck. The emperor awoke in the morning to find that thousands of his soldiers lay dead. He could do nothing but gather together his few remaining troops and go home.

192
The King's Illness
ISAIAH 38

At the very time that Assyria was threatening Jerusalem, King Hezekiah fell ill. He had a painful boil that spread poison through his whole body. Isaiah visited him with a message from God.

'God says that you must put your affairs in order, because you are going to die,' he told the king.

When Isaiah left, Hezekiah felt sad and worried. He did not know what would happen to his people if he was not there to lead and defend them.

'Please God, help me,' he prayed. 'You know that I have tried to do what you want and be loyal to you.'

God said to Isaiah, 'Go back to Hezekiah and tell him that I have heard his prayer. In three days' time he will be in the temple again and he will live for another fifteen years. I will also rescue this city from Assyria.'

Isaiah told the palace servants to pound up some figs and make a hot paste, and to spread it on the king's boil.

While they were preparing the poultice, Hezekiah asked the prophet, 'How can I be sure that God will make me better?'

'God will give you a sign,' Isaiah answered. 'The shadow on the sundial stairway will go back ten steps.'

Hezekiah's father, King Ahaz, had built a special stairway for telling the time. As the sun shone, the shadow moved from one step to the next. By giving him extra years of life, God seemed to be making time go backwards for Hezekiah, as well as for the sundial.

Hezekiah was so thankful to God that he wrote a song to sing in the temple. This is how it ends:

'Lord, you have healed me. We will play harps and sing your praise,

Sing praise in your temple as long as we live.'

193
The Great Find
2 KINGS 22

When King Hezekiah died, his son Manasseh became king. He was as wicked as his father had been good. He rebuilt the baal altars that his father had pulled down and even filled God's temple with idols. He sacrificed some of his sons to Baal by burning them alive. The streets of Jerusalem ran with the blood of innocent citizens. The people of Judah followed their king's bad example.

Manasseh ruled for forty years. His son, the new king, was just as wicked, so some of the palace officials put him to death and made his eight-year-old son, Josiah, king instead.

Josiah learned to love and obey God, and as he grew up he tried to bring the people back to serving God.

When Manasseh was king, the temple had grown shabby and broken down. Josiah decided to repair it. He sent his secretary, Shaphan, to tell the High Priest, Hilkiah, to hand over the money from the repair fund to the builders and carpenters and masons, so that they could begin work.

While the workmen were clearing out, they came across a scroll. When they took it to Hilkiah, he recognized it as a long-lost copy of God's law.

He decided that the king should see it and handed the scroll to Shaphan, who read it out loud to the king. As King Josiah listened, he grew worried and upset. He began to realize just how many of God's laws the kings and people of Judah had broken and how much they deserved his punishment.

'Find a prophet who can tell us what God has to say to us about it,' he ordered.

Shaphan went to a woman prophet, called Huldah, and told her all about the finding of the book and the king's distress.

'Tell him that God is going to punish Jerusalem,' Huldah replied. 'The people are set on disobeying God. But Josiah has made up his mind to serve and love God, so he will enjoy peace during his lifetime.'

194
Josiah Lights a Bonfire
2 KINGS 23

When Shaphan brought Huldah's
message to the king, Josiah decided to
do all in his power to bring the people
back to God. He took the new-found
book of the law to the temple, where
everyone was gathered. The
important officials and priests as well
as the ordinary citizens had come to
hear what the king would say.

First the king read to them from the
scroll. Then he said:

'This book of the law tells us about
the covenant that God made with our
people, after he had brought them out
of Egypt. God has kept all the
promises he made to us but we have
broken our side of the agrement. I am
determined to make a fresh start and
promise to obey God and keep his
laws.'

All the people shoulted, 'We will
promise to obey God, too!'

Then Josiah ordered Hilkiah to
clear out the inside of the temple. It
was no good making the outside as
good as new, if the inside was still full
of images and all the horrible things
that went with the baal worship. The
idols were smashed to pieces and
burned in a huge bonfire. Josiah
stopped the people sacrificing their
babies to the baals.

When all the evil things had been
taken away, Josiah organized a great
festival to God.

The first Passover feast had been
held on the night that the people of
Israel left Egypt, hundreds of years
before. Moses had taught them to
celebrate it once a year, to remember
how God had saved them from
slavery and from the death of the
first-born. But in the days of the bad
kings, no one had remembered to
keep the Passover.

Now Josiah planned a magnificent
Passover feast, to be held in
Jerusalem, in just the way that God
had instructed through Moses.
Everyone in Judah flocked to
Jerusalem to join in the fun and
rejoicing.

But although Josiah did all he could
the people did not really share his
heartfelt wish to trust and obey God.

The Last Days of Judah

📖 195
'Don't Send Me!'

JEREMIAH 1

When King Josiah was a young man of about twenty, another young man, called Jeremiah, was preparing to serve God as a priest in the temple at Jerusalem. But God had other plans for him.

One day God spoke to him and said, 'Jeremiah, long before you were born, I chose you to be my prophet, passing on my words to the people of Judah and the nations around.'

'Please don't ask me to do that,' Jeremiah replied. 'I'm too young for such an important job. I'm not even any good at talking.'

'I will be with you to help you,' God said. Then he reached out and touched Jeremiah's mouth. 'I will give you the words to speak.'

Jeremiah knew that it was no good arguing with God. Even if his work was going to be difficult, he must do as God said.

'What can you see?' God asked him.

Jeremiah looked hard. He saw a big cooking-pot, set to heat on a crackling fire. As he watched, the soup in the pot came to the boil and began to pour over the top in a stream of scalding hot liquid.

Then God said:

'In just the same way, an enemy is going to overflow Judah, and destroy Jerusalem. Your job is to warn the people. If they stop their worship of Baal, and begin to obey my laws, they will escape disaster. If they don't listen, the enemy will surely come.'

Jeremiah wondered who the unknown enemy might be, for by now the great Assyrian Empire had grown weak and powerless. But he believed God's warning and began to tell the people to turn back to God. He knew that, although King Josiah truly loved and obeyed God, the people were half-hearted. They had not really changed their ways.

Josiah was killed, fighting against Egypt, when he was only thirty. The victorious Egyptians took Josiah's son off to Egypt and put a king of their own choice on Judah's throne. He was another son of Josiah, called Jehoiakim. He had to do as Egypt told him.

196
Jeremiah at the Pottery
JEREMIAH 18—19

One day, God said to Jeremiah, 'Go to the potter's workshop, I will give you my message there.'

Jeremiah set off for the quarter of the town where the potters made and sold their wares. He watched silently as the potter skilfully shaped the clay and turned the pot on his wheel. Then something went wrong and the pot was ruined. Perhaps there was a small stone in the clay. The potter kneaded the soft clay into a ball and patiently began again.

God's voice came softly to Jeremiah: 'I can do with my people what the potter has done with his clay. If only they will say they are sorry and be ready to change their ways, I can begin again to make something good and useful of the nation.'

God had another lesson to teach Jeremiah.

'Buy a clay jar,' God told him, 'and carry it to the city dump. Take some of the older priests and leaders with you.'

The little procession wound its way out of Jerusalem, Jeremiah in front, with his water jar on his head. A crowd of inquisitive people followed.

Men never carried water pots—they thought that was women's work! What *would* this strange prophet do next?

When Jeremiah arrived at the dump he hurled the jar down with all his might, smashing it into hundreds of pieces.

'Listen,' he told the crowd, 'God has waited long and patiently for you to turn back to him. He wanted to give you good things. But instead of being soft like the clay which the potter can shape, you have grown hard and disobedient. If you do not turn back to God, you will be broken like the pot. An enemy will come and defeat us.'

Then Jeremiah climbed the steep path back into the city and preached the same sermon in the temple. The important priests and leaders were furious. How dare Jeremiah say that the country would be conquered? One of them gave orders that Jeremiah should be arrested, beaten and left in chains until the morning.

📖 197
The King's Penknife
JEREMIAH 36

For more than twenty years Jeremiah went on warning the people of Judah to turn back to God before an enemy destroyed Jerusalem.

Now God said to him:

'Write down all the messages that I have ever given you, from the time when Josiah was king, up to the present. Perhaps the people will listen to them and be sorry that they have disobeyed me. Then I can forgive and rescue them.'

Jeremiah bought a papyrus scroll and Baruch, his helper, began to write down what Jeremiah dictated. When they had finished at last Jeremiah said:

'Go to the temple and read the scroll to the people. I am not allowed to go there, so *you* must tell them God's words.'

Baruch waited until crowds were flocking to the temple for a holy day. Then he read to them all that he had written.

One listener told some of the palace officials about the scroll and they asked to see it, too.

When they heard Jeremiah's stern words, they knew that he would be in trouble once the king found out.

'You and Jeremiah must hide while we take the scroll to the king,' they told Baruch. It was winter and King Jehoiakim was sitting beside a blazing fire, to keep warm. As his secretary read the first part of Jeremiah's scroll to him, the king's face grew dark. He snatched the scroll and, with his penknife, slashed away the part that had been read. He threw it onto the fire and watched it burn up.

As his secretary read on, the king listened, then cut off and burned the part he had heard, until the whole scroll had gone up in flames.

'Arrest Jeremiah!' the king ordered. But by this time Jeremiah and Baruch were safely hidden.

'Begin again,' God told Jeremiah, 'and write everything once more on a fresh scroll.' Again Jeremiah dictated and again Baruch patiently wrote, until God's word was in writing for all to hear or read, from that day to this.

Babylon's Yoke

2 KINGS 24; JEREMIAH 27—28

When King Jehoiakim burned Jeremiah's scroll, he showed plainly that he did not care about God. But God wanted so much to forgive his people and make them happy, that he waited a long time before he sent the threatened enemy.

By now, Jeremiah had guessed who that enemy would be. The new empire of Babylon had overpowered Egypt and conquered Assyria. King Nebuchadnezzar of Babylon had forced King Jehoiakim to obey him, too.

For three years Jehoiakim did as he was told, then he began to plot against Babylon. Nebuchadnezzar set off for Jerusalem at once, to teach the king a lesson.

Jehoiakim never saw the enemy arrive. He died and his son, who was no better than his father, was king when the Babylonian army burst into Jerusalem in triumph.

Nebuchadnezzar took the new king and his court to Babylon, along with the best of Jerusalem's citizens. The strongest and cleverest young people and the most skilled workmen were carried off. Nebuchadnezzar stripped the temple of its golden treasures and took them, too.

Jeremiah stayed in Jerusalem, where the new king, chosen by Nebuchadnezzar, now reigned. Zedekiah had to do what Nebuchadnezzar ordered and make no trouble, if Jerusalem was to be left in peace.

Most of the people who remained in the city were cheerful. 'The captives will soon be back from Babylon, bringing the temple treasures with them,' they said. But Jeremiah knew that this was not true.

He made a wooden yoke, the kind that oxen wore for ploughing, and put it on his own neck. 'Listen,' he told the people, 'be obedient to Nebuchadnezzar and serve under his yoke. If you do this, God says that you will escape the terrible trouble that will come to this city.'

But another man roughly pulled the yoke from Jeremiah's shoulders and broke it.

'There!' he said triumphantly. 'That is what will happen to Babylon's rule. We can soon break free, then the captives will return in no time.'

'How I wish you were speaking the truth!' Jeremiah said. 'But seventy long years must pass before any of our people come back!'

The Baskets of Figs

JEREMIAH 24

The people who stayed in Jerusalem after King Nebuchadnezzar had carried off his prisoners felt very self-satisfied. They thought that God musl be pleased with them to let them stay in the land and angry with those who had been taken away to Babylon.

But the people of Jerusalem who were now far from home had begun to learn their lesson. They were sorry that they had disobeyed God.

One day, God said to Jeremiah, 'Look at those two baskets of figs in front of the temple. What do you think of them?'

'One basket is full of choice, ripe figs,' Jeremiah answered. 'They look delicious. But the figs in the other basket are all rotten. They aren't fit to eat.'

'The people of Jerusalem are like those baskets of figs,' God went on. 'The people who have been taken away to Babylon are like the good figs. I am going to take care of them and watch over them, and in the end I will bring them back to their own land. They are learning to trust and obey me.

'But King Zedekiah and his court and all the people left here in Jerusalem are like the rotten figs. They are bad through and through and will not change their ways. They are still plotting and scheming against the king of Babylon. They will end up like the rotten figs—not fit to keep.'

200
Rescue Party
JEREMIAH 38

Time after time, Jeremiah passed on God's message to King Zedekiah.

'Don't plot with Egypt against Babylon,' he pleaded. 'Keep your promise to King Nebuchadnezzar.'

But Zedekiah would not listen. At last, his schemes came to Nebuchadnezzar's ears and he sent his army to Jerusalem once more.

Then the Babylonians left Jerusalem to fight an Egyptian army, and everyone breathed a sigh of relief.

But Jeremiah warned King Zedekiah:

'Don't think your troubles are over. The Babylonian army will soon be back. But God can still help you, if you do as he says and give in to Nebuchadnezzar.'

No one liked that advice and Jeremiah was unpopular. One day, when he was going out of the city, he was arrested. 'You were running off to the Babylonians, weren't you?' they asked.

'I was *not* deserting,' Jeremiah protested but no one believed him. They beat him and locked him up. But people still came to hear his messages from God, so his enemies at court asked the king if they might throw him down a well, out of everyone's way.

They let him down by ropes through the narrow opening, into the deep, hollow pit, now empty of water. As Jeremiah's feet touched bottom, they sank into deep mud. The sides of the pit were slimy and slippery and it was dark and damp. Jeremiah's feet stuck fast in the cold, smelly mud.

Ebedmelech, a black official at the palace, heard about the fate of his friend Jeremiah, and hurried to the king.

'Your Majesty,' he said urgently, 'your servants have done a very wrong thing. They have left Jeremiah in the well, where he will starve to death.'

'Take some men with you and haul him out,' the king ordered.

Ebedmelech went first to the palace store-room and collected some old clothes. Then the rescue party made its way to the well.

'Jeremiah! Hello there!' Ebedmelech called. Heads blocked out the small circle of daylight that filtered down to the prisoner.

'We're sending down some rope and a bundle of rags. Put the rags under your arms first, to stop the rope cutting. Then fix the rope and we'll have you out in no time.'

When Jeremiah was ready, the four men at the top pulled hard. At last Jeremiah's feet came free and he began to go up. Soon he could see the sunlight and breathe clean, fresh air. How he thanked God for Ebedmelech!

201
The Last Days in Jerusalem
2 KINGS 25

All that Jeremiah had told King Zedekiah happened at last. The Babylonian army soon returned and camped outside Jerusalem once again. The king sent for Jeremiah.

'Please give me God's message—I want the truth,' he said.

'If I tell you the truth, you will have me put to death and if I give you advice you won't take it,' Jeremiah replied.

Too often Zedekiah had asked for God's message, only to ignore it completely.

'I promise you'll be safe,' the king said.

'Then this is God's word,' Jeremiah told him. 'Give in to the king of Babylon now.'

'I'm afraid of what he'll do to me,' the king said.

'God promises that he won't hurt you, if you surrender. But God has shown me what awful things will happen if you resist, or try to escape.'

Once more, Zedekiah disobeyed God and went on defying Nebuchadnezzar.

For two years the Babylonians besieged Jerusalem, while the people starved. At last their army broke through the walls and entered the city. King Zedekiah fled with his soldiers in panic, escaping through the palace garden and out of the city by a secret way. But the Babylonians soon caught him. Because of his treachery, they showed him no mercy. He ended his life in Babylon, blinded and in chains.

Then the Babylonians pulled down the city walls and burned the temple, the palace and all the fine houses of the rich. They took off the citizens to Babylon, leaving only the poorest people behind.

Jeremiah stayed with them.

The kings and people of Judah had refused to listen to God's words through his prophets once too often. Now they would live in exile, far from their homeland, for many years to come.

Daniel and his Friends

📖 202
Special Training at the Palace

DANIEL 1

When Nebuchadnezzar first marched into Jerusalem, he arrested the king and his court and took them back to Babylon. He told his chief official, Ashpenaz, to pick out all the young people who could be trained to become advisers at the Babylonian court.

Ashpenaz searched for teenagers who were healthy, good-looking and at the top of the class at school. He ordered them to be ready to set off for the court of King Nebuchadnezzar, far away.

One of the chosen young people was Daniel. He was glad that three of his best friends had been picked too.

Once they arrived in Babylon, Ashpenaz explained to them what would happen. The Babylonians were not cruel like the Assyrians, and the captives were well treated.

First of all, Ashpenaz himself would teach them to read and write in the Babylonian language. Then they would begin a three-year university course, studying philosophy, literature, astrology and the Babylonian religion. Once they had qualified, they would become advisers at court.

'You will live well,' Ashpenaz told them. 'You are to have the same choice food and wine that is served to the king himself.'

Although Daniel and his friends were far from God's temple in Jerusalem they were determined to be loyal and true to God. They did not want to live a life of luxury, accepting special treatment from the king and making themselves his chosen people. They decided to ask for a more simple way of life.

'Please let us have a plain vegetarian diet,' Daniel asked Ashpenaz. 'We don't want the royal luxuries.'

'I dare not do as you say,' Ashpenaz answered. 'If you looked pale and underfed, I'd be blamed and might be put to death.'

When Ashpenaz had gone, Daniel repeated his request to the guard who was in charge of them.

'Please give it a try,' he begged. 'Give us plain vegetables to eat and water to drink, just for ten days. Then see how we look compared with the other students.'

The guard agreed. *He* would be able to enjoy the special rations set aside for Daniel and his friends.

After ten days, the guard examined the four closely. He had to admit that they looked healthier and more full of energy than any of the other young people.

So, for the three years that they were students, the four Jewish boys kept to their simple diet and stayed loyal to God and their own people far away.

📖 203
The Forgotten Dream

DANIEL 2

All the time they were students at the Babylonian court, Daniel and his three friends were at the top of the class. They all worked hard. God also gave Daniel special skill in understanding dreams. The Babylonians believed that dreams foretold the future. Wise men studied huge books which had been written especially to explain the meaning of dreams.

When the batch of newly qualified students was presented to the king, he talked to them and asked them questions. He was more pleased with Daniel and his friends, Shadrach, Meshach and Abednego, than with any of the others. He chose them to stay at court. Whenever he had a problem, these four always gave the best advice.

One day, when Daniel and his friends were absent, the king called his advisers in a great hurry.

'I'm very worried,' he said. 'I've had a dream and want to know what it means.'

'Tell us your dream, your Majesty, and we will explain it,' the wise men answered.

'I won't!' the king said stubbornly. 'You must tell me what my dream was about and then explain it.'

The wise men were horrified at this unreasonable request.

'Tell us the dream, your Majesty,' they repeated patiently, 'and we will explain it.'

The king flew into a rage.

'You are playing for time,' he stormed. 'Either you tell me, or I'll have the lot of you torn limb from limb.'

'But no one on earth could do as your Majesty asks,' the advisers reasoned.

'Have them all executed!' Nebuchadnezzar shouted, and the wise men left quickly.

Daniel and his friends were soon told. They were among the king's advisers, so they too would be put to death.

The God who can Explain

DANIEL 2

As soon as Daniel heard the news that he and his friends, along with all the court advisers, were to be put to death, he went to Arioch, the officer in charge of the executions.

'Please tell me why the king has given this order,' he asked.

When Arioch explained, Daniel went immediately to ask for the executions to be put off until the next day, so that he had time to give the king his answer. Then he went to find Shadrach, Meshach and Abednego.

'Pray, all of you,' he told them urgently. 'Ask God to tell me what the dream was about and what it means, so that all our lives can be saved.'

Then Daniel went home to bed. He trusted God to hear their prayers.

During the night God told Daniel all that he needed to know. He felt so full of praise to God that he burst out singing:

'I give you praise, God of my ancestors.
You have given me wisdom and strength;
You have answered my prayer and shown us what to tell the king.'

The next morning Daniel returned to Arioch.

'Don't put the king's advisers to death,' he said. 'Take me to the king and I will tell him about his dream.'

Arioch led the way.

'I have found one of the Jewish exiles who is able to tell your Majesty his dream,' he announced.

'Can you tell me my dream and explain what it means?' Nebuchadnezzar asked Daniel.

'No one on earth could do that, your Majesty,' Daniel answered fearlessly. 'There is no wise person, fortune teller or astrologer clever enough to do that. But there is a God in heaven who knows all things. He has made the mystery plain.'

broke off the cliff, without anyone touching it. It collided with the feet of the statue and broke them to pieces. Then the whole statue began to crumble into dust. The wind blew and the dust was scattered. Not a trace of that great statue remained. But the stone began to grow and grow until it was big enough to fill the whole world.'

Nebuchadnezzar nodded excitedly. Daniel was absolutely right. That had been his dream. But could he explain what it meant?

'I will tell you the meaning of your dream,' Daniel went on, as if in answer to Nebuchadnezzar's unspoken question.

'The statue represents the empires of the world. You, your Majesty, are the head of gold and your empire the greatest and most splendid of all. Others, less noble, will arise, like the other parts of the statue. But however strong and mighty they may look, none will endure for ever. The unimportant looking stone, that grew bigger and sent all the empires flying, stands for the empire that God himself will set up. One day, in the future, God is going to put his king on the earth. His kingdom will never come to an end but will grow greater and greater until it fills the whole world.'

Nebuchadnezzar was very quiet as Daniel finished speaking. Then he said: 'Your God is very great and wonderful. He deserves worship and praise. I know this because you alone have been able to tell me my dream and its meaning.'

Then the king made Daniel chief of all his advisers. He gave the three friends important jobs in different parts of the empire. But Daniel stayed at court.

📖 205
The Meaning of the Dream
DANIEL 2

Daniel began at once to tell Nebuchadnezzar his dream.

'Your Majesty, your dream was about the future. God has told me its meaning, not because I am wiser than anyone else, but so that he could let you know what is going to happen.

'In your dream, you saw a giant-sized statue of a man, bright and shining. Its head was made of gold. Down to the waist it was of silver and below the waist it was of bronze. The legs were iron and the feet were of iron mixed with clay. As you were gazing at the statue, a great stone

206
The Giant Statue

DANIEL 3

Nebuchadnezzar did not forget the statue he had dreamed about. The more he thought, the better he liked the idea of making a statue himself and setting it up for everyone to see. His would be *all* of gold—at least on the outside—and it would be enormous.

The king gave instructions to the craftsmen and soon workmen could be seen in the large open space outside Babylon, setting up the statue. It gleamed in the bright sun, fifteen times taller than a man.

Nebuchadnezzar invited everyone of any importance to the opening ceremony. Crowds of ordinary citizens would come too. All the peoples of his empire would be united in worshipping the image.

Row upon row of people packed the open ground. The king's chief ministers and officials were at the front. The royal band waited, ready to strike up. Then a herald came forward with an announcement.

'People of the empire!' he proclaimed, 'in a moment you will hear the trumpets sound, and the playing of oboes, lyres, zithers and harps. As soon as the music begins, you are to fall down with your faces to the ground and worship the statue that the king has set up. Anyone who disobeys this order will be thrown into a blazing furnace.'

There was a tense stillness among the crowd. No one stirred. Then a fanfare of trumpets shattered the silence. At once, all the people, from the highest to the lowest, fell flat on their faces before the golden image.

All—except three.

Daniel's three friends stood boldly upright. They would not bow down to any image. They would be true to God and his commandment to worship him alone.

Four Men in the Fire

DANIEL 3

Many of Nebuchadnezzar's officials at court were jealous of Daniel and his friends. They were delighted to find a way to get rid of them. They hurried to the king and told him about the three men who had dared to disobey his order.

The king was furious.

He sent at once for Shadrach, Meshach, and Abednego.

'Is it true?' he asked, 'that you refuse to bow down to my statue? I am prepared to give you one more chance to show your loyalty to me. Bow down and you will not be thrown into the furnace.'

'We do not want another chance, your Majesty,' the three replied. 'We

will never bow down to anyone but our God. He is even able to rescue us from the fire. But whether he chooses to save us or not, we will be loyal to him.'

The king's face turned scarlet.

'Make the furnace as hot as you can!' he ordered. Servants stoked the brick kiln with charcoal until it glowed white-hot.

'Tie them up and throw them in,' the king said. By now the furnace was so hot that the guards who threw the three men into the fire were themselves scorched to death.

The king watched moodily. It was a just punishment for those who would not admit his greatness.

Suddenly his face changed. With a look of horror, he pointed to the door of the furnace, as if unable to believe his own eyes.

'How many men did you throw into the fire?' he asked.

'Three, your Majesty,' the servants replied.

'But there are four men there. They are not tied up but walking free in the fire. The fourth man is different—he looks like an angel of God.'

Then Nebuchadnezzar went closer and called out:

'Shadrach, Meshach and Abednego, you who serve the great God—come out!'

The three men stepped out of the furnace. Their skin was not burned and their clothes were not singed. They did not even smell of smoke. Only the ropes that tied them had gone up in flames.

Nebuchadnezzar looked again into the furnace, but the fourth person had gone.

'Your God is great and deserves praise,' he said in wonder. Then he turned to his officials:

'Their God sent his angel to look after the three men who risked their lives to be loyal to him. No one is ever to say a word against him, for no other god could rescue his followers like this.'

208
Nebuchadnezzar's Madness
DANIEL 4

Nebuchadnezzar was feeling pleased with himself. Everything was a great success, both in war and peace. He was happy.

Then his peace of mind was shattered by another dream. He sent for his wise men and begged them to explain it to him, but not one of them could. When Daniel arrived, the king said:

'I know that God explains things to you. I will tell you my dream. I saw a big tree that kept growing and growing until it reached the sky. Everyone in the world could see it and enjoy its good fruit. Wild animals sat in its shade and birds built nests in its branches.

'Then, suddenly, an angel flew down. "Cut down that tree," he ordered. The tree was felled and only a stump was left. Then the stump changed into a man. "This man will live in the open like an animal," the angel declared. "His mind will become like an animal's too. All people everywhere must learn that God rules in the world."

'Whatever *can* my dream mean?' the king asked.

For a moment Daniel was too upset to answer.

'Please don't be worried,' the king said kindly.

'How I wish that the dream was not meant for you, your Majesty!' Daniel exclaimed sadly. 'You are that tree, so strong and tall, giving food and protection to all. But unless you recognize God's greatness he will take away your power. You will be cut down and become mad. You will live like a wild animal. But if you turn back to God, he will give you greatness again. Please be warned by your dream, your Majesty. Treat the poor people kindly. Be just and be humble and this disaster need never come.'

But Nebuchadnezzer soon forgot Daniel's warning. One day he was walking on his palace roof, looking down on Babylon, with its beautiful hanging gardens and soaring ziggurat temples.

'What a wonderful city I have built!' he exclaimed proudly. 'This is all my own work. It shows how great and powerful I am!'

Then a terrible madness took hold of the king. He did not know who he was. He roamed in the fields, growing rough and wild, living like the animals. His madness lasted for a long time.

One day his mind grew clear again and he knew who he was. When he saw how he had been living he realized that he was not all-powerful. Only God deserved that title. Humbly he returned to his palace and his throne.

209
The Mysterious Hand

DANIEL 5

Kings came and went in Babylon, but Daniel remained at court, even though he was unknown to the new young king, Belshazzar.

One night, Belshazzar held a banquet for all the nobles and their wives. They ate and drank to their hearts' content. The more they drank, the noisier the party grew.

Then Belshazzar said:

'Send for the gold cups and bowls that were taken from the temple at Jerusalem. We will drink to our own gods and goddesses.'

Even the servants were shocked that the king should use sacred cups so carelessly. But Belshazzar was too drunk to listen.

So the servants brought the sacred temple treasures and filled the golden cups to the brim. The guests laughed and drank greedily.

Suddenly the king stopped dead. With a trembling finger, he pointed to the white plaster wall in front of him, where the lamp shed its light.

'Look!' he called out in horror. The noise and laughter sank at the sound

of terror in the king's voice. He was shaking with fear.

'I can see a human hand writing on the wall,' he said slowly. 'It must mean something terrible. Send for my counsellors to tell me what the words mean.'

Hurriedly the king's advisers were ushered in.

'Anyone who can read and explain the words on the wall will be richly rewarded,' the king promised. 'He shall have purple robes, a gold chain, high office—all he can ask for. Only tell me the meaning!'

The wise men shook their heads slowly. Not one had any idea what the king was talking about.

News of the king's distress spread through the palace and soon his mother appeared at the door.

'I know someone who can help you,' she told Belshazzar. 'Daniel is an exile from Judah. He was Nebuchadnezzar's chief adviser. God's spirit is in him and he will give you your answer.'

210
Weighed in the Scales
DANIEL 5

Daniel was sent for at once. When he arrived, the king feverishly offered him riches and a high position if he would only explain the terrifying writing on the wall.

Daniel replied in a clear, quiet voice.

'I do not want your gifts, your Majesty. Give them to others. But I will read and explain the writing to you. God has sent you a message tonight. You have not listened to him before, even though you could have learned about his greatness from King Nebuchadnezzar. Instead, you took the sacred cups from God's temple to use at your drunken party.

'Three words are written on the wall. They are, Number—Weight—Division. This is what they mean.

'*Number* means that God has numbered the days of your rule. Your empire is coming to an end.

'*Weight* means that you have been weighed in God's just scales—and found too light to meet his standards.

'*Division* means that your empire is going to be divided between the Medes and the Persians.'

Belshazzar kept his word and insisted on rewarding Daniel. But his heart was heavy, for he knew that Daniel spoke the truth. Even while he was holding his party, enemy troops were storming the walls of the city. That very night they burst into Babylon and killed Belshazzar. They put their king, Darius the Mede, on the throne.

Plot Against Daniel

DANIEL 6

The armies of the Medes and Persians conquered Babylon, and King Darius, ruler of a vast empire, set up his headquarters in the city. Darius organized his empire well. He chose one hundred and twenty governors to rule the many regions and put three supervisors over the governors, to make sure that they were loyal to the king.

One of these three was Daniel. The king soon found that Daniel was so much better than all the others that he planned to put him in complete charge.

The governors and other supervisors were determined that he should do no such thing. They were bitterly jealous of Daniel and decided to find some way of getting him into the king's bad books. But, however hard they tried, they could not catch Daniel doing anything wrong. 'We shall have to find something about his Jewish religion that will get him into trouble,' they decided. Although Daniel had lived in Babylon many years and had grown from a teenager

to an old man, he had stayed loyal and true to God. Three times a day he went to his window and looked in the direction of Jerusalem, where the temple had stood. Then he knelt and prayed to the God who was with him, even though he was far from home.

At last the jealous officials came up with a scheme to get rid of Daniel.

'Your Majesty,' they said to the king, 'we have drawn up a new law for you to pass. It states that anyone who wants anything at all during the next month, must ask for it from you alone. He must not make his request to any other person or god. Please sign this law with the seal of the Medes and Persians, for everyone knows that such a law may never be changed or broken. Anyone who disobeys your law shall be thrown into the pit of lions.'

Darius did not realize that they were setting a trap for Daniel. He agreed, and signed the law with his own royal seal.

212
Daniel Keeps Praying
DANIEL 6

The governors and supervisors thought carefully when they drew up the law for the king to pass. They knew that Daniel prayed every day, asking God for all he needed. They would soon find him guilty. They knew too that the laws of the Medes and Persians were binding. The king would not go back on his word.

When Daniel heard about the new law, he guessed that they were plotting against him. But he would not stop praying to God—or even pretend to stop. He would rather die.

He knelt by his open window, as usual, and prayed aloud to God.

When his enemies saw him, they rubbed their hands in glee. Daniel had fallen into their trap—and so had the king.

'Your Majesty,' they said to Darius, 'do you remember the law you passed? Daniel is breaking it, three times a day.' They could scarcely hide their satisfaction. 'He makes requests to his God and defies your law.'

Too late, Darius realized that he had been tricked into condemning his best and well-loved minister to death.

All that day he tried to think of some way of saving Daniel. By evening his officials were back.

'Your Majesty knows that the law of the Medes and Persians cannot be broken,' they reminded him.

The king knew that he was caught in their trap. Unwillingly he gave orders for Daniel to be arrested and taken to the pit where hungry lions were kept, to make short work of troublesome criminals. The king himself went with Daniel.

'You have been loyal to your God, Daniel,' he said. 'I hope he keeps you safe.'

Daniel was dropped down the narrow opening into the pit, where the lean lions paced restlessly up and down in their enclosure. Then a large stone was put over the top.

213
The Morning After

DANIEL 6

The king returned to his palace with a heavy heart. He waved away the servants who ran forward to serve him.

'No food!' he said. 'No music!'

Then he went to bed.

All night long he tossed and turned, unable to sleep. He knew that he had condemned to death a good and honest man, who had served him well.

As soon as the first pale light of dawn crept in at the window of the royal bedroom, Darius sprang out of bed. He could bear the suspense no longer.

He summoned his servants and was soon on his way to the lion pit. The huge stone was removed and the king called down into the evil-smelling darkness.

'Daniel, servant of the living God, was your God able to save you from the lions?'

With a thrill of relief he heard Daniel's voice, echoing from within the pit.

'Your Majesty, God sent his angel to close the lions' mouths, so that they would not hurt me. He did so because I am innocent and have done your Majesty no wrong.'

The king was overjoyed.

'Hurry! Hurry!' he ordered impatiently. 'Get ropes and pull Daniel out.'

They hauled Daniel up and looked at him hard. There was not even a scratch to be seen. Then the king's relief turned to anger against the men who had tricked him and tried to murder Daniel.

'Throw those wicked conspirators to the lions!' he commanded, and his orders were quickly obeyed.

This time the lions did not keep their mouths shut.

Ezekiel's Message

📖 214
Wheels and Wings
EZEKIEL 1—2

When Nebuchadnezzar marched into Jerusalem for the first time, he carried off the best young men to Babylon. One of these was Ezekiel. He had been longing for the day when he would be old enough to begin his duties as a priest in the temple. Now his dream would never come true.

The Jewish exiles began to settle down in a strange land. Their captors were kind and let them live freely and build rough homes on the sandy plain outside Babylon, by the side of a broad canal.

One day, Ezekiel saw a black thunder cloud coming out of the north. He knew it meant that a storm was on the way. The edges of the cloud were tipped with the red of the desert sun and bright streaks of lightning flashed across it. At the centre of the storm cloud was something bright and shining.

As Ezekiel watched, it broke loose from the cloud and darted towards him. It seemed to be a huge moving machine, made up of four live creatures. They were joined together into one complete whole by the tips of their outstretched wings.

Ezekiel stared hard. Each of these four strange creatures had four faces—a human face, a lion's face, a bull's face and the face of an eagle. The whole living machine moved at lightning speed in all directions without having to turn. It swooped to the earth, then took off into the air again.

Ezekiel saw that each creature had two sets of wheels with which to move along the ground as well as wings to fly with. At the centre of the machine, a ball of fire glowed, and above was a dome which sparkled as if it was made from ice crystals.

As the creatures flew, the beating of their wings filled the air with a noise like the roaring of the sea. They were terrible and wonderful, but far more terrible and wonderful was the throne that they carried on high above the crystal vault. It gleamed deep blue like sapphire. On the throne sat a human figure, shining with dazzling brightness and glowing with every shade of the rainbow.

Then Ezekiel knew that he was in the presence of God. He bowed low to the ground in fear and awe. God spoke.

'Ezekiel, I have called you to be my prophet. You must pass on my words to my people here in exile. Give them my message, whether they are willing to hear it or not. Do as I tell you and be my faithful messenger.'

215
Silent Sermons
EZEKIEL 3—5

God told Ezekiel that Judah's troubles were not over. There was much hardship to come to Jerusalem and he must tell the exiles in Babylon about this.

'Do not speak to them,' God said, 'but show them what is going to happen.'

Ezekiel listened to God's instructions and obeyed them.

He took a large brick and scratched a picture of Jerusalem on it. He sat down in the open with the brick in front of him, and began to mould the sand into little models of an army surrounding the city on the brick. He put a big baking tin between himself and the brick, as if it were a wall.

A crowd soon gathered, staring and pointing at the objects. What *could* it all mean? They recognized the picture of Jerusalem and began to guess the rest.

Next day, when the crowd came back, they found Ezekiel preparing his meal beside the brick. He carefully weighed out a small amount of cheap flour and made himself a tiny loaf. Then he measured two bare cupfuls of water as his daily ration.

Every day he did the same, until the crowd guessed that he was showing them what the hungry people of Jerusalem would soon be doing.

One day Ezekiel was sharpening his sword on a stone when the crowd arrived. Then, as his horrified audience watched, he slashed off his thick head of hair and sheared off his flowing beard. He gathered up the pile of cut hair and weighed it on his scales. He divided it into three parts.

One part he threw on the fire. The second, he chopped into tiny pieces with his sword.

The last, he scattered to the wind.

It looked as if the hair was all lost, but Ezekiel stooped down and rescued every stray hair that he could find, gently wrapping them in his cloak.

The people whispered together, wondering what the strange prophet could mean this time.

Some guessed that what he did with his hair was a picture of what would happen to the people of Jerusalem. They would be roughly removed. Some would die in the siege, others would be killed by the sword and the rest would be scattered far from home. But God would take care of a few people, like the hairs that Ezekiel wrapped in his cloak. One day God would bring them safely home and give them a new beginning.

Dry Bones Come Alive!

EZEKIEL 37

Ezekiel had warned the captives about the bad times ahead, but he had also given them a glimmer of hope. God told him more about that bright future for the captives.

One day, Ezekiel had another vision. He found himself in a valley, and looking around he saw that the ground was littered with human bones, of all shapes and sizes.

'Ezekiel,' God asked, 'can these dry bones come alive again?'

'Only you know the answer to that,' Ezekiel replied.

'Tell the dry bones to listen to my voice,' God went on. 'Tell them that I am going to make them come alive again.'

Ezekiel spoke God's words out loud.

As his voice died away, he heard a rustling that turned to a rattling. Then he saw the bones begin to move towards each other. As he watched, the bare skeletons joined together with muscles and ligaments. Then they grew a new covering of skin. The noise stopped and Ezekiel saw silent human forms lying lifeless all around him.

'Tell the winds to blow breath into these bodies,' God said. So Ezekiel commanded the winds as God had ordered.

Gently the bodies stirred. Their breath rose and fell. Then they stretched and began to move their limbs. At last they stood on their feet—a huge host of people. Then the vision faded away.

'Ezekiel,' God said, 'my people are like the dead bones. But they too will live again one day. I will breathe new life into the nation. I am still their God and I have power to bring them back to their own land and give them a new beginning and new life once more.'

God's People Go Home

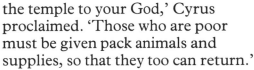

217
The Long Trek Back

EZRA 1—3

Nearly seventy years had passed since King Nebuchadnezzar took the very first batch of captives from Jerusalem to Babylon. Only a few of them could even remember their own land. But they had listened to the tales their parents told of the fine city and, above all, the beautiful temple.

Then Cyrus became king. His Persian empire stretched far and wide. He wanted the people he ruled to be happy and give no trouble, so he decided to let all exiles return to their own lands.

The captives from Judah realized that God was keeping his promises through Jeremiah and Ezekiel that one day they would go back to the Promised Land.

'Go back to Jerusalem and rebuild the temple to your God,' Cyrus proclaimed. 'Those who are poor must be given pack animals and supplies, so that they too can return.'

There was great excitement among the Jewish exiles as they go ready for the long trek back. They were led by Zerubbabel, the grandson of King Jehoiachin, who was helped by Joshua the priest.

Before they left, Cyrus handed back to them the temple treasures that King Nebuchadnezzar had seized.

Many Jews remained in Babylonia. Only a small party set off, compared with the huge crowds of dejected captives who had left their homeland long before. They were like the few hairs that Ezekiel had rescued when he cut his beard.

But they were full of excitement and joy. As they went, they sang praises to God and laughed and joked. Their wildest dreams were coming true.

When they arrived in Jerusalem their excitement turned to despair. Everything was in ruins. There was rubbish and rubble everywhere. There were no city walls and nothing remained of the temple.

Worst of all, the people around were unfriendly. When the northern kingdom of Israel had been conquered by Assyria, the Assyrians had taken away the Israelites and settled strangers in the land. These Samaritans had learned something about God but still went on with their own idol worship. They did not want these Jews to come back to their land and rebuild the city.

Zerubbabel and Joshua knew that they had a hard time ahead.

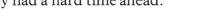

📖 218
Building Begins

EZRA 2—3

As soon as the leaders who had
returned from Babylon saw the
terrible state of ruin in Jerusalem,
they decided to start a fund. It would
be for the most important job of all—
the rebuilding of God's temple. All of
them gave as much gold and silver as
they could possibly spare, so that
materials could be bought and the
work begun.

But first of all they had to decide
where everyone would settle and
make some kind of temporary homes
to live in. Joshua and Zerubbabel did

not want to wait for the temple to be
built before God's worship could
begin again. So they put up an altar in
the very spot where it had stood
before.

Meanwhile the fund for the new
temple was growing steadily.
Ordinary people, who had no gold,
gave anything they could. Grain and
wine and olive-oil were all offered to
be used in payment for cedar wood.
This was shipped by sea from
Lebanon, just as it had been for King
Solomon, when he had built the first
temple, many years before.

The Levites were put in charge of
the whole project, but everyone,
including the priests, joined in with

the hard work. Once the foundations were laid, the people gathered for a great thanksgiving service. The priests blew their trumpets with a flourish; the Levites clashed their cymbals and then burst out singing:

'The Lord is good and his love for Israel is eternal.'

All the people shouted for joy and praised God. But some of the old priests and leaders remembered the glory of Solomon's temple. When they thought about the terrible fire and destruction that had befallen it, they burst out crying. Some were wailing with grief while others were laughing and shouting for joy. No one could tell which was which, but the noise could be heard far and wide.

219
The New Temple
EZRA 5—6

Everyone imagined that the new temple would soon be built. But they had reckoned without the Samaritans. At first they asked to help.

'We will build with you, because we worship the same God as you do,' they told Zerubbabel. But Zerubbabel refused, because he knew that was not true. The exile to Babylon had been God's punishment because the people of Judah had deliberately mixed with those who worshipped false gods and disobeyed God's laws. They were not going to make the same mistake twice.

The Samaritans were angry at being refused and made up their minds to do all they could to stop the work going ahead. They tried to frighten and upset the Jews. They gave bribes to Persian officials to persuade them to hinder the building, and even wrote letters to the emperor with untrue complaints against the Jews.

For sixteen years, work on the temple stopped altogether. But God sent two prophets to encourage the people to go on.

Zechariah reminded them that God loved them and would help them in spite of enemies. But they must obey God and not harm or cheat each other, if they were to have his blessing.

Haggai told them to put God first. It was more important to build God's temple than to make their own homes comfortable.

Zerubbabel and Joshua took these messages from God to heart, and with the help of the two prophets, the work began again.

Seventy years after King Solomon's splendid temple had been utterly destroyed, the new temple was completed. It might not be as rich and magnificent as the first one, but everyone rejoiced and celebrated on the day that it was dedicated to God.

Once more the priests and Levites took up their duties. When Passover time came, all the people flocked to the temple to keep the festival. And those others living in the land, who truly worshipped God, were invited to join in too.

The King's Wine Steward

NEHEMIAH 1—2

Nehemiah was one of many Jews who still lived in Babylonia. He held an important post as the Emperor Artaxerxes' wine steward. Every day he would taste the king's wine before serving it to him, to make sure that it was not poisoned. The wine steward had to be a man the emperor trusted completely.

One day, one of the Jews who had returned to Jerusalem came back to Babylon and visited Nehemiah. He had a sad tale to tell.

'Things are bad,' he said. 'The walls are still not built and there are no city gates. The people of the land make life impossible for us.'

When he had gone, Nehemiah felt very depressed. He went off alone to pray.

'O God,' he prayed, 'we have disobeyed you and don't deserve your kindness. But please help us, because we want to turn back to you. Please soften the emperor's heart, so that he is willing to hear me when I ask for his help.'

For four months Nehemiah prayed and waited. Then, one day, his opportunity came. He was serving Artaxerxes with wine in his winter palace at Susa. The emperor looked at him sharply.

'What is the matter?' he asked. 'I know you aren't ill but you look miserable.'

Nehemiah's heart missed a beat. No servant was supposed to show his feelings in front of the king. But he made up his mind to risk the emperor's anger.

Before he answered he breathed a quick prayer to God for help. Then he said:

'I am sad because my own people are in trouble. Would you allow me to return to my own land to help rebuild the city?'

The emperor looked across at the empress, sitting beside him. She was smiling kindly at Nehemiah.

'How long would you be?' he asked.

Nehemiah had all the answers ready. He had made careful plans. When the emperor gave him permission to go, he asked him for

timber from the royal forest for the building work, and a travel pass so that no enemies could arrest him. Then, protected by a guard of the emperor's own soldiers, Nehemiah set off for Jerusalem.

221
Rebuilding the Walls
NEHEMIAH 2—4

When Nehemiah arrived in Jerusalem he waited quietly for a few days, taking careful note of all that went on. Then, one night, when everyone was asleep, he set off on his donkey to have a thorough look at the whole city. He and a few friends went all around the outside of Jerusalem, noting where the damage was worst. In some places there was so much brick rubble and rubbish that the donkey could not pick her way through.

Nehemiah realized how much there was to be done.

The next day, he began to encourage the leaders to begin rebuilding. He told them how God had answered his prayers. He put new heart into them.

He called together all the volunteers and split them into groups. He gave each group one section of the walls or gates to work on. Sometimes a family would work together, or those who lived in the same village would form a team. The goldsmiths all banded together to build one bit of the wall and the priests another.

But as soon as they began building in earnest, their enemies, the Samaritans, came to watch and laugh at them.

'What do these miserable Jews think they can do?' their leader jeered. 'Even a fox could break through that wall!'

But the people went on working, determined to finish the job, whatever the difficulties. Sometimes they sang as they worked:

'There's so much rubble to take away,
How can we build the wall today?'

When the wall had grown to half its full height, the Samaritans grew anxious. They did not want Jerusalem to be safe and strong again. So they planned to attack the unsuspecting workers.

Nehemiah heard of it, and divided the people into two groups. One half he armed, so that they could stand guard, while the other half went on building.

'Don't be afraid,' Nehemiah told them. 'God will fight for us.'

Then he issued all the workmen with a sword to strap at their side and gave each man a weapon to hold. Each builder held his trowel in one hand and his weapon in the other. Nehemiah also stationed a bugler to sound an alarm if he spotted the enemy. Then the builders far and wide could hear the alarm, stop work and prepare for an attack.

They worked fast and furious from early morning until the stars came out at night. Nehemiah did not go to bed for nights on end. They were all determined to work on until the walls and gates were finished and Jerusalem would be safe from all danger.

Learning God's Law

NEHEMIAH 8

At last the walls of Jerusalem were completed and the strong city gates in place. Now it would be safe for the people to gather in the city square and listen to God's message.

Nehemiah called everyone to come. Fathers and mothers brought all their children who were old enough to understand.

'Please read to us from the Book of the Law,' the people asked Ezra, the teacher.

So he fetched the scroll and stepped up onto the large wooden platform that had been set up. He had thirteen Levites to help him with the readings.

'Praise the Lord, the great God!' Ezra called out and all the people got to their feet, held their hands high and called back, 'Amen.'

Then they humbly bowed down to worship God, before getting up to listen intently to what Ezra would say.

First he read a section from the scroll and then some of the Levites went up and down among the crowd, helping them to understand what they had heard.

From dawn to midday Ezra and his colleagues read and explained. The more they heard, the more the people realized that they had broken God's laws. They began to get very upset and many of them started crying.

Nehemiah and Ezra calmed them down.

'Today is a happy day because it is holy to God,' they said. 'Go home now and have a feast. Share your food and wine with any who haven't enough. God's joy will make you strong!'

Next day, all the leaders came back, so that Ezra could teach them God's laws more thoroughly. For two weeks he taught them.

Then the people assembled again. They told God how sorry they were and thanked him for keeping his covenant with them. Then they promised once more to keep their side of the covenant and be God's people, trusting him and obeying his laws.

The Story of Esther

📖 223
A New Queen is Chosen
ESTHER 1—2

Xerxes was ruler of the great Persian Empire that had conquered Babylonia. He had many wives in his harem, but none to take the place of his first queen, Vashti, who had been banished in disgrace.

She had dared to say 'No', when the king ordered her to show off her beauty to the guests at his royal banquet. The king's pride was still hurt.

'Round up all the pretty girls throughout your empire,' his ministers suggested tactfully, 'and choose a new queen.'

Mordecai was a Jew who was still living in Babylonia. Like many others, he had not returned with the first trickle of exiles to his own land.

Mordecai had adopted his beautiful orphan cousin, Esther, who was sent with a batch of girls to the palace, to take part in the beauty parade.

'Don't tell anyone that you are Jewish,' Mordecai advised Esther.

The palace official in charge of all the girls liked Esther. She was gentle and pleasant. She did not put on airs or expect everyone to make a fuss of her. He was especially kind to her.

Mordecai came to court to be near his cousin. Esther was kept strictly inside the women's quarters, but Mordecai would walk up and down outside, waiting his chance to find out how Esther was.

At the end of a long course of beauty treatment, the girls were to choose a new outfit of clothes. Then, one by one, they were taken to the king.

The moment Xerxes set eyes on Esther, his mind was made up.

'This girl shall be my new queen,' he announced.

Esther was both excited and frightened. Emperors were self-willed and fickle. She knew that at any time she might displease the king, as the last queen had done.

By this time, Mordecai had been given a job in the royal household, so the cousins could send messages to each other more easily.

One day Mordecai, who had ears for everything, learned of a plot against the king's life. He quickly passed the information to Esther, who told the king. The culprits were charged and hanged.

'Write an account of the whole affair in my royal records,' the king ordered.

📖 224
Plot Against the Jews
ESTHER 3—4

Haman, King Xerxes' new prime minister, was pleased with himself. He was next in importance to the king himself and everyone should know it.

All the people and all the king's ministers bowed to the ground when Haman passed by. All except one.

Mordecai stood defiantly upright.

'Why don't you bow to Haman?' the others asked him.

'I am a Jew,' Mordecai answered. 'I will give homage to no one but God.'

Haman was furious with this

Jewish rebel. He was determined to punish not only Mordecai but the whole Jewish race.

He asked his astrologers to calculate a lucky day for his scheme. Then he went to the king.

'Your Majesty,' he said, 'there is a race of people in your empire who disobey your laws. Issue a decree for all of them to be killed on the day I appoint. If you do, I will guarantee you a vast sum of silver.'

Haman planned to loot the silver from the Jews themselves.

The king liked the idea. He set his seal to Haman's order and sent copies to every part of his empire.

Mordecai and his fellow Jews were shocked and horrified. They fasted and prayed.

Then Mordecai sent a message to the queen, telling her of the king's edict.

'Go to him and plead for us,' he wrote. But that was not as easy as Mordecai seemed to think.

'Anyone who goes into the king's presence without being sent for, can be put to death,' Esther replied. 'I dare not go to him uninvited. It is a month since the king sent for me and he may no longer be pleased with me.'

Mordecai knew that Esther was the Jews' only hope. 'Don't you realize that you will die anyway?' his next message read. 'You are Jewish and will not escape the massacre. Go to the king. He may receive you. Perhaps you became queen for this very purpose—to save your people.'

225
The Queen's Request
ESTHER 4—6

Esther's heart beat fast and her thoughts whirled. But her mind was made up. She would take her life in her hands and go to the king.

She had one chance. If he was in a good mood, he might hold out to her the gold sceptre in his hand. That would be a sign that her life would be spared. She sent to Mordecai, asking the Jews to fast and pray while she did the same.

Then she put on her royal robes and went trembling to the doorway of the throne-room. The king looked up and saw her.

'How lovely she looks!' he thought. 'How could I have forgotten her for so long!'

With a smile, he held out his sceptre. Esther was safe. 'What is your request?' he asked.

'Please come to dinner with me tonight and bring Haman,' Esther stammered out.

The king was delighted and so was Haman. That night Esther gave them an invitation to dinner for the next evening.

'I will tell you my request then,' she told the king.

'Even the queen respects me!' Haman told his wife. Then he added: 'But I can never be happy as long as Mordecai lives!'

'Then build a gallows and hang him,' his wife suggested.

Haman set to work at once, then went to the palace to ask the king's permission for the execution.

That night the king had not been able to sleep.

'Read me the royal records,' he ordered.

When the servant read about the plot on the king's life, which Mordecai had foiled, Xerxes asked: 'Was Mordecai rewarded?'

'No,' his servants replied. Haman, waiting to be admitted to the king, was quickly sent for.

'What should be done for the man I wish to reward?' the king asked him.

'He must mean me!' Haman thought. So he suggested a royal procession around the city, on the king's own horse.

'Good,' the king agreed. 'Find Mordecai and conduct him through the streets yourself, announcing that he is the man I wish to reward.'

Haman was boiling with rage but he dared say nothing against his enemy now. When at last Haman reached home, his wife shook her head sadly.

'Your luck has turned!' she said. 'That Mordecai is going to get the better of you in the end, after all.'

226
A Day to be Remembered
ESTHER 7—8

At Esther's second banquet, Haman was silent and sick at heart. But the king was in good spirits. He smiled at Esther and sipped his wine, then asked: 'What is it you want, Queen Esther? You shall have anything you ask for—up to half my kingdom.'

'I ask only for my life and the life of my people, your Majesty,' Esther answered quietly. 'Through one man's wicked plot, my whole race has been condemned to death.'

'Who dares to do such a thing?' the king asked angrily.

Esther pointed to Haman, sitting white-faced and speechless.

'There is the man!' she said.

The king got to his feet in a fury and stormed out to the garden, where he paced up and down. Haman fell at the queen's feet, begging for mercy, but the king returned and roared out: 'How dare you approach the queen!'

'Haman has already built a gallows taller than the city walls to hang Mordecai on,' a servant told the king.

'Then hang Haman on it!' the king shouted. 'Mordecai shall be prime minister in his place.'

Haman was dragged from the room, half dead with terror.

Then Esther begged the king to change his order to massacre the Jews.

'Once made, my laws can never be changed,' Xerxes replied. 'But you may add what you wish to the law and it shall be sealed with my seal.'

Mordecai drafted an added order, giving all Jews the right to arm and defend themselves on the day appointed for their murder.

When that day at last arrived, many people were afraid to attack the Jews. They knew that Mordecai and Esther were both Jews, and they had the king's protection.

The Jews showed no mercy to their enemies.

The Jews have never forgotten Esther's courage in risking her life for her people. To this day the book of Esther is read on the anniversary of Haman's chosen day of vengeance.

The Story of Job

227

Troubles for Job

JOB 1—2

Job was a very rich man who lived in the days of Abraham. His wealth was not in silver or gold but in sheep and oxen, camels and donkeys.

Everyone admired Job. He was not selfish or grasping. He loved God and gave help to anyone in trouble or need. He prayed constantly for his large family of sons and daughters.

God noticed Job's goodness and kindness and was pleased.

But someone else was watching Job. It was Satan, God's enemy and the source of all evil.

'Job only loves you for what he can get out of you,' Satan told God.

'If things went wrong for him, he would soon change his tune.'

God was sure that Job would be true to him. 'You may put Job to the test,' he said. 'Take away anything he owns. But you must not hurt Job himself.'

One day soon after, one of Job's servants came hurrying to him with terrible news. Raiders had swooped down and made off with all his oxen and donkeys.

The servant had scarcely finished speaking when another came running up to tell Job that lightning had killed all his sheep and the shepherds who were looking after them.

A third messenger arrived to say that Job's camels had all been stolen.

Worst of all, a servant told Job that his sons and daughters had all been killed when a desert storm blew down the house where they were feasting.

Job was shattered. But he did not blame God for his misfortune.

'I was born with no possessions at all,' he said. 'Everything I had was given to me by God. Now he has taken it away. I will still praise him.'

'My servant Job has stood the test,' God told Satan. But Satan replied:

'That is because you have not harmed Job himself. If he is ill, he will soon change his mind.'

'You may bring illness on Job,' God said, 'but you must spare his life.'

Soon Job's whole body broke out in horrible boils. He did not know what to do for the pain and irritation.

'It's all God's fault!' his wife complained. 'Hush!' Job answered, 'You are talking nonsense. We are glad enough when God gives us happy times. We should bear it patiently when God sends trouble.'

228
Cheering Job Up?
JOB 2—37

Soon everyone was talking about Job's misfortunes. Three of his best friends came to visit him, to try to cheer him up. But when they saw him sitting by the rubbish dump in rags, covered with sores, they were horrified. They sat in shocked silence for a long while.

Then, one by one, they began to give him advice.

'You must have done something very wrong that we know nothing about,' one said. 'God certainly would not send such pain and suffering to a man who is good and just. God is punishing you for your sin.'

But Job's conscience was clear. He knew that he loved God with all his heart and had been honest and kind. He insisted that he was innocent. But his friends only said:

'Stop pretending! Own up and tell God you are sorry for what you have done. Then he will forgive you and everything will go well for you again.'

'Won't you believe me and have pity on me?' Job begged. 'I need loyal friends in my trouble. You are no comfort to me.'

Job knew that his friends were wrong. But he began to feel that God was being very unfair and he told God so.

'Why won't you give me a hearing and then answer my questions, God?' he exclaimed.

Then a fourth person interrupted. 'I've kept quiet until now because I am so much younger. I thought you would all be wiser than I am. But you have got it wrong! Just look at the stars in the sky, Job! Think how great God is! Can you expect him to be interested in whether you are good or bad?'

But the thought of a great faraway God brought no comfort to Job either. If only God would listen to him and answer his questions!

229
God Talks to Job

JOB 38—42

When all five men had stopped talking, a storm began to rage. Lightning flashed across the sky, thunder crashed and rain lashed down.

Out of the storm, God spoke: 'You have been asking *me* all kinds of questions, Job. But you must answer my questions to *you*.

'Where were you when I made the world? Were you there when the stars first sang for joy at creation? Or when I drove the sea back, so that its powerful waves could not go beyond the limits I set? Can you tell me where the light comes from? Where do I keep my treasures of snow and ice? Answer me!

'Are you able to make the rain fall, to give life to plants and animals? Can you teach the birds to fly, or provide food for the wild beasts? Answer me!

'Have you the strength to catch the crocodile with a fish hook? Would you be able to tame the animals, or play games with the huge hippopotamus? Answer me!'

Job had nothing to say. He felt very ashamed. He had lived a good life and kept God's laws, but he had thought he could argue with God as if he had his power and skill. He had expected to understand everything God did.

God did not explain to Job the reason for his troubles. But he made Job realize that he could safely trust such a great and wise God to do what was right.

'I never really knew you before,' Job admitted. 'I only knew what others told me about you. Now that you have spoken to me, I realize how great and wonderful you are. I am bitterly ashamed that I was so full of myself and my own importance.'

Then God turned to Job's three friends.

'You have done wrong. You did not give a true picture of me to Job. You did not speak the truth about me as Job did. But Job will pray for you and I will forgive you because of his prayers.'

Job was not bitter or unforgiving towards his friends, although they had been so unkind and unfair to him. He prayed for them.

Then God made Job well again. He gave him back the wealth that he had lost. He even had more children. He had seven sons and three beautiful daughters, called Jemimah, Keziah and Keren Happuch. Job lived to be very old and died at a great age.

The Hymnbook of Israel

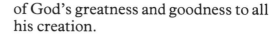

📖 **230**

Praising God

PSALMS 117, 100, 103

The people of Israel loved singing songs and hymns, just as we do today. The Book of Psalms was their hymnbook. They had a temple choir and orchestra to lead the singing.

The psalms were written over many years, by many different poets. Some were sung at religious festivals or on special national occasions, to give God thanks or ask for his help. Other psalms describe the writer's own feelings.

King David was a poet and singer and many of the psalms fit the events in his life. The psalms describe the way we feel today, too, when we are happy or sad, gloomy or cheerful.

Best of all, they give us words to tell of God's greatness and goodness to all his creation.

'Praise the Lord, all nations!
Praise him, all peoples!
His love for us is strong
and his faithfulness is eternal.'

'Sing to the Lord, all the world!
Worship the Lord with joy;
come before him with happy songs!
Never forget that the Lord is God.
He made us, and we belong to him;
we are his people, we are his flock.
Enter the temple gates with thanksgiving,
go into its courts with praise.
Give thanks to him and praise him.
the Lord is good;
his love is eternal
and his faithfulness lasts for ever.'

'Praise the Lord, my soul!
All my being, praise his holy name!
Praise the Lord, my soul,
and do not forget how kind he is.
He forgives all my sins
and heals all my diseases.
He keeps me from the grave
and blesses me with love and mercy.
He fills my life with good things,
so that I may stay young and strong
like an eagle . . .
The Lord is merciful and loving,
slow to become angry and full of
constant love . . .
He does not punish us as we deserve
or repay us for our sins and
wrongs . . .
He knows what we are made of;
he remembers that we are dust . . .
Praise the Lord, all his creatures
in all the places he rules.
Praise the Lord, my soul!'

231
Songs to Comfort and Help

PSALMS 23, 121, 46

'The Lord is my shepherd;
I shall not want.
He maketh me to lie down in green
pastures:
he leadeth me beside the still waters.
He restoreth my soul:
he leadeth me in the paths of
righteousness
for his name's sake.
Yea, though I walk through the valley
of the shadow of death,
I will fear no evil;
for thou art with me,
thy rod and thy staff
they comfort me.
Thou preparest a table before me
in the presence of mine enemies:
thou anointest my head with oil;
my cup runneth over.
Surely goodness and mercy shall
follow me
all the days of my life:
and I will dwell in the house
of the Lord for ever.'

'I lift up my eyes to the hills.
From whence does my help come?
My help comes from the Lord,
who made heaven and earth.
He will not let your foot be moved,
he who keeps you will not slumber.
Behold, he who keeps Israel will
neither slumber nor sleep.
The Lord is your keeper;
the Lord is your shade on your right
hand.
The sun shall not smite you by day,
nor the moon by night.
The Lord will keep you from all evil;
he will keep your life.
The Lord will keep your going out
and your coming in
from this time forth and for
evermore.'

'God is our shelter and strength,
always ready to help in times of
trouble.
So we will not be afraid,
even if the earth is shaken
and mountains fall into the ocean
depths;
even if the seas roar and rage,
and the hills are shaken by the
violence . . .
The Lord Almighty is with us;
the God of Jacob is our refuge.'

Proverbs

📖 **232**

Wise Words

When God offered to give Solomon whatever he wanted, the young king asked for wisdom. He knew that he could not manage to rule by his own skill and cleverness alone. In the Bible, wisdom means knowing the best way to manage every part of life. The Book of Proverbs is full of advice on how to be wise in this way. Solomon, and all the other writers of Proverbs, agree that the first step to wisdom is love and reverence for God.

Here are some wise words taken from the Book of Proverbs on the subjects of Friendship and Family, Cheerfulness and Kindness, Laziness and Gossip.

'Some friendships do not last, but some friends are more loyal than brothers.'
'Friends always show their love. What are brothers for if not to share trouble?'
'Do not forget your friends or your father's friends.'

'Children are fortunate if they have a father who is honest and does what is right.'
'A wise son makes his father proud of him: a foolish one brings his mother grief.'
'Anyone who thinks it isn't wrong to steal from his parents is no better than a common thief.'

'When hope is crushed, the heart is crushed, but a wish come true fills you with joy.'
'Being cheerful keeps you healthy. It is slow death to be gloomy all the time.'

'If you want to be happy, be kind to the poor; it is a sin to despise anyone.'
'Kind words bring life, but cruel words crush your spirit.'
'Be generous and you will be prosperous. Help others, and you will be helped.'

'A lazy man who refuses to work is only killing himself; all he does is think about what he would like to have.'
'If you are lazy you will never get what you are after, but if you work hard, you will get a fortune.'

'A gossip can never keep a secret. Stay away from people who talk too much.'
'Gossip brings anger just as surely the north wind brings rain.'
'Without wood, a fire goes out; without gossip, quarrelling stops.'

Jonah's Story

📖 233
Running Away from God

JONAH 1

One day God told the prophet Jonah: 'I have a message for you to take to the people of Nineveh. You know how cruel and wicked they are. You must tell both king and people that unless they are sorry for their wrong doings and change their ways, I am going to punish them.'

Jonah did not want to do as God said. He was ready to preach to God's own people in Israel, but he did not see why he should go to a foreign nation. And what a nation! Nineveh was the capital of the great Assyrian Empire. Everyone knew the cruelty of the Assyrians. They showed no mercy to those they conquered.

'If I go to Nineveh and tell them about God,' Jonah thought, 'they may be sorry for their sins and tell God so. Then he will forgive them and decide not to punish them. They deserve to be punished without any early warning from me!'

Jonah decided to get as far from Nineveh—and God—as he could. He set off for the sea port of Joppa, where ships tied up, waiting to sail to places near and far. One, Jonah found, was due to sail to Tarshish, a land so far away that the land-dwellers of Israel heard of it only from sailors' tales.

Jonah paid the fare and climbed on board. Tired out with his long walk and his struggle against God, he went below to sleep. When he woke up he would be far away from the impossible mission that God had set for him.

📖 234
Storm at Sea
JONAH 1

Jonah soon fell fast asleep. The shouts of the crew as they got ready to sail and cast off the ropes did not wake him up. At first the gentle rise and fall of the ship on the sea soothed his tired body and mind.

But before they had gone far, a strong wind began to whip up the water. The waves rose higher and higher, then came crashing against the sides of the ship and breaking over the deck.

The sailors worked with all their strength to try to keep the ship on course. In desperation they threw some of the cargo overboard, to make the ship easier to control. But the ship's strong timbers seemed thin as matchwood in the teeth of the storm.

Soon, they knew, it would break up and they would all drown.

The terrified crew began to cry out to their various gods for help.

The captain went below, and found to his astonishment that Jonah was still asleep. He shook him by the shoulder urgently and shouted:

'Wake up! Pray to your gods! If this storm goes on, we are all lost!'

On deck the sailors talked and planned.

'I reckon we've got a villain on board,' one said. 'The gods are angry with him and have sent this storm to punish him. Let's draw lots to find out who is to blame.'

The rest agreed. The names of everyone on board were written down and one name drawn out. The name of the culprit was Jonah!

'Own up, Jonah!' they begged. 'Tell us who you are and what you have done to bring such trouble on us all.'

'I am a Jew,' Jonah answered. 'I worship the God who made heaven and earth. You are right. I have sinned against God. I am his prophet but I have disobeyed his orders and I am running away from him.'

'That is terrible!' the sailors exclaimed.

'But how can we put things right and stop this storm?'

'By throwing me overboard,' Jonah said bravely.

The sailors were kind men. They did not want Jonah to drown, so they made one last attempt to get the ship to land by taking to the oars. But they were helpless against the force of the storm. They would have to take Jonah at his word.

'Please, Jonah's God,' they prayed, 'don't blame us for throwing him out. We don't want to harm him but it's our only hope, and it was you who sent the storm.'

Then they picked Jonah up and tossed him over the side. At once, the wind began to die down, the waves subsided and soon the sea grew calm.

The crew knelt on the deck in awe and prayed again to Jonah's God.

'We believe that you are the only true God. From now on we will serve and worship you alone,' they promised.

235
The Lesson of the Big Fish
JONAH 1—3

Jonah had shown great courage when he told the sailors to throw him into the raging sea. But as he began to fall from the side of the ship straight into the angry, foaming water, he felt terrified.

Down, down, down he went. Green fingers of seaweed caught at his neck and feet. He heard a roaring in his ears, felt his mouth and lungs fill with water and prayed to God to rescue him.

A huge shape loomed up from the depths of the ocean floor and the next moment Jonah found himself inside the most enormous fish he had ever imagined.

He had not drowned!

He was still alive!

Jonah did not think about what might happen next. He felt full of thankfulness to God. He was certain that the arrival of the big fish was just as much God's doing as the violent storm.

'Thank you, God!' Jonah sang out in the suffocating darkness. 'You have saved me from death!'

On the third day, the fish swam close to land. At God's command, it brought Jonah up safely onto the beach.

'Go to Nineveh, Jonah,' God said for the second time.

Jonah had learned his lesson.

He obeyed.

236
The Lesson of the Little Worm

JONAH 3

When Jonah arrived at Nineveh, its size took his breath away. It took him three days to walk the length and breadth of the city with its suburbs.

As he went, he preached. He told both king and people about the God of earth and heaven, who would no longer let their cruelty and wickedness continue. They must admit how wrong they had been, tell God they were sorry and then change their ways, or else God would punish them and their proud city.

The people listened and paid attention.

From the king down, they turned to God, asking him to forgive them. God was glad. He did not want to punish Nineveh.

But Jonah was very angry.

'Didn't I say this would happen?' he told God. 'I ran away the first time because I was afraid that you would forgive these dreadful Assyrians. You are ready to show mercy to our worst enemies, who showed no mercy to us. It makes me wish I were dead!'

Then Jonah walked out of Nineveh. He settled down a little way off, to watch the city. He hoped God might decide to send down fire or brimstone after all. But the heat of the midday sun soon grew unbearable and Jonah felt more wretched than ever.

Then God, who had provided both the storm and the fish, prepared a big, shady plant to protect Jonah from the sun's blazing rays. As Jonah cooled down, he felt better.

But God told a little worm to nibble at the roots of Jonah's plant and by next morning the plant had withered and died.

As the sun grew hotter and Jonah missed the plant's shade, he grew more angry and wretched than ever.

'What right have you to be angry that the plant has died?' God asked him.

'Every right!' Jonah answered back. 'At least it made my life bearable. I'm so miserable now that I'd like to die!'

'Jonah,' God said gently, 'you are angry because the plant has died, yet you did nothing to make it grow or keep it alive. It was here one day and gone the next. How do you expect me to feel at the thought of bringing punishment and death to all the people of Nineveh? They are men, women and children that I have made and have cared for over many years. They never had a chance to know or love me until you came. Shouldn't I have pity on them and spare them, and all their animals too?'

Malachi

237
'My Messenger is Coming!'
MALACHI

Nothing exciting seemed to happen any more. The Jewish people looked back wistfully to the days when their parents had first returned in happy triumph from the captivity in Babylonia.

Years of hard work had followed before the temple and the city had been rebuilt, but even that time seemed better than the dull routine of their own lives.

They worked hard all week, but no one was well off. On the Sabbath they went to the temple, but the services seemed dreary and boring.

Then Malachi, God's prophet, spoke to them:

'God still loves and cares about you!' he told them in warm, ringing tones.

'It doesn't seem like it,' the people grumbled back. 'Those who don't worship God are better off than we are. It doesn't pay to serve God.'

'Give God the place he deserves in your lives,' Malachi told them. 'God would rather shut the temple doors for ever than put up with the way you carry on. You only go there out of habit, not because you love God. You mumble your prayers without

meaning a word you say. Instead of giving God the pick of your flock, you get rid of any sick and lame animals as your gifts to him. How can you expect God to bless you? Turn back to him! Give him the best you have! Then he will shower you with blessings—just you see!

'You keep complaining that God does not work wonders any more. I have news for you—God himself is going to visit this temple of his. God notices those who truly love him and when he comes he is going to sort out the good from the bad. He will make you pure, just like a goldsmith who burns off the dross to get pure gold.

'But before God comes he will send his messenger to prepare for his visit. He will be another Elijah, telling you loud and clear what God requires. So look out—God's messenger is coming!' The people listened. When would God's messenger arrive, they wondered? Would he come soon, or would they have a long time to wait for him?

THE NEW TESTAMENT

The New Testament is the story of Jesus and how he came to bring a new covenant between God and all people everywhere. Jesus, God's Son, died so that everyone could have forgiveness through trusting him. After Jesus came alive again, his followers spread the good news about God's promise of new life in Jesus far and wide.

The Promised King

238
Hoping and Praying
LUKE 1

Over four hundred years had passed since Malachi had warned the Jewish people to be ready for the day when God would visit them. And they had been hard times. Greek conquerors had followed the Persian emperors. After one glorious burst of independence under the great Jewish freedom fighter, Judas Maccabeus, the Jews were now, once more, under foreign rule. Rome had conquered Greece and the Roman emperor had marched into Jerusalem itself. Roman soldiers were stationed throughout the land.

How the Jews longed for another national hero, who would throw out the hated Roman legions and set up a Jewish kingdom again! If only God would send his promised King to bring them freedom!

Others in the land were more concerned about justice and obedience to God's ways. They too longed for God's anointed King, but they looked for a just and good ruler, rather than a great warrior.

Zechariah was a priest, and he and his wife Elizabeth prayed that God would send a king like that. When they had first been married they had longed, like all married couples in those days, to have a family of their own. But the years had passed and no baby was born.

Now they were growing old. But together they still talked about the scripture verses that told of the King God would send to save his people and they prayed that one day soon God would make his promises come true.

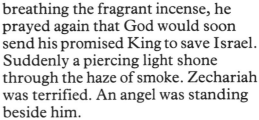

239
The Promise of a Baby
LUKE 1

The priests who served God in the Jerusalem temple were divided into twenty-four groups. Every group had two turns a year, a week at a time, to serve God in the temple. The most sacred and important duty that the priest had to perform was to burn incense on the altar inside the holy temple itself. Every priest longed to do this, but because there were so many priests, names were drawn to see who should have the privilege. Some priests might never be chosen and none was given a second chance.

Zechariah was excited and a little nervous when at last his name was drawn. He knew that he must go inside the holy place while the crowds waited quietly outside. When he had burned the incense he would come out again and bless them.

As Zechariah stood at the altar,

breathing the fragrant incense, he prayed again that God would soon send his promised King to save Israel. Suddenly a piercing light shone through the haze of smoke. Zechariah was terrified. An angel was standing beside him.

'Don't be frightened,' the angel said. 'God has heard your prayers. You and Elizabeth will have a son. He will be the messenger sent by God to make ready for the coming of the King himself. Name him John. He will grow up to be good and great, like the prophet Elijah himself. God's own Spirit will be upon him and he will bring the people back to God.'

Zechariah could not believe his ears or eyes.

'How can I be certain that you are telling me the truth?' he asked.

'I am Gabriel,' the angel replied. 'I stand in God's very presence and he sent me to you with this good news. But because you do not believe, you will be unable to speak until after your baby is born.'

Outside, in the temple court, the people shuffled and whispered. Why was the priest so long?

Zechariah appeared at last, white-faced and trembling. He opened his mouth to speak the blessing, but no words came. He could only point upwards and then touch his silent lips.

'He's seen a vision!' the people said.

When the week's duties were over, Zechariah went home. He wrote down for Elizabeth all that had happened. She had no doubts. She was bubbling over with happiness and excitement. After years of waiting and disappointment she would have a son. He would help bring God's promises to pass.

240
Journey to the Hills
LUKE 1

Mary was a relative of Elizabeth. She lived in Nazareth, a town in the northern hills of Galilee. She was young but already she had been betrothed to Joseph, the local carpenter. Soon they would be married.

One day, as Mary sat quietly, a strange brightness fell on the cloth she was sewing. Startled, she looked up. Gabriel, the mighty angel of God, was standing in the little room.

'God is with you, Mary,' Gabriel said, 'and he has blessed you greatly. Don't be frightened, for I come with good news. You are going to have a son. He will be very special. He will be the long-awaited King, the descendant of David, whose kingdom will last for ever.'

'How can such a thing happen to me?' Mary asked in wonder. 'I am not yet married.'

'God's power will rest on you and his Holy Spirit will come to you. That is why your child will be God's own Son. Nothing is too hard for God. Elizabeth, your relative, thought that she could never have a child, but she is going to have a baby in three months' time.'

'I don't understand,' Mary said quietly. 'But I am God's servant and ready for anything he asks me to do.'

When Gabriel had gone Mary thought for a long time. She knew that the only person she could confide in was Elizabeth. So she set off to visit her.

Elizabeth saw her coming and hurried out to meet her. She hugged and kissed her. She knew Mary's wonderful news already.

'How happy and blessed you are!' she exclaimed. 'You will be the mother of the King we have waited for so long, the one who is coming to save us!'

Mary hardly knew whether to laugh or cry. She was so full of thanks to God that she burst out singing, praising God's goodness. What great things he had done! He was choosing ordinary, poor people to bring about his wonderful plans.

The two women had so much to talk about. Both knew that the babies they would bear would be very special. Through them God would visit and save his people.

Mary stayed with Elizabeth until just before Elizabeth's baby was due to be born. Then she made her way back to Nazareth.

241
'Call him John!'
LUKE 1

There was great excitement when a son was born to Zechariah and Elizabeth. When he was one week old there was a special celebration at which the baby would be given his name. Friends and relatives came from far and wide.

'Of course you'll call him Zechariah, after his father,' they said.

'No,' Elizabeth replied firmly. 'His name is to be John.'

'Why call him that?' they asked. 'It's not a family name.'

' "The Lord is gracious"—that's what John means,' Elizabeth murmured. Then she added out loud. 'See what his father says.'

They turned to Zechariah. He still could not speak but he made signs to them to pass him his writing-tablet.

'His name is John,' he wrote clearly.

At that very moment Zechariah's speech returned. He began to thank and praise God for all his goodness. Then he spoke to them all about his little son and about the even greater child who was soon to be born.

'God has kept his promises, made so long ago,' he began. 'The long night of waiting is over and morning has dawned. God is shining on us with his presence. His Rescuer is going to bring us light and guide us into ways of peace.'

Then he took his baby son from Elizabeth's arms. He smiled as he looked down at him.

'You will be special, too, my little one,' he said. 'You will go ahead of God's King. You will bring the message of God's love and forgiveness to his people and make all things ready for the coming of our King.'

242
Joseph
MATTHEW 1

Joseph was the carpenter in Nazareth. He was proud of the fact that he belonged to the royal tribe of Judah and he was actually descended from King David himself. Like all Jews, Joseph took a keen interest in the long line of his family ancestors. He knew that not all in that famous family tree were pure Jews.

Rahab's name appeared far back in the line. She was the woman in Jericho who trusted in the God of Israel and kept the Israelite spies safe. She had married a Jew.

Ruth was the great grandmother of David. She was a girl from the country of Moab, who left her own people to go with her mother-in-law to Bethlehem.

God's care and love went beyond the chosen people of Israel to all who put their trust in him.

Joseph had been looking forward eagerly to the day when he and Mary would be married. But when he found that she was going to have a baby, he was bitterly upset. He thought that Mary had been unfaithful to him and to their solemn betrothal vows. He decided to break off the marriage. Because he was a kind and gentle man, he planned to do it as quietly as possible, to save Mary from shame and disgrace.

That night, God spoke to Joseph in a dream. 'Don't be worried and upset,' he said. 'The baby that Mary is going to have will be born through God's power and his Spirit. Name him Jesus—the one who saves—for he is God's promised King. Marry Mary and bring her child up as your son and part of your own royal line.'

Joseph woke up feeling very happy. Mary was good and true, as he had always believed. Now he must do all he could to make things easier for her.

They were married as soon as possible, so that Joseph could take care of Mary even before her baby was born.

God's Promise Comes True

📖 **243**

Jesus is Born

LUKE 2

The great Augustus, emperor of Rome, wished to know just how many subjects he had and how much tax he could hope to collect. He ordered a numbering (or census) of everyone in his empire. Every Jewish man had to report to his home town to see that his name was added to the electoral roll.

News of the census reached Nazareth not long before the time when Mary's baby was due to be born. Joseph would have to make the journey south to Bethlehem, the birthplace of his ancestor King David, to put his name on the Roman register. He decided to take his young wife, Mary, with him, rather than leave her alone at Nazareth.

The journey took nearly a week. In the day-time they walked. At night they slept in the open. How glad they were when at last Bethlehem came into sight on the hill-top, surrounded by its peaceful fields.

The inn would be a rough and ready place, they knew. There would be no comforts, just a bare room to sleep in, and a courtyard for the animals. At least it would provide shelter for Mary that night. But, when they arrived, the inn was full. There was no possible space for two more weary people to lie down.

Someone noticed their tired, disappointed faces and realized that Mary's baby would soon be born. He offered Joseph a cave, where he usually kept his animals. It was a dirty, smelly place.

Joseph cleared a space and cleaned it as best he could before helping Mary to lie down. Someone brought water for her to drink and wash.

Then, in the dimness, among the smells and dirt, Mary's baby was born. Joseph and Mary forgot everything else as they gazed with joy at the tiny baby boy.

'We shall call him Jesus,' Joseph said, 'as the angel told me. He is the one God has sent to save us.'

Mary wrapped the baby up, as mothers did in those days, with long, bandage-strips of cloth, to keep his small legs and arms firm and safe.

They had no cradle, so Joseph laid him to sleep in the manger, the feeding-trough for the animals' hay.

The Shepherds' Story

LUKE 2

For the shepherds in the fields around Bethlehem, that night began like any other night. They must take good care of their sheep because soon they would be sold in the nearby capital of Jerusalem. There they would be bought as offerings to God, at the beautiful temple. They had to be in perfect condition, with no scratched ears or torn legs.

As the shepherds kept guard, warming themselves at their fire, they told stories to while away the time and keep themselves awake.

Suddenly the quiet night sky was a blaze of light and the glorious shining figure of an angel bent over them.

The shepherds were terrified but the angel said, 'Don't be frightened. I have come with good news for you. It

will bring joy to the whole world. This very day a baby was born in Bethlehem. He is Christ the Lord! Go and see him for yourselves. You will find him tightly wrapped and lying in a manger.'

At once the whole sky came alive with angels and the air was filled with their singing. They poured out a hymn of praise and thankfulness to God.

'Glory to God in the highest,' they sang, 'peace on earth to those with whom God is pleased.'

Then, as suddenly as they had come, the angels disappeared. Slowly the sky sank back into darkness and silence. The shepherds looked at one another, scarcely able to believe that they had not been dreaming.

'Come on,' they said. 'Let's go and find out if it's true.'

They raced across the fields toward the sleeping town. When they found Joseph and Mary and saw the baby lying in the manger, they fell on their knees to worship him. Then they told Joseph and Mary all that had happened and the message that the angel had brought to them.

Mary said nothing but she thought hard about the wonderful things that had been said about her little son.

As the shepherds hurried back to their sheep, they could not help bursting out singing too, in praise of God. Everything had turned out just as the angel had said.

245
'Where is the Prince?'

MATTHEW 2

It was not only the Jews who were looking for a great king, promised by God. Tales of a coming king, anointed and sent by God, had spread far and wide. Wise and learned men in distant lands waited for such a king to be born in the land of the Jews, who would rule the world in justice and peace.

Scientists in those days studied the stars and the planets. They accurately charted their courses, because they believed that they could learn from them about future happenings.

At the time when Jesus was born in Bethlehem, some of the astrologers from far away discovered a star in the sky that shone with special brightness. Such a star, they believed, must be the sign that a great king had been born. Could it mean that the ancient prophecies had at last come true and a king had indeed been born in far-off Judea?

Quickly they packed up provisions for a long journey and, taking with them rich gifts, suitable for a king, they set off with a camel caravan towards the land of Israel.

When they arrived at the border, they thought that their quest was nearly ended. They would go straight to the palace in Jerusalem, the capital city. The baby would certainly be there.

But at the palace Herod reigned as king. He had been given his power by the Roman rulers and he held it greedily. He was madly jealous of any who might, he suspected, try to take his throne from him.

When news reached him that wealthy strangers had arrived, inquiring for a new king, he was alert at once.

He knew, too, about the Bible's prophecies of a coming Messiah and he hastily sent for the religious teachers.

'Is there any scripture that foretells where the promised King will be born?' he asked in agitation.

'Yes, your Majesty,' the learned teachers replied. 'The prophet Micah writes that he will be born in Bethlehem, the city of great King David.'

Herod ordered his servants to summon the strangers to a meeting. He listened politely to their story, carefully hiding his own fear and anger.

'Go to Bethlehem,' he advised them. 'That is where the Messiah is to be born. Come back and tell me exactly where he is,' he added, 'for I shall want to visit him and take him presents too.'

Night fell as the wise men set off towards Bethlehem. As they journeyed, their own special star came into sight once more. How excited they were! God was surely guiding them to his King.

246
Presents Fit for a King
MATTHEW 2

By the time the wise men from the east had arrived in Bethlehem, Joseph had been able to move Mary and the new baby from the rough shelter of the cave to a house. There was always work for a good carpenter and he must earn enough to feed the family.

When the wise men arrived at the little house they had to stoop low to enter the simple, one-roomed dwelling. There were no rich tapestries or expensive hangings on the walls, no servants to wait on the mother, or to take care of the baby.

All they could see in the dim light was a simple peasant girl nursing her little son. But they did not doubt for one moment that they had found the long-promised king. They knelt low in worship, their rich robes sweeping the bare earth floor. They knew that someone far greater than they lay sleeping in his mother's arms.

Soon they brought their gifts from the camels' packs and held them out to Jesus with reverence and awe. Mary took them in wonder.

There was gold, a fit gift for a king. There was frankincense, the sweet-smelling incense offered in worship in the temples of their lands.

Last came the gift of myrrh. Mary thought this strange, for myrrh was the fragrant spice used in burying the dead.

Now that they had found the King the visitors were satisfied. They would begin the long trek home. But that night, as they were sleeping, God warned them not to return to King Herod.

The next morning they set off by another route to their own land.

Escape to Egypt
MATTHEW 2

That same night Joseph too had a dream.

'Take Mary and Jesus and set off at once for Egypt,' God's angel warned him. 'King Herod will soon be sending his soldiers here to search for the baby, in order to kill him. You must all stay in Egypt until you are told that it is safe for you to come back again.'

Meanwhile Herod had waited impatiently at his palace. Would those strangers never return with news about the baby king?

As the time passed, he grew more and more anxious and angry. At last he realized that they had deceived him. They must have discovered his evil scheme and gone straight home.

Now he would have to think of a plan to make absolutely certain that the rival king did not live. He would order the death of every single baby born in Bethlehem since the date when the wise men first saw their star.

He gave the order to his army officers:

'Kill every boy child under two years, born in Bethlehem or anywhere near.'

What sadness and tears there were because of Herod's cruelty!

But by this time Joseph and Mary, with baby Jesus, were on their way to Egypt. God kept them safe.

Not very long afterwards, King Herod himself died.

'Go back home now,' the angel told Joseph. 'The ones who wanted to kill the child are dead.'

The little family started out but Joseph was still afraid that it might not be safe to go to Bethlehem. He learned that Archelaus, Herod's cruel son, had become king instead of his father. But he had been given only the southern part of the country to govern.

So Joseph took his family back to the north and they settled once again in Nazareth. Joseph opened up his carpenter's shop and began work in the town once more.

Jesus Growing Up

📖 **248**

The Boy in the Temple

LUKE 2

Every year, when spring came, Jewish families began to plan an exciting trip. They would soon be going to Jerusalem to celebrate Passover, the festival that reminded them of God's wonderful rescue of his people from Egypt, long ago.

Those who came from a distance enjoyed picnics on the way and nights in the open. Gradually they would meet up with pilgrims from other towns and together they would join the great, surging crowd that thronged the narrow streets of Jerusalem, on the way to the temple.

When Jesus was twelve, he went with Mary and Joseph to the Passover festival.

When at last the week of celebrations was over, the mothers started for home with the children, leaving the men to catch up with them later. It was evening before Joseph and Mary met again.

'Where's Jesus?' Joseph asked.

Mary's heart missed a beat. She had thought he was with the men. At twelve he was nearly a man, by Jewish law, and too old to travel with the little ones.

They checked with everyone in the party but Jesus was nowhere to be found. They would have to retrace their steps to Jerusalem, hoping they would find him there.

As they hurried back, breathless and fearful, they wondered where to look for him. Had he gone home with some new-found friend? But all their inquiries were met by blank faces, until at last someone said, 'I saw Jesus with the teachers in the temple.'

They hurried to the temple court, where the Jewish rabbis, or teachers, regularly taught any who wished to listen, and discussed the scriptures among themselves.

Mary's quick eye soon caught sight of her son. He was listening eagerly to the white-bearded teachers. He leaned forward to ask a question. Mary could see the surprise on their faces that anyone so young could join in their discussions so wisely.

Then Joseph strode into the circle. He took Jesus firmly by the arm and led him to his mother.

'How could you behave like this?' Mary asked. 'Your father and I have been so worried.'

'I thought you would guess that I must be in my Father's house,' Jesus replied.

Then they all began the journey home to Nazareth.

Although Jesus knew already that God was his Father in a special way, he still did as he was told by his earthly parents.

Mary thought hard about it all. She knew that her son was different. She must wait to discover what this was going to mean.

John the Baptist

📖 249

Show You Are Sorry!

MATTHEW 3

The years passed. John, son of Zechariah and Elizabeth, and Jesus, son of Mary, both became men. Although their mothers were related, they were very different from each other.

John left home and went to live a rough, outdoor life in the hot, bare desert near the River Jordan. He wanted to be alone and find out God's purpose for him.

He was a plain, outspoken man, like the prophet Elijah, and he dressed like him, too. He wore a rough camel-skin coat, tied round the waist with a leather belt. He ate the desert food of wild honey and locusts.

God gave him a message to preach and crowds soon came flocking out to hear him.

'Listen!' John thundered. 'God's kingdom is on its way! See that you are ready for it. Put your lives right with God.'

'Why should we do that?' the people asked. 'We are God's chosen people—he must be pleased with us.'

'Don't rely on that!' John warned them. 'Being born an Israelite isn't good enough. You must tell God how sorry you are for doing evil and begin to live lives that please him.'

Many people knew that it was God's voice speaking to them. They were really sorry for breaking God's laws and wanted to please God. So John baptized them in the River Jordan, by dipping them under the water. It was a sign to show everyone that God had forgiven them and given them a clean, new start.

'Now change your ways,' John urged. 'Don't be greedy and grasping. If you have more food and clothes than you need, share with others. Do your jobs well and without grumbling. That is what God wants.'

250
Jesus is Baptized

MATTHEW 3

John warned the people that God would punish them if they did not repent and change their ways, but he also brought them good news.

'I'm preparing the way for a very important person, who is coming soon,' he announced. 'He is so much greater than I am that I'm not good enough to be his meanest slave. I'm only baptizing you with water—he will bring you all God's blessing and power. He will be God's awaited King.'

One day, Jesus came to see John.

'Please baptize me, too,' Jesus asked him.

'I couldn't do that!' John exclaimed. He had known Jesus since they were boys. 'You have never gone your own way and disobeyed God. You have nothing to be sorry for. You are a better person than I am.'

'But I believe that it's what God wants,' Jesus persisted.

So John baptized him.

As Jesus came up from the water, a strange thing happened. When John tried to describe it afterwards, he said:

'I saw something that looked like a dove alight on Jesus.'

Then, in a sudden blinding flash, John realized that the relative he had known and admired for so long, was none other than the King he had been preaching about. Immediately he heard God's voice speaking to Jesus:

'You are my own dear Son,' God said. 'I am wholly pleased with you.'

251
A New Leader
JOHN 1 AND 3

Some of the people John baptized became his friends and followers. They would come and listen to him whenever they could. They longed to hear more about the coming King.

One day, while John was talking to some of these friends, he saw Jesus walking along the path.

'Look hard at that man,' John told them. 'He is the one chosen by God to carry away the sins of the whole world.'

Two of John's friends hurried after Jesus. Something about him made them want to get to know him. Suddenly they felt shy and stopped still. But Jesus stopped, too, and invited them to come and spend the day with him.

When they went home that night, one of them, called Andrew, was full of excitement. He rushed to find his brother, Simon, bursting with news.

'I've found the Messiah!' he exclaimed. 'God's anointed King! Come and meet him.'

When Jesus saw Simon, he gave him a long, searching look. Then he said: 'I'm going to give you a new name, Simon. I shall call you Peter— the rock. For that's the kind of man you will one day be.'

Preparing to Start

252
Temptation
LUKE 4

As soon as John baptized Jesus, he was certain that he was the long-expected King that God had promised to send to his people. Jesus knew, too, that from now on he must carry out God's plan for him and preach the good news that God's rule on earth had begun. His time in the carpenter's shop at Nazareth was over for ever.

But, before he began his special life-work, Jesus wanted to think hard and to pray to his Father about it. He went away on his own into the desert. The sun glared down on bare rocks and dry sand. There was no fresh grass or green trees to be seen. There was no food to eat, and the only sound to be heard was the howling of the wild beasts.

Jesus realized that he would not be

like other kings. He would not have fine clothes, a rich palace and slaves to obey his orders. He was going to be poor and badly treated and at the end he would be cruelly killed. All this was part of God's loving plan to rescue the whole world from the power of evil. And Jesus willingly accepted God's plan.

But Satan, the enemy of God and the source of all evil, was determined to try to stop Jesus from obeying God, just as he had made Adam and Eve disobey God long ago.

When Jesus was hungry and exhausted, after many days of prayer and going without food, Satan suggested to him:

'God has said that you are his Son, so why go hungry? Just order these little rocks to turn into loaves!'

'The Bible says that man cannot live by bread alone,' Jesus answered. Jesus refused to use his power to satisfy his own needs. He knew, too, that food is not the most important thing in life.

Satan went on: 'This world belongs to me. Recognize my power and do things *my* way and I will give it all to you.'

A glimpse of all the glittering empires of the earth flashed before Jesus' eyes in a moment. But he shook his head.

'The Bible says that God is the only one we should obey and worship,' he replied. 'I will do things *God's* way.'

Once more Satan tried to make Jesus give up God's plans for him.

'Do something daring and spectacular,' he suggested. 'If you throw yourself down from the top of the temple you will be a popular hero. You need not worry, because God says in the Bible that he will take care of you and save you from hurting yourself.' '

The Bible also says that it is wrong to test God and then expect him to get you out of trouble,' Jesus replied.

In no way could Satan persuade Jesus to turn from God's plan and go his own way. For a while Satan left him alone and God sent angels to help and strengthen Jesus, after his long struggle against evil.

253
'Follow Me!'
MARK 1, 2, 3

The time had come for Jesus to begin to tell everyone that God's Kingdom had arrived on earth. He did not announce himself as the king but showed God's great love and power in everything he did and said.

Jesus knew that he would need people to help him and he asked God to show him the men he should call to follow him and help in his work.

As Jesus walked one day along the shore of Lake Galilee, he caught sight of his old friends, Andrew and Simon Peter.

'Come with me!' he called to them.

At once the two fishermen dropped their nets and raced across the beach to join him. A bit further on, two other brothers, John and James, were cleaning and mending their nets, ready for the next night's fishing.

'Follow me!' Jesus called, and they gladly left the servants to help their father Zebedee and went with Jesus, too.

'No more looking for fish!' Jesus told them. 'From now on I shall teach you how to fish for people who need to be caught for God!'

Jesus chose twelve men altogether to be his close disciples, or followers. They were a mixed bunch.

As well as fishermen there were freedom fighters, who had tried to rid their people of Roman rule. One, called Matthew, was a tax collector for King Herod. He collected customs duty from everyone bringing goods into Herod's province of Galilee. Tax collectors were hated and despised by the Jews. Most worked for the Roman conquerors, often they took more money than the Romans demanded and kept the extra for themselves.

Although there were many other men and women who became Jesus' disciples as time went by, these twelve were special. Jesus also called them 'apostles' or 'messengers' because he sent them out to tell others the good news about the kingdom of God.

These are their names: Simon (called Peter), James and John (the sons of Zebedee), Andrew, Philip, Bartholomew, Matthew, Thomas, James (the son of Alphaeus), Thaddaeus, Simon (the patriot) and Judas Iscariot.

254
Doctor for the Sick
MARK 2

Matthew had been sitting in his little hut at the lakeside when Jesus called him. He collected customs duties on goods brought in and out of the province. He gladly gave up his well-paid job to go with such a wonderful leader. He wanted all his friends to meet Jesus, too, so he gave a huge party and invited them all. Plenty of uninvited guests joined in as well.

The religious leaders were puzzled. They could see what a bad lot of people were at the party. If Jesus was really a good man, how could he mix with them?

'Why does your master share a feast with such wicked people?' they asked the disciples. Jesus overheard them.

'When do you go to the doctor?' he asked them. 'When you are well, or when you are ill? It's the people who are sick who need the doctor. I'm God's doctor to heal and forgive those who are sick, because they have done

wrong and broken God's laws. I must
go where they are, if I'm to help them.
Those who are good and have done
nothing wrong don't need me.'

The religious people were really
just as much in need of Jesus'
forgiveness as those they called
'sinners'. But Jesus was only able to
help those who were willing to admit
that they had broken God's laws and
who asked for his forgiveness.

Jesus' Mission Begins

📖 **255**

Wine for the Wedding

JOHN 2

One day, Jesus and his disciples were invited to a wedding. It was to be held at Cana, a little village in the hills of Galilee.

While the guests were enjoying the feast there was panic behind the scenes. There was no more wine and nothing to give the guests to drink. Jesus' mother was helping and she beckoned to Jesus.

'Please do something!' she begged him. 'If we can't get some more wine somehow, the feast will be spoiled and the bridegroom and his family disgraced.'

Jesus knew that his time at home, doing as his mother wished, was over. Now he must take his orders only from God, and follow his plan.

'I must wait until the right time to act has come,' he told her.

'See that you do everything my son tells you,' Mary whispered to the servants.

She was sure that Jesus would help their friends out of their difficulty and save them from disgrace.

Everyone likes to wash before eating but some people did much more than that. Because of strict religious rules, they washed their hands over and over again. Jesus could see the row of huge water-pots that had held the large quantity of water the guests had needed. Now they stood empty.

'Fill up those jars,' he told the servants. 'Then draw the water from them to take to the guests.'

The servants did just as Jesus had said. As they poured for each guest, they saw rich red wine filling the cups.

The chief guest took a satisfying drink, then exclaimed to the bridegroom:

'You've left the best wine until last!'

He did not know where the wine had come from, but Jesus' disciples had watched all that had happened. They were full of wonder at their new leader. They believed that he was someone very special. In place of strict rules, Jesus would bring God's love and joy wherever he went.

256
Screams in the Synagogue

MARK 1

Once or twice a year, Jewish families went up to the beautiful Jerusalem temple, but every Sabbath day they flocked to the synagogue in their own town. The synagogue was a plain building, used the rest of the week as the school and the law court. In every synagogue stood a chest, holding the scrolls of holy scripture. At synagogue services, men sat on one side and women on the other, while the scriptures were read and prayer was made to God.

One Sabbath, Jesus and his disciples went to the synagogue at Capernaum, the fishing-town on the shores of Lake Galilee, near to where Peter and Andrew lived.

Jesus was invited to preach. The people listened intently. Usually the preacher explained scripture by quoting what other people had said, but Jesus told them himself exactly what God's word meant.

Suddenly there was a great commotion and a piercing scream rang out. Everyone turned around and saw, with horror, a wild-looking man staggering towards the front. He shouted at Jesus:

'What are you doing here? Do you want to destroy us? I know who you are—you are God's holy messenger!'

Jesus knew that this man was not just excited or even hysterical. An evil spirit from Satan had taken charge of his body and mind. Satan was determined to fight God's chosen king in every way he could.

'Be quiet, evil spirit!' Jesus ordered. 'Come out of the man and leave him in peace!'

Jesus was stronger than the most powerful force of evil, and the demon had to obey.

The man shook violently, gave another piercing scream, then lay completely quiet and at peace.

An excited chatter soon broke the silence.

'Who can this new teacher be?' the people began to ask one another.

'He explains God's word in a wonderful way,' some said.

'Yes, and he's even powerful enough to make evil spirits obey his orders,' others replied.

Jesus Makes People Well

MARK 1

When the synagogue service was over, Peter and Andrew took Jesus home with them, and the other disciples went too. When they arrived, Peter's wife came to meet them with a worried face.

'Mother is so ill,' she began. 'The fever is getting worse and I don't know what to do.'

Jesus can help,' one of them said.

They led Jesus to the corner of the room where Peter's mother-in-law lay tossing and moaning. Jesus took her thin, wasted hand in his strong one and began to help her sit up. At once the burning flush died from her face and she smiled at Jesus.

'I should be up and looking after *you*,' she said. She got to her feet, feeling well and strong. She soon had dinner ready for Jesus and the tired disciples.

The people next door caught sight of her and could not believe their eyes. The news soon spread and by evening there was a large crowd outside Peter's house.

All kinds of sick people were patiently waiting for Jesus to help them. There were deaf and blind people, those troubled by evil spirits and many who could not walk. Friends and relatives had helped them there.

Jesus went out to the crowd and healed them all. He showed them that God's great power was at work in the world, now that he had come. He also made them realize that God loved and cared for every one of them.

258
It's Only Joseph's Son!
LUKE 4 AND MARK 6

On another Sabbath, Jesus went to the synagogue at Nazareth, where he grew up. Relatives and friends who still lived there were sitting in the congregation. Some remembered Jesus as a little boy and others knew him as the carpenter who made the cradle for their baby or yokes for their oxen.

Jesus was invited to read the scriptures and explain them. The official in charge handed Jesus the scroll of Isaiah's writings. Jesus began to read Isaiah's words:

'God has chosen me to bring good news to the poor, to proclaim liberty to the captives and recovery of sight to the blind; to set free the oppressed and announce that the time has come when the Lord will save his people.'

The Jews believed that in these verses Isaiah was describing the wonderful day that would come when God's kingdom would be set up on earth.

When Jesus had finished reading, he sat down, as rabbis always did when they were going to teach. Everyone's eyes were fixed on him. They wondered how he would explain Isaiah's words.

They could scarcely believe their ears when Jesus said, 'This very day the verses I have read to you have come true.' Jesus was claiming to be God's Messiah-King.

There was a low rumble of complaining whispers.

'How can he talk like that? He's just Joseph's son.'

'He's the village carpenter,' others agreed.

Jesus broke in on their discussion.

'You won't believe me because you know me too well,' he said. 'God's prophets have never been accepted in their own home towns. While Elijah was in Israel his life was in danger. He had to go out of the country to find a widow who would care for him. Later on it was Naaman, a Syrian, not one of the Israelites, who believed Elisha and was healed by him.'

The people were furious at what Jesus said. How dare he suggest that foreigners were readier to hear and obey God than God's own people!

They rushed from their seats, seized Jesus and dragged him out of the building and up the steep hill on which their town was built. They meant to hurl him headlong over the cliff. But Jesus slipped quietly through the angry crowd and went on his way, unhurt.

259
John in Prison

MARK 6 AND LUKE 7

John the Baptist had spoken bluntly to the crowds of ordinary people who flocked to hear him. He had also had the courage to speak the truth to the king himself. (King Herod, who ruled in Galilee, was the son of wicked Herod the Great, who ordered the death of the babies in Bethlehem when Jesus was born.)

John told Herod plainly that he did wrong to take away his brother's wife and marry her himself. Although Herod's conscience was pricked when John talked like that, he could not help admiring him for his courage and honesty and for the simple life he lived. It was very different from the luxury and shallowness of life in his palace.

But his wife, Herodias, hated John. How dare he tell them what they ought to do! She nagged Herod so much that at last he had John arrested. He shut him up in the grim rock fortress of Machaerus. Far below lay the Dead Sea and there was not a green tree or blade of grass to be seen on the deep and desolate ravines on every side.

John had lived a life of freedom in the open air. Now he was chained to the walls of a dark, airless dungeon.

As he lay there, day and night, he began to wonder whether his vision of the coming King had been no more than a dream. At last he sent some of his friends to find Jesus and ask him the truth.

When they arrived, Jesus was surrounded by a crowd of sick people. He was busy giving them back their sight and hearing and making them fit to walk again.

'John wants to know if you really are the Messiah,' the friends asked.

'Go back and tell John what you have seen,' Jesus answered. He knew that John would recognize his wonderful acts of healing as true signs that God was at work and that his chosen Messiah had come.

When John's friends had gone, Jesus talked to the crowds about John. 'I wonder what you thought you were going to see when you went to listen to John,' he said. 'Not a courtier in fine clothes—but a true, honest messenger of God. John is the greatest prophet that has ever lived.'

Reward for the Dancing Girl

MARK 6

Time passed and John the Baptist still lay chained in his dark dungeon. One day it was Herod's birthday, so he decided to have a party. Lavish supplies of food and wine were prepared and everyone of importance was invited.

After the guests had eaten and drunk all they could, they lay back ready to be entertained.

Salome, Herodias' beautiful daughter, came into the hall and offered to dance for the king and the men who were his guests.

The audience was entranced by her performance and when at last the music died down and Salome sank gracefully at the king's feet, wild clapping and shouts broke out. Herod was flushed with wine and excitement.

'You must have a reward for your dancing!' he exclaimed. 'Choose anything on earth you want and I swear to give it to you.'

Without a word Salome slipped quietly from the room and went to look for her mother. What should she ask for? Herodias did not need to stop and think.

'Ask for John the Baptist's head,' she ordered her daughter, with grim relish.

Salome hurried back to the crowded banquet-room. 'Please give me the head of John the Baptist on a dish—now, at once,' she said.

Herod was horrified. He was afraid to kill such a good man. But he would feel a fool if he went back on his word when all his servants and his guests had heard his promise to Salome.

Regretfully, he sent a soldier to John's dungeon with the terrible order to behead him.

Herodias was satisfied. She had succeeded in silencing the man who had spoiled her happiness by telling her of her wrongdoing.

John's friends were very sad. Gently they took his body to give it a reverent burial. Jesus was sad too. He had loved John dearly.

Lessons out of Doors

261
The Sermon on the Mount
MATTHEW 5 AND LUKE 6

Some of the religious leaders soon made it clear that they did not want to listen to the things that Jesus taught about God. They had their own ideas of what God is like and how they could please him. They were very strict about keeping the law that Moses had given, and added to it many hundreds of rules of their own.

Jesus taught that the way we think and act towards others is more important than how we wash our hands or the kind of food we eat.

When the religious leaders refused to have Jesus in the synagogues, he taught his disciples and the crowds who listened in the open air.

One day, as they sat on the hillside, Jesus said: 'If you want to be God's children you must take after him and do as he does. God is good to all. He sends sun and rain to everyone—not only to those who deserve it. You must be generous like that. Be loving and giving even to those who are spiteful to you or treat you badly. Pay them back with kindness!'

The religious teachers were strict about keeping the Ten Commandments, including the one that says, 'Do not murder'. But there were murderous thoughts against Jesus in some of their hearts. Jesus said that God looks deep into a person's thoughts. When he sees hatred and anger, that is like committing murder, too. God wants people to be right inside, as well as on the outside, where others can see.

'The truly happy person,' Jesus went on, 'is the one who knows just how much he needs God's help and forgiveness. He knows that he will never be good enough for God, yet he wants to love and please him with all his heart. God will satisfy that person.

'Real happiness comes from being kind and patient toward others, not from pushing and grabbing for yourself.

'The happy ones are those who try to stop quarrels and make peace.

'The happy person puts God first and stays true to him, whatever the cost.

'If people bully you and say unkind things about you because you are my followers, then be happy! God has a wonderful reward waiting for you in heaven!'

262
'Lord, Teach us to Pray!'
MATTHEW 6; LUKE 11; MARK 11

Late at night and early in the morning, when the disciples were dropping with tiredness, Jesus went off alone to pray. He seemed to need prayer as much as they needed sleep.

One day they asked, 'Master, will you teach *us* how to pray?'

'How *not* to pray is important too,' Jesus explained. 'Don't copy the people you see around, who are really only putting on an act. They say their prayers for the benefit of others, not God. They find a place where plenty of people are about, then stand up and pray out loud at great length, so that everyone else will be impressed. Don't do that. Find somewhere to go on your own, where only God can see and hear you.

'Don't imagine that your prayers have to be long and full of high-sounding words if you are to make God listen. And don't keep saying the same words over and over, without thinking about what they mean. God knows all about your needs before you pray to him. But he wants you to talk to him about them in plain, honest words.

'This is the way to pray:

'Say, "Our Father"—for God is great and holy but he is also your father.

'Then ask: "May your name be kept holy. May your kingdom come soon. May we obey you on earth as those in heaven do." God's glory and God's kingdom must come first in your thoughts and prayers.

'Then pray for your own needs:

' "Please give us today the food we need. Forgive us the things that we have done wrong, as we forgive the people who wrong and hurt us. Please keep temptation away. But, whatever happens, rescue us from the power of evil."

'Never forget that it is impossible to ask God to forgive you if you are not ready to forgive others. God can only hear and forgive you when you have love and forgiveness in your hearts for one another.

'Above all, never come to God full of doubt. Believe that he is listening to you and trust him to give you the best possible answers to your prayers.'

263
The Two Prayers
LUKE 18

There were two very different groups of listeners in the crowd around Jesus. In one group were the Pharisees who kept as separate as possible from the ordinary people who made up the rest of the huge throng.

The Pharisees stood a little apart, their robes drawn carefully about them. They spent much of their time keeping every tiny regulation that had been added over the years to the law of God.

They were often good men, but they were also very pleased with themselves. They were certain that God was pleased with them, too. How much better they were, they thought, than the common people, who sat, open-mouthed, drinking in every word that Jesus spoke.

Jesus looked at both kinds of listener and told them this story:

'Two men went up to the temple to pray. One was a Pharisee and the other was a tax collector. ThePharisee took care to stand well away from the

tax collector and then began to pray to himself like this: "O God, I thank you that I am not greedy or dishonest, or the kind of person who breaks your commandments, as everyone else does. I thank you that I am nothing like that tax collector over there. I fast two days in every week and I give a tenth of all I possess to you."

'The tax collector stood at a distance. He hung his head in shame and cried out to God in utter despair at his own badness. He prayed, "Please God, hear me and give me help! I know that I am a sinner— please have mercy on me!"

'Let me tell you,' Jesus said firmly, 'it was the tax collector who went back home put right with God. He was the one that God heard and accepted—not the Pharisee.

'Everyone who makes himself great and important will be brought low. But those who humbly recognize their own need will be helped and made great by God.'

264
The Friend at Midnight
LUKE 11

'When you pray to God,' Jesus said to his disciples, 'tell him plainly what you need. Ask, and he will give to you; look for him and you will find him; knock, and God himself will open the door to you.

'Imagine that you have been woken up in the middle of the night by the arrival of an old friend. He is on a long journey and has called on you for a meal and a rest. But you find to your dismay that there is no food in the house—not even a loaf of bread. So you set off to a nearby house to borrow some bread.

'You knock hard on the door, calling out, "A friend of mine has arrived and I haven't even a slice of bread to offer him. Please lend me three loaves!"

'Silence follows. Then, as you keep on knocking, a sleepy voice growls back, "Go away! We're all in bed and the house is locked up for the night. I can't get up and give you anything!"

'But you refuse to give up. You just keep on knocking and asking, because you must have food for your friend. In the end, the man in bed gets up, finds the loaves and thrusts them at you—just to get rid of you. With a smile and a big thank you, you hurry back to your hungry guest.

'Remember,' Jesus ended, 'how different it is when you pray! Even that man who was reluctant to help was persuaded to do so at long last because his caller kept asking. But when you pray you are coming to a loving, heavenly Father. How ready and willing he is to hear you call and to provide you with the things you need and ask for!'

265
Building the Right Way
MATTHEW 7

'Once upon a time,' Jesus began, 'two people began to build a new house for themselves and their families. Before the first one began to build, he chose his site carefully.

He found a place where there was a solid shelf of rock beneath the soil and there he built his house. Winter came. The wind blew and the storms beat about the house, but it stood firm, because of the rock that lay beneath and held it firm.

'The other person did not stop to think about a foundation. He chose a pretty, sheltered hollow where his house would look its best. He did not realize that he was building on the dried-up bed of a stream. In summer all was well. But soon the winter rains came. The wind blew and floods of water began to fill the sandy hollow. They rushed beneath the house and soon the whole building collapsed into the roaring torrent.'

Jesus looked hard at his disciples, who had been listening to all he had been teaching them.

'Be wise,' he warned them. 'Build your lives on the teaching I have given you. If you obey what I have said, you will be like the wise builder who built on a rock foundation. Nothing that can happen will shake you. You will stand firm.

'But if you take no notice of what I say and live your lives your own way, doing as you think best, you will be like the stupid builder. He did not bother to find a safe foundation and his fine house fell in ruins.

'Your life will go to pieces when trouble and difficulties come, if it has no solid foundation. Build your lives wisely by obeying my teaching and doing as I say.'

Jesus' Enemies

266
Four Friends Find a Way
MARK 2

Everyone was beginning to talk about the new teacher, who did and said such wonderful things.

When Jesus came back to Capernaum, the little house in which he was teaching was soon packed with people. Outside, crowds pressed close to the open door, straining their ears and craning their necks to see.

Four men came slowly down the road, each one holding a corner of a sleeping-mat on which a sick man lay.

As they came near the house they tried to elbow their way through the crowd, but no one was willing to stand back and let them through. For a moment they put down their burden, while they thought what to do next. They were determined to get their friend to Jesus somehow.

Suddenly one of them had an idea. He climbed the outside steps leading to the flat roof and began with his hands to scrape away at the hard-packed earth that filled the space between the wide roof beams. A little hole appeared and he grunted with satisfaction. It would be easy enough to patch up the mud roof afterwards. He signalled to his friends to give a hand. Before long they had dug a gap big enough for their friend and his mat to squeeze through.

Next came the difficult job of carrying him up the steps. When they were all ready, they gently and skilfully lowered their friend through the gap in the roof, bending over the hole as they guided the mat to the

ground, right at Jesus' feet. There
was a shout of laughter from some in
the crowd at the man's unexpected
arrival, but the religious leaders who
were there frowned and scowled at
such a rude interruption to their
serious conversation.

Jesus smiled. He was delighted that
the four friends had such trust and
faith in him that they would go to any
lengths to find a way of bringing their
sick friend to him for help.

Who Can Forgive Sins?

MARK 2

The crowd in the room watched eagerly. They wanted with their own eyes to see Jesus perform a miracle. But, turning to the man who lay still and white on the mat at his feet, Jesus said, 'My son, your sins are forgiven.'

Even though he had never seen this man before, Jesus knew that there was something he needed more than a cure for his illness. The people may have been disappointed, but the sick man himself felt a surge of happiness and relief. The wrong things that had been preying on his conscience for so long had been taken away by Jesus' power.

The religious leaders were horrified.

'How dare he forgive this man?' they whispered to one another. 'God is the only one who can forgive sin. Who does he think he is?'

Jesus knew exactly what they were thinking and saying, and he answered their question out loud.

'When I say "I forgive your sins" there is no way of proving that I have really been able to do so. But you will soon see my power if I heal this man's body too.'

Then he turned again to the figure on the mat.

'Get up!' Jesus told him. 'Pick up your mat and go home!'

Then the man, who for so long had been unable to walk or even move, got to his feet and bent easily to pick up his mat. With a broad grin he pushed through the crowd and out of the door.

If Jesus is really able to cure a paralyzed man like that, the crowd thought, perhaps it's true that he can forgive sins too.

Not on the Sabbath!

MARK 3

Jesus had quite a different way of teaching God's laws from the religious leaders.

One group of these called themselves Pharisees, which means 'separated ones'. They kept themselves separate from anything or anyone that might not be pure according to their rules.

They tried very hard to be good and spent their lives keeping every tiny little rule that had been added over the years to the law that God gave through Moses.

Hundreds of extra rules had been tacked on to the commandment that says, 'Remember to keep the Sabbath day holy'. The Pharisees taught that anything that *they* called work was forbidden on the Sabbath. Healing was work, so no one could call the doctor—unless the patient was going to die before the Sabbath was over.

One Sabbath, Jesus came into the synagogue and saw a man whose hand was paralyzed. He could not use it to do his daily work and earn his living.

Some of the Pharisees in the congregation watched Jesus with eagle eyes. Was he going to break their rules by healing this man?

Jesus knew exactly what they were thinking. He had already been in trouble with the Pharisees for not making his disciples observe their rules. He called the man to the front, then turned to the people and asked a question.

'Do you think that the Sabbath should be a day for helping others, or doing them harm?' he asked them. 'Which does our law really mean us to do?'

No one answered. They knew that Jesus had the right idea about God's law but they were afraid of their leaders. Then Jesus looked at the hard, uncaring faces of the Pharisees and he was angry. He knew that they did not want to help the man. They were only trying to find a way of getting Jesus into trouble. But he was not afraid of them.

'Stretch your hand out!' he told the man.

At once, the man found that he was able to hold out the hand that had been useless and lifeless before. Now it was as good as the other hand.

The Pharisees got to their feet and walked out. They would look for others to join them in their campaign to get rid of Jesus.

He did not scold them or despise them like the Pharisees but told them that God loved them. But some thought he should have stayed put in the carpenter's shop.

'We can't think what's come over him,' they told Mary and the rest of his family. 'He must be mad!'

The religious teachers at Jerusalem had heard all about Jesus by now and some had come to listen to what he had to say. They were jealous of him because he was popular and for the wonderful things he did. They disagreed, too, with the things he taught about God. Instead of admitting that God was giving him power to help and heal, they spread the lie that he got his power from Satan.

Jesus called them across and said, 'Does it make sense to talk of Satan fighting against himself? Illness of body and mind come from Satan, who wants only to give pain and sadness. Would he get rid of them as I do? You have seen God at work and made the mistake of thinking it is Satan. That is a sin that cannot be forgiven. I have come to break Satan's hold over people and to set them free by God's power.'

269
'He's Mad!'

MARK 3

Jesus was kept busy from morning to night. A never-ending stream of people came to stare and to listen to Jesus, and crowds came for help.

Mothers and fathers carried sick children, and friends helped those who were too ill to walk by themselves, or guided those who could not see. Others hobbled along on their own to be cured by Jesus.

The disciples were rushed off their feet, too, helping Jesus and seeing that everyone had a fair turn. In the end, there was no time to stop even for meals.

Most ordinary people loved Jesus.

Stories About God's Kingdom

📖 **270**
Sowing Seed

MARK 4

People pushed and elbowed to get close to Jesus as he taught them on the beach at Lake Galilee. So Jesus climbed into a boat and the disciples pushed it a little way out, where everyone could see him.

'Listen!' Jesus began, and his voice carried over the still water.

'A farmer set out to sow his grain. He walked across his field, scattering the grain as he went.

'Some fell on the hard footpath. The birds swooped down and pecked it all up.

'Some fell on thin soil, which covered a shelf of hard rock. The seed sprang up quickly there, but because it could not put down deep roots, it soon withered and died in the hot sun.

'Some seed fell among the thorns at the border of the field. As it grew it was choked by the tough thorns.

'But some of the farmer's seed fell on rich, fertile soil. He had a good harvest from that seed.'

There was a little silence, then Jesus added,

'If you have ears, then use them!'

'We don't know what that story means,' the disciples complained later. 'How can we use our ears, if we don't understand what we hear?'

'I teach by telling stories,' Jesus said, 'so that those who really want to learn will be able to discover all kinds of things about God's kingdom. But the people who are just inquisitive and don't want to hear and obey God's message, will remain in the dark.

'I'll explain this story for you. The farmer stands for the person who spreads God's message. The seed is God's message and that is always good. But it falls on the ears of different kinds of hearers.

'Some have hard hearts and minds and won't accept God's word. They are like the hard, worn pathway. Satan soon makes them forget all about the message they have heard.

'Others are like the rocky soil. At first they are delighted to receive God's word. But when it costs a lot to obey it, they give up.

'The seed sown among thorns is like people whose lives are full of their own worries and wants. God's word is quickly choked and smothered by their own affairs.

'But some people have hearts and minds ready to receive and obey what God has to tell them. They are like the good soil. They go on showing by their lives that they have listened to God and are obeying him. That is what God calls a good harvest!'

271
Making Bread
MATTHEW 13

When Jesus talked with the clever religious leaders, who thought they knew all about God, he used the kind of words and arguments that they used. But when he taught the ordinary people, he told stories to explain God's kingdom to them.

We call these stories 'parables'. Those who think hard can discover in every story a picture that helps us understand more about God's kingdom.

'I'll tell you what God's kingdom is like,' Jesus said one day. 'It's like a housewife making bread.'

Everyone nodded, knowingly. The mothers in the crowd made bread every day and the children helped. Even the men had watched their mothers when they were little.

'You know how she does it,' Jesus went on. 'She takes a tiny bit of yeast and buries it in a big crock of flour. Before long, an amazing change takes place. The whole mixture begins to froth and then to heave and rise to double its size. That's like God's kingdom. God is at work beneath the surface. You may not see how it's happening, but lives will be completely changed and God's kingdom will grow and grow by God's power.'

272
Finding Treasure
MATTHEW 13

'Once upon a time,' Jesus began—
and everyone pricked up their ears.
He was going to tell them another
story to help them understand about
God's kingdom.

'Once upon a time, a man was
digging in the field where he had been
sent to work, when his spade hit
something hard. He bent to brush the
earth away and found a pot full of
treasure. Gold coins, rings and
brooches spilled out on the earth and
gleamed in the sun.

'The man hurriedly covered up the
treasure again. He leaned on his
spade, thinking fast. If he could

buy that field, the treasure would
belong to him. He knew it would cost
everything he had. But he went and
sold each stick of furniture and
everything else he owned, so that the
field could be his. It was worth it! The
treasure was his own.'

Jesus had hardly finished, when
one of the children in the crowd called
out, 'Tell us another story—please!'
Jesus smiled and began again.

'Once there was a merchant, a
dealer in fine pearls. He went to every
seaport market, far and near, to add to
his fine collection. One day he caught
sight of a pearl so large and so
beautiful that it made him catch his
breath. He had never seen one like it.
He asked to look at it more closely
and, as it lay in the palm of his hand,

he realized that he had found the perfect pearl. It was without flaw.

'But when he asked the price he knew that, rich as he was, he had not enough money to buy it. But he *must* have it! The rest of his pearls, once so treasured, must go. Only that way could the pearl beyond compare become his own.'

Some of Jesus' listeners began to understand something more about God's kingdom. To belong to it and to have Jesus as king would be so wonderful and so worthwhile that nothing else in life mattered compared with that. To have Jesus would be to have the most precious thing in the world.

273
The Big Dinner Party
LUKE 14

Many people longed for the day when God's kingdom would arrive on earth. Some pictured it as one long feast—for God's chosen people.

One day, when Jesus was at dinner with a very religious family, one of the guests said:

'Won't it be wonderful to be at God's banquet, when his kingdom comes?'

'Let me tell you a story,' Jesus replied.

'There was once a man who planned a big dinner party. He invited the guests and then began to prepare the feast. When everything was ready, he told his servant: "Go and call the guests to dinner!"'

'At the first house, the owner was just hurrying away. "Tell your master I'm sorry not to be at his party," he called out, over his shoulder. "I've just bought a field and I'm going to have a look at it."

'The second guest on the list was just as busy. "I can't spare time to come," he said. "I've just bought some oxen and must try them with the plough."

'The disappointed servant made his way to a third house. "I've just got married," the owner announced, beaming. "Your master won't expect *me* to come."

'One after another the invited guests made excuses. Not one would keep his promise to be there. The servant returned sadly home.

'When the master heard what had happened, he was very angry. "There are plenty of people who would be only too glad to come to my banquet," he told the servant. "Go and invite *them*. Search the back streets of the town for all the poor and hungry people and bring them here."

'In no time the servant was back, leading a string of thin, ragged people. The grubby children skipped with excitement and the older ones hobbled behind. The master welcomed them all. But when they were all seated at the huge, laden table, there were still empty seats.

' "I want my dinner table to be full," the master told his servant. "Go off to the country lanes and bring back all the tramps and the people who travel from place to place. Then my party will be complete." A shadow passed over his kind face as he added, "Not one of those friends I first invited will share my feast." '

There was an awkward little silence as Jesus finished his story. Could he really be saying that good, religious people might miss God's kingdom celebration? Would God welcome instead the very people they looked down on and despised?

Jesus, Friend in Need

📖 **274**

The Storm on the Lake

MARK 4

It had been a long, tiring day. Jesus had been teaching and healing the crowd on the lake-shore since early morning. Now the deep blue of sky and water was fading. Night was near.

'Let's cross the lake,' Jesus said, and the disciples thankfully climbed into the familiar boat and got busy with the sails. Most of the people began to drift off home.

'Rest there in the stern, on the cushion, Master,' they told Jesus. With fishermen to sail the boat, Jesus was in good hands. His head had no sooner touched the cushion than he was fast asleep. Quietly the disciples got the boat under way.

But even the most experienced fishermen on Lake Galilee feared the storms that could blow up within a few moments. Suddenly the wind began to moan and then to howl and shriek as if it were struggling to escape from the narrow lake, locked in among the high hills all around.

The waves rose high, toppling over the sides of the little boat. The tame, gentle lake had changed into a wild, snarling beast.

The disciples worked with all their might, baling out the foaming water as it swirled around their feet and legs. But however fast they worked, more water kept pouring over the sides. Soon, they knew, the boat would fill and sink. They would all be in the water, fighting the fierce currents below.

They turned to find Jesus. To their astonishment, they saw that he was still asleep. Two of them shook him by the shoulder.

'Wake up!' they shouted, above the noise of the wind. 'Don't you care that we're all going to be drowned?'

Jesus stood up at once. He spoke directly to the wild, shrieking wind.

'Be quiet!' he ordered.

Then he looked out at the waves. 'Be still!' he said to them.

At once, with scarcely a last whimper, the wind died down and the

waves subsided into a melting froth of foam.

Then Jesus turned to the disciples.

'Why were you frightened?' he asked them. 'Didn't you trust me?'

But they didn't answer. They were almost as scared by what Jesus had done, as by the storm itself.

'Who is he?' they whispered.

'Whoever heard of a man who could give orders to the weather—and be obeyed!'

275
Madman Among the Tombs

MARK 5

Soon the boat crunched on the far shore of the lake. Jesus and the disciples were safely across. There were no crowds here. But all at once they heard a piercing wail. Then scream followed scream, as the sound came nearer to them.

The disciples had heard stories about the mad, wild man who had been banished from the town to live among the rock tombs in the surrounding hills. No chains had been strong enough to stop him from hurting and cutting himself.

They clustered together nervously, as the man lurched into sight. His eyes stared wildly. His hair was matted and tangled and his bare body was covered with cuts and bruises.

Jesus was quite unafraid. He walked towards him, and at once the man broke into a run. He dropped to his knees in front of Jesus.

'Don't torment and punish me, Jesus!' he whimpered. 'I know who you are. You are the Son of the Most High God!'

Jesus felt very sorry for the man. He knew that it was not his fault that he behaved as he did. It was Satan's evil power that had possessed him.

'What is your name?' he asked him.

'Legion,' the man replied. 'That's because there's a whole army of demons inside me.'

'Evil spirits, come out of this man!' Jesus commanded. Nearby a herd of pigs was rooting for food on the hillside.

'Send us into those pigs,' muttered the demons.

'Very well,' Jesus agreed. 'You may go into the pigs.'

At once the whole herd of pigs charged helter-skelter down the hill, tumbling into the lake.

Then the man knew for certain that Jesus had set him free from Satan's power for ever. The wild look had gone from his eyes. He smiled happily up at Jesus.

Jesus helped him to his feet and the disciples took him down to the lake to wash his face and hair. One of them gave him a cloak to wear.

Meanwhile, the men who had been looking after the pigs rushed off to the town to tell everyone what had happened, and a little stream of sightseers soon arrived.

They looked in amazement at their madman as he sat, calm and dressed, talking quietly with his new friends. But they did not welcome Jesus. They did not want this mysterious newcomer who could send their pigs into the lake.

'Please go away,' they said to Jesus. Without delay the little party returned to their boat.

'Let me come too!' Legion begged.

'I need you here,' Jesus told him gently. 'You can serve me best by telling the people all around how kind God has been to you and by letting them see what he has done.'

Two Very Important People

MARK 5

When Jesus and his friends arrived back on the busy side of the lake, a big crowd began to gather. Everyone was pushing to get nearer to Jesus but, at the sight of one particular man who was trying to reach him, they all stepped aside.

They had recognized Jairus, the president of their synagogue. He was a very important man in the town. As the crowd parted he ran up to Jesus and then dropped down humbly at his feet.

'Please come quickly!' he begged. 'My little daughter is very ill. She will die if you don't come soon.'

Jesus turned at once and began to follow where Jairus led. The crowd jostled and hurried along with them. Jairus was looking back to make sure that Jesus was close behind, when Jesus suddenly stopped.

'Who touched me?' he asked.

'What a question to ask, in this crowd!' the disciples objected. 'Everyone is bumping into you!'

But Jesus still waited, his eyes searching one face after another. At last a small, white-faced woman stepped timidly forward. She was trembling as she knelt at Jesus' feet.

'I was the person who touched you,' she confessed. 'I was sure that if I did I would be healed.'

'Tell me all about it,' Jesus said.

'I have been ill for twelve long years,' the woman went on. 'I've spent all the money I had on doctors but I've grown worse instead of better. I believed that if I could touch even your cloak, I should be cured—and so I was!'

Jesus looked at her with great kindness. She was just as important in God's sight as president Jairus.

'My daughter,' he said quietly, 'your trust in me has made you well. Go and begin a new life of health and peace.'

Jesus watched her dart swiftly from the crowd and make her way home, her face alight with thankfulness and joy.

Awake from Death

MARK 5

While Jesus was giving his whole attention to the woman who had touched his cloak, there was a stir nearby, where Jairus was waiting impatiently. Some servants had arrived from his house. They brought the message he had dreaded to hear.

'Your daughter has died,' they told him. 'There is no point in bothering Jesus now.'

Poor Jairus! His heart sank. He had tried so hard to get Jesus before it was too late. If only he had not stopped to talk to that woman! Surely she could have waited! It was no good now.

But, at that moment, Jesus turned from watching the woman and put his hand on Jairus' shoulder.

'Don't be frightened or worried,' Jesus said. 'Go on trusting me.'

The two of them strode quickly towards Jairus' grand house. The hired mourners were already wailing noisily outside.

'What is all the noise about?' Jesus asked them. 'The little girl is only sleeping.'

But they laughed at him. They knew that she was dead.

Jesus walked past them into the house. He gave orders that no one was to come into the little girl's room except her parents and his three close friends, Peter, James and John.

Jesus went across to the still, dead figure lying on the mattress. He took the cold, white hand in his.

'Get up, little one,' he said. At once the girl opened big brown eyes and smiled at him. Then she was out of bed in a moment and hopping about the room in excitement. Tears were streaming down her mother's face.

Jesus did not want the girl to be upset. He spoke quickly to her parents.

'Your daughter is feeling hungry now. Why not get her something to eat?'

278
'Don't Cry!'
LUKE 7

Jesus and his friends were making their way up the steep path to Nain. They stood aside to make way for a stream of people coming towards them out of the city. It was a funeral procession, winding its way down towards the rock tombs among the hills.

In front walked the mourners, some playing a doleful tune on their flutes, while others wailed loudly. Next came the men, carrying the stretcher on which lay the dead body of a young man. His mother walked beside them, her tears falling fast. Friends from the town followed behind.

As Jesus looked at the mother, his heart was full of sympathy. She was a widow and now that her only son was dead she would have no one to care for her or provide for her.

'Don't cry!' Jesus said gently.

Then he stepped across and touched the stretcher. At once the men who were carrying it stood still. All eyes were on Jesus. What would he do next?

'Young man, get up!' Jesus said, and the man sat bolt upright, his face flushed with pink.

'Who are you?' he asked. 'What's happening? How is it that I feel so well?'

Jesus took the boy to his mother and put his hand into hers. Everyone was talking excitedly. One pointed to the nearby town of Shunem.

'Remember how Elisha brought a boy back to life there?' he asked.

'Yes,' his friend answered.

'Jesus must be another great prophet like him.'

'God has come to us again and will rescue us from all our troubles,' his wife added.

They did not realize yet who Jesus was, but they saw God's love and kindness in all that he did and recognized that God was working through him to help everyone in need. He cared even for the poor people whom religious leaders ignored or despised.

Jesus and his Disciples

📖 279
Two by Two
LUKE 9 AND 10

Jesus and his friends went from one place to the next, telling people the good news that God's kingdom had arrived. Even when he was asked to stay longer, Jesus knew that he must move on to the next town, so that others would have the chance to hear God's message.

One day he told the disciples, 'I want you to go off on your own to spread the good news to the villages around. That way many more will hear it.'

At first the disciples felt scared of going alone, but Jesus put them in pairs so that each one had a partner to help him.

Then he promised, 'I am giving you my power, so that you will be able to cure those who are ill and drive out evil spirits.' He gave them instructions, too.

'Don't go weighed down with baggage. Carry as little as possible and you will travel more easily and quickly. When you arrive in a town, stay with whoever invites you in. Pray that God will bless the homes where you are made welcome. Give freely to everyone, because God has given generously to you. If the townsfolk won't listen to you, leave that place well alone. They will be responsible for refusing to hear God's invitation.'

The disciples set off nervously on their preaching tour. But when they arrived back they were full of excitement and enthusiasm. They told Jesus everything that had happened.

'It was wonderful!' they exclaimed. 'Even the evil spirits obeyed us—just as they obey you!'

Jesus thanked God for such a victory against evil and suffering. But he warned the disciples not to get carried away by the things they had done.

'The most important thing is not that you have power to do wonderful things,' he reminded them, 'but that God has chosen you to belong to him for ever.'

📖 280
Who is the Most Important?
MARK 9

Jesus and his friends were walking along the dusty road. Jesus went ahead and the disciples dawdled behind. They were arguing as they went and getting hotter and more irritable by the minute.

When at last they reached the cool of the house, Jesus had already arrived. He gave them an inquiring look.

'What were you so busy arguing about on the way?' he asked. There was an awkward silence. They were ashamed to tell Jesus what the quarrel had been about. Each one of them had been trying to prove that he was more important than the others. Soon, they felt sure, Jesus would be crowned king and they all wanted to make sure in advance of the best job at court.

Jesus knew very well what had been going on.

'Come over here,' he said, and the disciples, shamefaced, made their way across to where their master was sitting.

'Now then,' Jesus began, 'which one of you would like to be leader—the most important of all?'

Again there was silence, but everyone was listening hard.

'I'll tell you how to be the most important person in *my* kingdom,' Jesus went on. 'The leader will be the one who is always looking after others—the one who never thinks about himself or his own needs.'

One of the children of the house had stolen across to sit beside Jesus and listen to him too.

Now Jesus gently pulled him to his feet and with his arms around him said, 'Look—great people are like children. They are not full of their own importance but ready to trust me and do as I say—like this lad here.

'Remember that every time you welcome a boy or girl for my sake, instead of sending them away, it's just as if you are welcoming me. And whoever welcomes me is welcoming God, my Father, himself.'

Salt and Light

MATTHEW 5

As well as preaching the good news of God's kingdom to the crowds, Jesus took time to teach his disciples, too. There were many more who had decided to trust Jesus and obey him beside the twelve special friends.

Jesus began to tell them all how they should live as his followers. He looked at the eager faces turned towards him and saw many different kinds of people. There were mothers and housewives, fishermen and shopkeepers, craftsmen, merchants, tax collectors and boys and girls, too.

'When you become my followers,' Jesus told them all, 'you can serve me in the places where you live and work. You will be like salt.

'Salt stops meat and fish from going bad. You will keep your little corner of the world wholesome and fresh. Because you love me you will be honest and fair, hardworking and kind to those in need. There will be no rottenness or corruption in your dealings.

'Salt gives taste to food, too. Because you live life with true enjoyment, your words and actions will add relish to the lives of everyone you mix with.

'Don't try to keep your loyalty to me a secret. Just look up there, at that town built on the top of the hill. It doesn't try to hide away and pretend it isn't there—everyone can see it, wherever they are. See that you stand out clearly as my followers.

'Let everyone know that you have found me, the light of the whole world. Then you will shine like lights, too. You will help others to find their way in life. You will bring comfort and help to those who are in the dark because they are lonely or sad, or puzzled by life's problems.

'Light and salt—these are pictures of every true follower of mine in this dark and evil world.'

Jesus in Control

📖 **282**

The Enormous Picnic

MARK 6; JOHN 6

The disciples were very tired after their preaching tour but the crowds around Jesus were as big as ever. There was not even time to stop for meals. When Jesus saw their exhausted faces, he said, 'We'll go off on our own for a rest.'

The disciples thankfully agreed, and they all clambered into Peter's boat and set off across the lake. But as they drew nearer to land they saw that the quiet spot they had chosen was thronged with people, all waiting for the first glimpse of Jesus. They had seen the boat leave and raced around the shore, arriving ahead of them.

The disciples groaned with disappointment but Jesus looked with pity at the people. They were in such need of his loving care.

All day he taught them but, when evening came, the disciples had had enough. 'Send the crowds away, Master,' they begged. 'There are no shops here and they'll have to hurry if they are to get to the town in time to buy food.'

'Why don't *you* give them a meal?' Jesus asked.

'However could we do that?' Philip replied. 'It would cost a small fortune to feed this number. There must be at least five thousand men, not counting their wives and families.'

Then Andrew spoke.

'There's a lad here who has offered Jesus his lunch. But it's only two little fish and five small bread rolls, so what good is that?'

Jesus did not answer Andrew's question.

'Sort the people into groups of fifty,' he told the disciples. 'Then get them to sit on the grass.'

As the disciples bustled off to organize everyone, Jesus turned to the boy, who was waiting shyly.

'Thank you,' he said with a smile, as he took the packed lunch from him.

When everyone was ready and waiting, Jesus held up the picnic food for all to see and thanked God for it.

No one understood what happened next. They only knew that the bread and fish that Jesus handed to each disciple to give to the crowd was more than enough for them all.

Even the children had to say, 'I'm full!' at last. But how good it had tasted!

Each of the twelve disciples was left with a basket full of food that had not been needed.

'That will do for our next meal,' Jesus said.

How wonderful their master was! He could satisfy their deepest needs, as well as seeing that they had enough food to eat!

283
Walking on Water

MARK 6; MATTHEW 14; JOHN 6

When the enormous picnic was over, Jesus sent the disciples ahead of him, back across the lake. Some of the crowd still clustered around Jesus, cheering and shouting. They wanted to make him king then and there. It would be a fine thing to have a king who could provide them with free meals!

Kindly but firmly, Jesus refused and sent them off home. Then, as night fell, he climbed the hill overlooking the lake, to be alone with God his Father.

Meanwhile, the disciples were struggling desperately against a strong wind. However hard they rowed, they made no headway.

From the top of the hill Jesus could see the little boat and picture his exhausted disciples. He would go to them.

But when the disciples saw a mysterious shadowy figure coming towards them across the lake in the moonlight, they were terrified.

'It's a ghost!' they shrieked. Their tired nerves could stand no more.

Then a familiar voice rang out.

'Don't be frightened! I'm coming to help you!'

They could not believe it.

'If it's really you,' Peter called back, 'tell me to come to you.'

'All right, Peter,' Jesus answered, 'come on!'

Peter climbed over the side of the boat and began to walk towards Jesus on top of the water. Suddenly he felt a strong gust of wind catch him and he looked down at the swirling waves. In that moment of panic he began to sink.

'Help! Save me, Lord!' he shouted. Jesus put out his hand quickly, caught Peter by the wrist and pulled him up from the foaming water.

'Why did you doubt me, Peter?' he asked.

Then the two of them climbed into the boat. Immediately the wind died down. The disciples were amazed. They could not understand how their master was able to do the impossible.

Questions and Answers

□ 284

The Man who Came at Night

JOHN 3

Nicodemus was a Pharisee. He tried with all his heart to keep God's laws and to obey all the many rules that had been added to them over the centuries. He was also a member of the ruling Jewish Council.

Nicodemus had heard all about Jesus, but he was not angry or jealous, as many Pharisees were.

'Jesus must be a good man,' he reasoned, 'or he could not do such miracles.' He wanted to talk to Jesus, so he decided to visit him at night, when no prying onlookers would tell his friends on the Council. *They* would not approve.

Jesus knew all about Nicodemus, long before he emerged from the dark shadows to talk to him.

'There is something important that I must tell you right away,' Jesus said. 'You will only enter God's kingdom if you are born again.'

'However can I be born, at my age?' Nicodemus asked. 'I can't become a baby all over again!'

'There is more than one kind of birth,' Jesus explained. 'You are born into this world through natural parents. But you are born into God's kingdom through his Holy Spirit.'

Nicodemus was a trained teacher but he had no idea what Jesus meant.

'God's Holy Spirit is like the wind,' Jesus went on. 'You cannot see him, any more than you can see the wind.

But just as you know when the wind is blowing by what it does, so you will know when the Holy Spirit is at work in your life. He is the one who can give you God's life. God loves every human being so much that he has sent his Son into the world so that all those who put their trust in him will be given God's eternal life.'

Nicodemus walked slowly away into the dark night. How different was Jesus' way from the teaching of the Pharisees! One day he would make up his mind which to follow.

285
The Woman who Came for Water

JOHN 4

The hot midday sun beat down as Jesus waited for his disciples by the well near Sychar, in Samaria. He was tired and very thirsty.

A woman came plodding wearily towards the well, her water-pot on her head. She was startled to see Jesus. No one was usually around at noon.

'Would you give me a drink of water?' Jesus asked her. Now the woman was *really* surprised. She could see that Jesus was a Jew, and Jews did not speak to Samaritan men—and certainly not to women.

'You mean you would be willing to accept a cup of water from me, although I'm a Samaritan woman?' she asked. 'Whoever can you be?'

'If you knew that,' Jesus told her, 'you would ask *me* for a drink. I would give you living water.'

'You haven't even got a bucket,' the woman said, laughing. 'How do you think you'd draw your wonderful water?'

'The water I give is different from the water in this well,' Jesus explained. 'If you drink the water I give, you will never be thirsty again. It will satisfy your deepest needs.'

'That sounds good,' the woman agreed. 'It would save me coming here every day.'

'Then why not get your husband?' Jesus suggested.

'Because I haven't got one,' the woman retorted sharply.

'I know that,' Jesus replied gently. He knew all about this unhappy woman. 'You have been married five times and you aren't even married to the man you live with now.'

The woman was astonished. Jesus knew all about her! She put down her water-pot and ran back to the town, full of the news.

'Come and see the most wonderful person!' she told everyone. 'He has told me everything about myself. I think he must be the Messiah.'

The townsfolk were full of curiosity and followed her back to the well.

'Please stay here a few days,' they invited Jesus. 'Tell us about the good news you have brought.' And Jesus did.

After they had heard all he had to say, they told the woman, 'You were right. Now that we've seen and heard Jesus for ourselves, we are certain that he is the Messiah, the one that God has sent to save the world.'

Stories About God's Love

📖 **286**

The Lost Sheep

LUKE 15

The Pharisees and strict religious teachers who came to listen to Jesus were outraged at some of the others they saw in the crowd. They were people who broke the rules and regulations of the law which the Pharisees observed so strictly. Such outcasts had no business to mix with respectable people like themselves.

'I'm told that he even goes to dinner with them,' one Pharisee exclaimed.

'He certainly can't be a teacher sent from God if he welcomes such people,' his friend remarked.

'God will have nothing to do with sinners like them,' the other agreed.

Jesus heard the muttered conversation. He turned to look at them, as they kept a little apart from the rest.

'Imagine,' he said, 'that you are the owner of one hundred sheep. One night, as you count them, you find that one sheep is missing. What will you do? Are you going to settle down for the night with the ninety-nine others, thinking that one lost sheep doesn't really matter?

'Of course not! You'll be up and away, however tired you feel, retracing the route you took that day with the flock. You'll look down over every steep rock and shine your lamp into every dark bush.

'At last—the sound of a faint, weak bleat! All tiredness gone, you hoist that stray sheep onto your shoulder and start for home, happy and lighthearted.

'When you get back, you throw an impromptu party for the rest of the shepherds and villagers, so that they can share your joy over the sheep you've found.

'That's the way God feels about people. There is more happiness in heaven about one lost person brought back to God than over ninety-nine good people who don't need to change their ways.'

The Lost Coin

LUKE 15

Before the outraged Pharisees had time to get their breath back, Jesus began another story.

'Imagine a housewife who owns just ten silver coins. One day she discovers to her distress that she has lost one of them. She doesn't shrug her shoulders and decide to make do with the remaining nine. She begins a thorough search of her little house.

'She shines her lamp into all the dark corners, then she gets a broom and carefully sweeps the floor. She watches keenly for the smallest gleam of silver.

'At last she sees a twinkle of brightness. She's found the lost coin! She is so happy that she invites her friends in and tells them the whole story. They share the celebrations.

'That is how God feels about a sinner who turns back to him. The angels join in the happiness and all heaven is filled with joy.'

The Lost Sons

LUKE 15

When Jesus saw that the Pharisees' faces were still proud and hard, he went on to tell them a third story about God's love for everyone, however good or bad.

'There was once a landowner who had two sons,' he began. 'One day the younger son said to his father, "I'm tired of being at home, doing as I'm told. I want to go away, so please give me my share of the family fortune now."

'Without a word, the father set about making all the arrangements and handed him his share of the estate.

'With money in his bag, the son started off for the bright lights of the town. He spent his money freely, enjoying himself and doing whatever he wanted.

'One bleak morning he woke to find that his money had all gone—and so had his friends. Worse still, there was a severe famine in the land.

'He was soon in real need. When at last he got a job, it was looking after pigs. He was so hungry that he would have been glad to eat the pig-food himself.

'At last he came to his senses. "Here I am, starving," he said to himself, "when back at home even my father's casual workers get plenty of food to eat. I shall go back and tell him how sorry I am. He won't take me back as his son, but he may give me work on the farm."

'He started off at once, painfully covering the rough ground on bare feet and pulling his ragged cloak around his thin body.

'When he was still a long way from home, his father caught sight of him and ran to meet him, full of pity and love. He threw his arms around him, tears of joy running down his cheeks. "I'm sorry, Father," the boy whispered, near to tears himself. "I'm not fit to be your son."

'But the father would not let him say another word. He turned to the servants.

'"Get my son the best robe and bring sandals for his feet. Put my ring on his finger. Then kill the calf we've been fattening up. We're going to have a party to celebrate."

'The party was in full swing by the time the older son arrived back from a day in the fields.

'"What's going on?" he asked the servants, as the sound of music and dancing came to his ears.

'"Your brother's come home," they replied. "We've killed the prize calf for the feast."

'The older brother was furious. He stormed up and down with a face like thunder.

'His father came out to find him. "Come and join the party!" he begged.

'But the older son scowled. "I've slaved for you all these years," he grumbled, "yet you've never given a party for me. Now this son of yours, who has wasted all your money, comes home and you kill the prize calf!"

'The father was sad to see his son so jealous and unloving. "Everything I possess belongs to you," he reminded him gently. "You are with me all the time. It is right to celebrate, for your brother was lost and now he's found. He was as good as dead, but now I have him home, alive and well."'

289
The Workers and their Wages

MATTHEW 20

'I'll tell you another story to show you what God's kingdom is like,' Jesus said one day.

'Once there was a man who went to the market-place early one morning to hire some men to help with his grape harvest. "I'll pay you a silver coin for the day's work," he told them and they gladly agreed to this fair wage.

'At nine o'clock he went back to the market-place to hire some more workers. "I'll pay you a fair wage," he promised.

'He hired another lot of workers at noon and more again at three o'clock in the afternoon. Then, only an hour before the working day ended, he returned to the market-place for the last time. A bunch of men was still loitering there.

' "Why aren't you working?" he asked them.

' "Because no one has employed us," they replied.

' "I'll give you work," he told them. "Join the others gathering my grapes."

'When work was finished for the day, the master told his foreman to pay all the men. The last batch was called up first and each was given a silver coin. When, last of all, the workers who had started work early in the morning lined up for pay, they expected to get more. But they were given one silver coin each, the same as all the others.

' "That's not fair," they grumbled. "We've worked through all the heat of the day. We deserve more."

' "Listen, my friends," the master said gently. "We agreed on the wage before you began work and I've kept to what I promised. It's my business if I choose to be generous to these latecomers." '

The disciples were puzzled. If that was what God's kingdom was like, then no one got what they deserved! But perhaps no one *could* deserve or earn God's generous love.

Jesus broke in on their thoughts.

'In God's kingdom,' he said, 'the people who think they are first end up last. And the last ones take first place.'

Jesus Teaches About Money

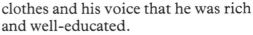

290
The Man with a Lot of Money

MARK 10

As Jesus was walking along the road, a man came hurrying after him, running to catch up with him. Breathless, he knelt in front of Jesus, saying, 'Teacher, please tell me what I have to do in order to have eternal life!'

The disciples were impressed with the newcomer. They could tell by his clothes and his voice that he was rich and well-educated.

'You know the commandments,' Jesus replied. 'Don't murder; don't commit adultery; don't cheat; show respect for your parents.'

'I've kept all those commandments since I was a boy,' the young man answered eagerly.

Jesus looked at him with affection. He knew everything about him. He was indeed a good young man, who had kept God's laws. But he had forgotten that the first and most important of all the commandments is to love God with all our heart and mind. There was something that he loved more than God.

'If you want to be rich in God's eyes, you must get rid of all your money,' Jesus told him. 'Give it away to people in need. Once that hindrance is gone, follow me.'

The young man's face fell. His eagerness had faded. He loved his money too much to part with it. With a sigh, he turned sadly away.

'It's very hard for a rich person to enter God's kingdom,' Jesus told the disciples. 'It's easier for a camel to get through the eye of a needle than for a rich person to get into God's kingdom.'

The disciples were astounded. It seemed to them that everything in life was easier for people with money.

'If rich people can't be saved, who can?' they asked.

'It's impossible for anyone to be saved—apart from God!' Jesus answered.

'But what men and women can't do for themselves, God can do for them. Everything is possible when God is at work.'

The Biggest Gift of All

MARK 12

One day Jesus sat in the temple court, watching people come and go. Thirteen big collecting-boxes stood nearby into which the passers-by could drop their coins. The money that was collected paid for the temple expenses.

Jesus watched the wealthy people throwing in large sums of money. Some slipped their gold coins in without fuss; others counted them out noisily, so that everyone would see how many gleaming coins they were giving to God.

Then a shabbily dressed woman came along. She was a widow, with no one to earn money for her. She dropped two tiny copper coins into the big treasury-box.

Jesus pointed her out to the disciples.

'Did you notice that widow who put two small coins into the box? She gave more to God than all the wealthy people, however many gold coins they poured in.'

The disciples couldn't understand that. Jesus' words didn't make sense. They knew enough arithmetic to work out who had given most money. Then Jesus explained.

'The rich people gave God what they could easily afford. It didn't cost them anything to part with those gold coins. They still had plenty left for themselves. That widow gave all she had. She kept nothing back for herself. That's what God calls the biggest gift of all.'

292
The Poor Rich Farmer
LUKE 12

A worried-looking man pushed his way to the front of the crowd to talk to Jesus. 'Teacher,' he said, 'my father has died and my brother won't divide the family property between us. Please tell him to give me my fair share.

'It's not my job to settle arguments like that, my friend,' Jesus replied. Then he turned to the crowd and said, 'See that you don't become greedy. Real life is not a matter of how many things you possess.

'I'll tell you a story about a rich farmer. One year his harvest was so good that he hadn't enough room to store it all.

' "I know what I'll do," he said to himself. "I'll pull down these small barns and build myself some really big ones. Then I can store all my grain and I'll have enough to live on for years to come. I shall be able to enjoy myself. I'll just take it easy and live in comfort."

'That night God spoke to him.

' "What a fool you have been!" he told him. "This very night you are going to die. What will become of all your money then? What good will it do you?"

'That's what happens,' Jesus ended by saying, 'to everyone who spends his life getting rich but never gives a thought to being rich in God's sight.'

'*We'll* never be rich!' one of the disciples murmured. Jesus smiled.

'Those who haven't any money sometimes spend as much time thinking about it as rich people do,' he told them. 'Don't keep worrying about where the next meal will come from, or how you will be able to afford new clothes for all the family. Think of the way in which God takes care of the birds—and they can't even earn their own living. God is your heavenly Father. If he provides for the birds, and clothes the flowers so beautifully, he will certainly see that *you* have the things you need.

'Put God first—always—and he will take care of all your other worries and provide for all your needs.'

Jesus Teaches About Himself

293
'You Are God's Messiah!'
MARK 8

Everyone seemed to be talking about Jesus, the new teacher from Nazareth. Tales soon spread about the little girl he had brought back from death and the picnic meal he had provided for thousands of people. If he was only a village carpenter, how could he do such wonderful things?

Jesus' disciples thought very hard about their Master, too. He always knew just what they needed and seemed to understand them better than they understood themselves. They watched him constantly, as he helped and healed everyone who came to him. Now and then they felt rather scared. How could an ordinary person give orders to the wind and sea, or bring someone back to life?

One day, as they were walking together, Jesus asked them, 'What are people saying about me? Who do they think I am?'

The disciples eagerly repeated some of the remarks they had overheard from the crowds.

'Some of them think that you are John the Baptist, alive from the dead,' one of them told him.

'Some think you are Elijah, come back to earth to be God's messenger, as the prophet Malachi said he would,' another added.

'They certainly believe that you are a prophet,' a third agreed.

Then Jesus gave his friends a searching look.

'Who do *you* think I am?' he asked.

There was a split second of silence.

Then Peter burst out:

'We believe that you are God's anointed King—the promised Messiah!'

Jesus' face lit up. He was glad that his disciples had at last discovered who he was. But he knew that it was really God who had opened their eyes to the truth.

'Don't tell anyone else who I am,' he warned them.

He knew that, once people realized who he was, they would want to make him into the kind of Messiah that they were looking for—a king to fight the Romans and provide them all with free meals. That was not the kind of king he was.

294
The Road Ahead
MARK 8

The disciples were glad and excited when they discovered that Jesus, their master, was God's chosen Messiah. But, like the crowds, they had dreams of a Messiah who would be a great Jewish deliverer and who would bring in a golden age of freedom. Once he was crowned, they felt sure that they would be chosen as his chief ministers.

Jesus knew the way that they were thinking. It was time for him to try to explain to them what kind of Messiah he was really going to be.

'Listen carefully,' he said. 'There are hard times ahead for me. All the religious leaders will turn against me. They will plot and scheme until they get me arrested. In the end they will sentence me to death and I shall be

killed. But I shall rise to life again three days later.'

Peter was fuming. He could hardly wait for Jesus to finish speaking.

'Don't talk like that, Master!' he blurted out. 'That's not what we want!'

'Be quiet, Peter!' Jesus said sternly. 'You are giving me Satan's advice. I have come to earth to follow the plan that God, my Father, has prepared for me. I shall go *his* way.'

Then Jesus beckoned to the people who were standing a little way off. When they had all gathered around, he said: 'If you really decide to follow me, be ready for a tough time. Being a follower of mine means doing as I do.

It will mean saying no to your own wants and choosing the hard way. The person who clings to all the things he has ends up by losing everything. The person who is ready to give up everything he has for my sake, seems to be throwing his life away, but he is the one who will keep most. He will win true life, the life that lasts for ever. That life is worth more than anything else in the whole wide world.'

The Transfiguration

295
A Glimpse of Glory
LUKE 9

One day Jesus set off with Peter and the brothers, James and John, to climb a steep mountain ridge. Jesus wanted to be alone with God, to find out what his Father wanted him to do. The sun was setting as Jesus prayed and the three friends, tired out, fell fast asleep.

Suddenly they were wide awake. At first they did not know what had disturbed them. Then they saw a warm, bright light shining through the darkness.

They looked across at Jesus. His face was dazzling bright and his clothes glistened with a light more beautiful than any on earth. Two men were talking to him. Somehow they recognized them as Moses, the great lawgiver, and Elijah the mighty prophet. They were discussing the way in which Jesus would follow God's plan and give up his life at Jerusalem.

James and John were silent in wonder but Peter felt that he would burst if he didn't speak.

'This is wonderful, Master!' he called out excitedly. 'Would you like us to put up three tents—one each for you and Moses and Elijah?' He really didn't know what he was saying.

At that very moment a cloud shone above them. It was the bright cloud of God's presence.

'This is my own dear Son,' God said. 'Listen to him.'

The disciples hid their faces, full of fear and wonder. Then they felt a gentle touch on the shoulder. They looked up fearfully, but it was Jesus, their own dear master, looking as he had always done. And he was quite alone.

As they walked soberly down the hill in the morning light, Jesus said, 'Don't tell anyone what you have seen until after I have been put to death and have come to life again.'

The disciples did as Jesus said. But they never forgot the time when they had caught a glimpse of Jesus' real glory.

Jesus the Healer

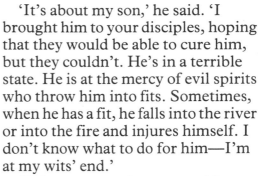

📖 296
The Frantic Father

MARK 9

It was the morning after Peter, James and John had seen Jesus, transformed and glorious, talking to Moses and Elijah. They walked down the hillside full of excitement and wonder, but when they joined the other nine disciples they found them talking and arguing with a little knot of Jewish teachers.

Jesus went up to them. 'What is the argument about?' he asked his disciples.

A man in the crowd stepped forward.

'It's about my son,' he said. 'I brought him to your disciples, hoping that they would be able to cure him, but they couldn't. He's in a terrible state. He is at the mercy of evil spirits who throw him into fits. Sometimes, when he has a fit, he falls into the river or into the fire and injures himself. I don't know what to do for him—I'm at my wits' end.'

'Bring your son here to me,' Jesus ordered. As soon as the boy was near he had another terrible fit. The father watched helplessly, as his son lay writhing on the ground.

'How long has he had this illness?' Jesus asked.

'Ever since he was a child,' the father replied. 'Please have pity on us and help him—if you can!'

'*I* can, if *you* can!' Jesus told him. 'You must put your faith in me and believe that I can help you, if I am to heal him.'

'I know I'm a doubter, but I have a little bit of faith,' the poor father cried out. 'Please help me to trust you more!'

All this time the inquisitive crowd had been coming nearer, until they had almost hemmed them in. When Jesus saw what was happening, he commanded, 'Evil spirit, come out of this boy and never go into him again!'

Immediately a change came over the boy. The convulsions stopped and he lay completely still.

'He looks as if he's dead,' someone at the front of the crowd remarked. Others peered more closely and nodded their heads.

'He *is* dead!' they announced.

But Jesus took the boy by the hand and quietly helped him to his feet.

Then he led him to his father, fit and well again.

'Why weren't *we* able to heal him?' the disappointed disciples asked Jesus later. They knew that they had failed Jesus in front of the jealous religious leaders.

'Only prayer can make healing possible in cases like this,' Jesus told them. 'You must put your trust in me and in God's power over evil.'

297
The Soldier's Servant

LUKE 7; MATTHEW 8

One day, when Jesus was in the little lakeside town of Capernaum, some of the leaders from the synagogue came to him with a request.

'We've come on behalf of a man who really deserves your help,' they explained.

'He is a Roman officer who is stationed in our town. He is a good man, with a great respect for the Jewish faith. In fact, he paid for the building of our synagogue. Now he badly needs your help.'

Jesus looked across to where the Roman centurion was standing respectfully to attention. He beckoned him over.

The officer's strict military bearing relaxed a little as he spoke earnestly to Jesus. 'Will you help me?' he begged. 'I have a slave who means a lot to me and he's desperately ill. He is suffering great pain.'

'Shall I come to your house?' Jesus asked at once.

'Certainly not, sir!' the centurion exclaimed. 'I do not deserve to have someone as great as you in my house. You have only to give the order, I know, and my servant will be healed. I am a soldier, under orders from Rome, and have soldiers under my command. I have only to say "Come here!" and a servant comes running— or "Go there!" and another is on his way. In the same way I know that you have only to give the word of command and my servant will be healed.'

Jesus was amazed that a Roman soldier should have such complete faith in him. He had not been brought up to know and trust God as the Jewish people had.

'No one else in the whole land has shown such faith in me as this man has,' he told the onlookers.

Then he turned to the Roman centurion and said, 'Go home now. You will find that your slave has been healed, just as you believed he would be.'

At that exact time the centurion's slave felt completely well again; his pain had gone.

298
'Open Up!'
MARK 7

One day, a little group of men arrived, bringing their friend to see Jesus. He was deaf and could not speak properly.

'Can you cure him, Teacher?' they asked. Jesus gently led the man away from the excited crowd. He saw how nervous and shy the man felt with everyone milling around and staring at him. When they were on their own, Jesus carefully mimed everything that he was going to do, so that the deaf man would understand what was happening, even though he could not hear what Jesus said.

First of all, Jesus lightly placed his fingers in the man's ears, to show that he was going to cure his deafness. Next he moistened his finger and touched the man's tongue. At that time people believed that spittle could heal. Jesus wanted the man to realize that he was able to cure his speech defect, too.

After that, Jesus looked up, as if he was praying, so that the man would know he was going to heal him by God's power.

Then Jesus spoke one word, 'Ephphatha!' In the Aramaic language that Jesus and his disciples spoke, that means 'Open Up!'

Jesus' command was obeyed at once. A thousand unfamiliar sounds burst on the ears of the man who had been deaf. How glad he was that the crowd was a little way off! He found, too, that he could speak clearly. At last everyone would understand what he was saying! He had a lot of talking to do, to make up for the years of silence—and he began at once.

When the people in the crowd heard him, they were amazed. 'Isn't Jesus wonderful?' they said to one another. 'How well he does everything! He can even make deaf people hear and dumb ones talk!'

299
Trees that Walk

MARK 8

Jesus was in Bethsaida, the lakeside town where Peter and Andrew grew up, when a little group of people arrived, bringing a blind friend with them.

'Please put your hands on him, Master!' they begged.

Jesus led the man by the hand, away from the curious bystanders, to a quiet place outside the town. He wanted to help the man to trust Jesus for himself, even though he could not see him. So he used the sense of touch. Gently Jesus touched the blind eyes and then put firm hands on the man's shoulders.

'Can you see anything?' Jesus asked.

The man peered around, uncertainly. The deep darkness he had known for so long had given way to a half-light. He could make out vague shapes but he could not be certain what they were. Some of the shapes suddenly loomed near enough for him to recognize them as people.

'I thought that they were trees,' he admitted, 'trees that walked!'

Once again Jesus placed his hands on the man's eyes. This time, when he took them away, the mist had cleared completely and everything was in sharp focus.

'Don't go back into the town,' Jesus told him. 'Go straight home to see your wife and children with your own eyes!'

Jesus Teaches about Obedience

📖 300
The Two Sons
MATTHEW 21; MATTHEW 7; JOHN 14

When Jesus went up to Jerusalem, some priests from the temple and leading religious teachers began to argue with him. They were sure that they were God's chosen people. How dare Jesus criticize them? He was not even a properly qualified teacher as they were.

So Jesus told them this story. 'There was once a father who had two sons. One morning he said to the older one, "I want you to go and work in my vineyard today."

'"I don't want to," the son complained. But later he changed his mind and went off to help his father after all.

'Meanwhile the father found his younger son and asked him to go and help in the vineyard, too. "Certainly, sir!" he answered politely, but he never went. He did not do as he had promised.

'Which of these sons, do you think, obeyed his father?'

'The older one, who did as his father wanted,' the leaders replied.

'Yes,' Jesus agreed. 'In the same way, the tax collectors and all the other people you despise, are changing their minds and beginning to obey God's commands. They will go into God's kingdom ahead of you. You may *say* the right things, but you are not willing to do what God asks.'

Another time Jesus told his followers, 'Those who enter God's kingdom will not be the ones who politely call me "Lord," but those who treat me as Lord, by obeying me.

'When the great Judgment Day arrives, plenty of people will claim, "We have preached about you, Lord. We have done all kinds of wonderful deeds, using your name." But I shall tell them, "I don't know you. Go away from me." For what matters is that a person keeps God's commands and is obedient to me.'

Jesus explained to the twelve close friends and disciples, 'Those people who really love me will obey me. If anyone does what I tell him, then I know for certain that he loves me.'

Stories About Loving Others

📖 301

The Man who Wouldn't Forgive

MATTHEW 18

One day Peter asked, 'Master, how many times should I forgive someone who keeps wronging me?' Religious people agreed that it was fair to forgive a person three times but Peter generously suggested, 'How about seven times?' Jesus smiled and shook his head.

'No, Peter,' he said, 'seventy times seven is nearer the mark. Listen to this story.

'There was once a king who decided to check the accounts of his officials, to see how much money they owed him. He had scarcely begun when one of them was ushered into his room.

' "This man owes you a huge sum," the king was told.

'The king consulted his books and found that indeed the servant owed him millions—enough for a king's ransom.

' "Sell him and his wife and children as slaves," the king ordered.

'But the official fell on his knees and sobbed out, "Please have mercy on me! If you will only be patient, I will pay it all back!"

'The king knew very well that he would never be able to pay back such a huge sum, but he felt sorry for him.

' "Get up," he said kindly. "I am going to write off your whole debt. You don't need to pay me any of it."

'The delighted servant jumped to his feet and bowed himself out of the king's presence.

'No sooner was he outside than he bumped into a fellow servant.

' "Here!" he shouted out, "Stop! You owe me some money!"

'His victim nodded miserably. "It's only a very small sum," he pleaded. "Give me time to pay you back!"

'But the other man caught him by the throat, half-throttling him. "Pay me at once, or you'll go to prison!" he threatened. Then he kicked the man out of the palace and threw him into prison.

'The rest of the king's officials were horrified. They told the king the whole story. The king was very angry. He sent for the first official.

' "You are a wicked, hard-hearted servant!" he said. "I forgave you that huge debt, yet you refuse to have mercy on someone who owes you such a tiny sum. Because of that, you will go to prison yourself, until you pay back everything you owe me."

'Remember,' Jesus said, as he finished his story. 'God will not forgive you, unless you forgive one another from the bottom of your hearts.'

📖 302
The Good Friend

LUKE 10

One of the teachers of the scriptures asked Jesus a difficult question, to try to catch him out.

'Teacher,' he said, 'What must I do to gain eternal life?'

'You know the scriptures,' Jesus replied. 'What do they say?'

'They tell us to love God with all our heart and mind and strength, and to love other people too,' he answered readily.

'You are right,' Jesus agreed. 'Go and do that and you will gain life.'

But the teacher of the law was not satisfied. He tried again. 'How am I supposed to love other people?' he asked. 'What does that mean?'

'One day,' Jesus began, 'a man set off down the steep and dangerous road from Jerusalem to Jericho. Suddenly, robbers sprang on him from behind the boulders. They beat him up, stole his clothes and money, then took to their heels, leaving him stripped and half-dead by the roadside.

'After a while, someone else came along. He was a priest, fresh from his duties in the temple at Jerusalem. When he saw the cloud of buzzing flies and the body covered in blood, he walked quickly past, on the other side of the road. For all he knew, the man might be dead, and no priest was supposed to touch a corpse.

'A little later a Levite came along. He too had been serving God in the temple. He went across to have a closer look at the victim. He guessed only too well what had happened. Suppose the robbers were still behind the rocks, ready to jump on him? He hurried off quickly.

'At last, a Samaritan came along. His people were not friends with the Jewish nation, yet he felt full of pity for the injured man. He went over to him, and began to clean up his wounds with antiseptic wine. Then he treated them with soothing oil and bandaged him up. He carefully lifted him onto his donkey and led him to the nearest inn.

'He gave the innkeeper two silver coins. "Take care of him until he is well," he said. "If you have any further expense, I'll pay you next time I call."

Jesus turned to his questioner. 'Which of the three passers-by showed love to the wounded man?' he asked.

'The one who was kind to him, I suppose,' the law teacher admitted grudgingly.

'Then go and be like him,' Jesus said.

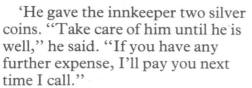

303
Sheep or Goats
MATTHEW 25

'When God's Judgment Day comes,' Jesus told his disciples, 'God's king will come with all the angels. He will sit on his throne to give justice. Everyone in the world will be brought into his presence and he will divide people into two groups, just as a shepherd separates the sheep in his flock from the goats.

'On his right-hand side he will put the righteous—those whom God has accepted.

' "Come and share my kingdom," he will say to them. "I was hungry and you fed me. I was thirsty and you gave me water. I had nothing to wear and you clothed me. I was in prison and you visited me. I was a stranger and you invited me into your homes."

'The righteous will reply, "When did we ever see you hungry or thirsty, in prison, or homeless and come to your help?"

'The king will answer, "Whenever you helped the least important of these followers of mine, you helped me!"

'Then the king will turn to those on his left.

' "Go away from my presence," he will command. "When I was hungry you gave me no food. When I was thirsty you gave me nothing to drink. When I had nothing to wear you did not clothe me. You never visited me in prison, or took me into your homes."

'They will answer indignantly, "Lord, when did we see you hungry or thirsty, homeless, or in prison and refuse to give you help?"

'The king will reply, "Every time you saw one of my followers—however unimportant—and refused to help him in his need, you were refusing to help me."

'Then the king will call the righteous to live with him for ever, but the others he will banish into the darkness, far from his presence.'

Jesus Welcomes Everyone

📖 **304**
The Loving Welcome
LUKE 7

Simon was a Pharisee who was curious to find out more about the new teacher from Nazareth. He decided he would ask Jesus to dinner, and see what he had to say for himself.

It was cool in the courtyard of Simon's house, where the guests reclined at table. A fountain was playing and the table was well-spread.

People from the street crept into the shaded garden, too, listening to Jesus.

Simon looked disapprovingly at one of these uninvited visitors. She was a woman with a very bad reputation in the town. As he watched, she slipped quietly behind Jesus' couch and began to pour perfume on his feet. Her tears fell fast, making his feet wet, too. So she shook out her hair and wiped them dry with the long tresses. Then she gently kissed his feet.

Simon watched in amazement. That settled the matter, he decided. Jesus could not possibly be a prophet from God. If he were, he would realize that this woman lived a sinful life, and would not have let her come anywhere near him.

Jesus looked directly at Simon, knowing very well what was going on in his mind.

'Simon,' he said, 'two men owed money to a money-lender. One owed him five hundred gold coins while the other owed only fifty. The money-lender freely forgave both men their debts. Which of the two, do you think, will show more love and gratitude to the money-lender?'

'I suppose the man who was forgiven the larger sum,' Simon replied in an offhand way.

'You are right,' Jesus agreed. 'When I arrived at your house, you did not offer me water to wash my feet, but this woman has washed them with her tears. You gave me no welcoming hug, but she has kissed my feet. You did not even offer me a drop of olive oil to refresh my head, but she has poured costly perfume on my feet.

'She has shown all this love because she realizes how much she has been forgiven. Those who do not think they need God's forgiveness, do not show gratitude or love.'

'Then Jesus turned to the tear-stained woman. 'Your sins are forgiven,' he told her.

There was a little stir among the guests at table. How dare Jesus say a thing like that?

But Jesus was still looking at the woman.

'Go and enjoy a life of peace,' he said. 'Your faith in me has saved you.'

📖 **305**
Families
MARK 10

Some mothers came to see Jesus one day, bringing their babies and small children with them. They wanted the Master to put his hands on them and bless them. Jesus was very busy with the crowds, and the disciples thought how tired he looked.

'Go away,' they said to the

mothers. 'The Master is too busy to spend time on children.'

Sadly the mothers turned away. One of the babies began to cry and soon there was a chorus of wails. Jesus looked up quickly and saw what had happened.

'Never turn children away!' he said sharply to the disciples. 'My kingdom is made up of people willing to become like children—those who are trustful and loving and humble too. Always let the children come to me.'

'Come back!' the disciples shouted to the retreating mothers. When the children and the toddlers saw Jesus' face, they ran towards him eagerly. The mothers shyly held up their babies for Jesus to bless.

He took the ones that were crying first. They stopped as soon as he held them, gazing up at him with big eyes.

When Jesus handed them back, they lay gurgling contentedly in their mothers' arms.

Then Jesus picked up the toddlers and gave them all a hug. Lastly he placed his hands on the heads of the older children, giving them God's blessing.

The disciples looked on in wonder. The Master would never cease to amaze them. He did not seem to think *really* important people, like the Pharisees, important at all! Yet he spent all this time and trouble on mothers and children.

Then the mothers said, 'Time to go home,' and the children laughed and sang as they skipped away. The baby brothers and sisters were already fast asleep in their mothers' arms.

306
The Man who Came Back
LUKE 17

When Jesus and his disciples were on their way to Jerusalem, they caught sight of a little huddle of men, standing outside a village. The disciples drew back quickly. They knew what was wrong with those men. They were suffering from a skin disease that everyone dreaded. Unless a priest could certify that they were free from the disease, Jewish law said that the victims had to live alone, far from any town and from their homes.

As soon as the men saw Jesus, they called out, 'Jesus, Master—have pity on us!' The disciples backed away further, but Jesus went forward to meet them, showing no fear or disgust at the state they were in.

'Go straight to the priest,' he told them. 'When he has examined you, he will pronounce you cured.'

The ten men set off, excitedly. As they went, they looked at one another in wonder. Instead of scarred, marked skin, they saw clean, healthy limbs and features.

With shouts of joy, they broke into a run. The sooner they saw the priest, the sooner they would be free to go home to their families.

But one of the ten stood stock still. Jesus had answered their prayer for help, and a flood of thankfulness swept over him. Then, turning around, he scrambled back the way they had come. Breathless, he threw himself down at Jesus' feet.

'Thank you, Master!' he burst out. Jesus looked at him and then looked around.

'I healed ten men,' he said. 'Where are the other nine? Are you the only one who has come back to say thank you? And you are a Samaritan, with none of the privileges of the Jewish nation.'

Then Jesus gently helped him up and said, 'Be on your way now. Your faith in me has made you well.'

Jesus Says 'I Am...'

📖 307
The Good Shepherd
JOHN 10

In the land where Jesus lived, a shepherd had a hard life. Every day he had to wander far and wide, looking for enough grass for his

sheep. Streams soon dried up in the hot sun and he must find running water for them to drink. Sometimes he risked his life rescuing a sheep that fell over the cliffs or into ravines, or driving off the wild animals that attacked his flock.

King David had once been a shepherd, and God's care for him reminded him of the way in which he had looked after his sheep.

'God is my shepherd,' David sang. 'I have everything I need.'

Jeremiah and Ezekiel had compared the leaders of the nation to shepherds. But often they ill-treated and neglected their charges, unlike true shepherds.

'I am the good shepherd,' Jesus told his listeners one day. 'I am willing to give my life for my sheep. A true shepherd is very different from one who is hired to help but does not really care about the flock. He soon runs off, if he sees a wolf coming. But the shepherd who loves his sheep will risk his life to save them. I am going to give my life for my sheep. My sheep are the people who know me and listen to my call. I know every one of my sheep and no one can snatch them away from my loving care. My sheep recognize my voice and come when I call.'

Jesus had come not only as the shepherd of Israel. He was going to give his life for all people, everywhere.

'I have many other sheep,' Jesus explained, 'who don't belong to God's fold yet. I am going to call them, too. They will follow me and become part of my one big flock. I shall be the loving shepherd of them all.'

The Real Vine

JOHN 15

In the Old Testament, the nation of Israel was sometimes pictured as a vine. One writer described how God had first planted a little vine-shoot in the Promised Land, and how it had soon spread and grown strong. But Isaiah realized what a disappointment this vine had been to God. Kings and people had chosen their own way, not God's. The prophet told the people how God had come looking for the fruit of loving thoughts and obedient deeds from his nation, but had found only the wild, sour grapes of self-will and disobedience.

'I am the real vine,' Jesus told his disciples. 'Those who love and trust me are like branches of the vine. I am the vine and you are the branches. If a branch wants to produce grapes, it must stay attached to the main stem of the vine.

'If you love me and obey my commands, you will stay close to me. Then you will be able to draw strength and life from me, just as the branches take life-giving sap from the vine itself.

'When you keep close to me, your lives will show the beautiful fruit of patience and kindness, gentleness and truth, humbleness and self-control. You cannot be that kind of person without my help. On your own, you will fail. Keep close to me, and my life and my strength and my goodness will flow into you.'

The nation of Israel, the vine, had failed God over and over again. Jesus, the real vine, was always true and obedient to God. Now he was going to give his followers the help they needed to be true and obedient to God, too.

Stories About Using Opportunities

309
The Fig-Tree Without Any Figs
LUKE 13

Thousands of people listened to Jesus, but not many were ready to take notice of what he said. They did not want to obey God and change to his ways.

Jesus explained that God is loving and patient, but he also made it plain that their chance to follow him would soon be gone. One day it would be too late, both for the nation and for the men, and women who belonged to it. He told them this story.

'There was once a man who planted a fig-tree in good soil. He waited patiently until it had grown big enough to have fruit. Then he looked eagerly for figs. For three years he searched and for three years the tree was bare. There was not one juicy green fig to be seen.

'He knew that if the tree had not borne any figs by this time it probably never would. So he called the gardener and said, "I've been looking for figs on this tree for three years and there hasn't been a single one. The tree is using up all the goodness in the soil without being any use to me. Cut it down."

'But the gardener pleaded to keep the tree. "Give it one more chance, sir!" he begged, "I'll do all I can to encourage it to bear fruit. I'll dig the soil all around it and give it some fertilizer. Perhaps it will have figs next year. If it fails again, then you may have it cut down."'

The Wise and Foolish Girls

MATTHEW 25

Jesus must have joined in many happy weddings when he was a boy. The bride and her friends would wait at her home for the bridegroom to come and get her. But no one knew when he would come. It might even be in the middle of the night! At last they would hear the shout—'The bridegroom is on his way!' And soon he would arrive, followed by a procession of excited people. Then all who were invited would return to the bridegroom's house for a week of feasting and celebration.

Jesus longed for people to follow him and come into his kingdom while they had the chance. He knew he would not be with them much longer. But a day was going to come when he would return to earth as king, in glory and power. It would be too late then for people to change their minds and choose to follow him.

'On that day,' Jesus told them, 'the kingdom of God will be like a wedding. Once there were ten girls who were waiting to join the bridegroom's procession. It was evening, so all had their lamps ready. But five of them had not taken any oil to burn. Night came on and all the girls slept.

'Suddenly at midnight, a cry rang out in the quiet street—"The bridegroom is on his way!"

'The girls started up and began to turn up their lamps. Then the five foolish ones realized their mistake. "We haven't any oil!" they wailed. "Please lend us some!" But the five wise girls had only enough for their own lamps. "We can't help you," they said, "go and buy some."

'While the five foolish girls were away, the bridegroom arrived. The five wise girls joined the procession and soon they were all safely inside the bridegroom's house. The door was shut.

'It was some time later when the five foolish girls came knocking on the door.

' "Let us in!" they shouted.

'But the bridegroom answered, "Certainly not! I don't know you." '

When Jesus had finished the story, he added, 'Be ready and prepared for the coming of the king. No one knows when that time will be.'

311
The Three Servants
MATTHEW 25

Jesus would not always be living on earth. His followers must learn to be loyal to him and use every opportunity to serve him, even when he was no longer with them.

'There was once a man who had to go away on a long journey,' Jesus told them.

'Before he started out, he called his servants together and put them in charge of all his possessions. He shared his money among them, according to how well each one would be able to manage it. He gave the first servant five thousand gold coins, the second servant two thousand, and the third servant one thousand coins. Then he went away.

'The first two servants at once began to use the money they had been given, in order to earn more. But the third servant dug a hole in the ground and buried his gold coins there.

'After a long while the master returned. He called the servants to ask them what they had done with his money.

' "I've doubled what you gave me," the first servant told him. "Here are ten thousand coins for you."

' "Well done!" his master said. "You have been a good and loyal servant. You have shown that you can be trusted in small ways. I shall give you the opportunity to serve me in bigger ways now. Come and join my celebrations."

'Then the second servant stepped forward. "I have also doubled what you gave me," he said, and he handed his master four thousand coins.

' "Well done! You too have been loyal and good and you shall be promoted, too. Join my celebrations."

'Last of all, the servant who had been given one thousand coins came forward.

' "Here are your coins," he said. "I know you are always out for what you can get. I wasn't going to risk losing your money, so I buried it. It's safe. You can have it all back."

' "You bad, lazy servant!" his master exclaimed. "If I'm really as mean as you make out, then you should have invested my money, so that at least I should have earned interest from it. Your gold coins shall be given to the servant who gained five thousand. Those who make full use of what they are given, end up being even better off. Those who refuse to make good use of the little they have, lose even that."

'Then the master turned to the other servants.

' "Turn this bad servant out," he ordered. "He has lost his opportunity. There is nothing for him to look forward to but misery and regret."

The Watcher from the Tree

LUKE 19

Jesus and his disciples were on their way to Jerusalem for the Passover festival. Jesus knew that it would be his last journey there. Other pilgrims joined them as they came near to the beautiful city of Jericho. All around was barren desert and the waste land by the Dead Sea, where no green thing grew. But because of its fresh-water springs, Jericho was green with sweet-smelling balsam trees and fruitful date palms.

Tax collectors made a good living in that city and none more than Zacchaeus, their chief. But he was not happy, although he was rich. Everyone despised and insulted him. They knew that he lined his pockets with their hard-earned money, as well as passing it on to the hated Roman rulers.

Zacchaeus had heard about Jesus, the wonderful teacher who changed people's lives. How he wished that he could see him! But crowds had already lined the city street and if he tried to squeeze through he would get nothing but kicks and sharp elbows. If he stayed where he was, at the back, he would see nothing. He was too short.

Zacchaeus glanced up at the fig-tree that grew beside the street, and decided what to do. A few minutes later, as the little procession was arriving, he was surveying the scene below from the vantage-point of a strong branch.

Jesus and his followers came level with the tree, and Zacchaeus held his breath.

Then Jesus stopped and, looking straight up at his hiding-place, called out, 'Come down, Zacchaeus! I'm having dinner with you today.'

Zacchaeus came down a good deal faster than he had gone up. Brushing leaves and twigs from his stained robe he went hesitantly forward. The unkind mutters of the crowd reached his ears: 'Why should Jesus go to dinner with him? Everyone knows he's a crook!'

But Jesus put his hand on Zacchaeus' shoulder, and together they went towards his fine home.

No one knows what Jesus said over dinner, but when they both came out again, the waiting crowd could see that Zacchaeus was a changed man.

He stepped boldly forward and said, 'Lord, I'm going to give half of all I have to help the poor. If there's anyone I've robbed (and his eyes went from one to another in the crowd), well, I'll pay him back four times as much as I took.'

Jesus turned to the amazed crowd. 'It's people like Zacchaeus I came to find,' he said. 'I came to look for those who have strayed away from God and bring them back to him.'

313
Beggar by the Roadside
MARK 10

Further along the Jericho street, another man sat waiting. But he sat waiting every day, hoping that passers-by might put some small coin in his beggar's bowl. Perhaps he would do well out of the pilgrims who were coming through the town today. They might feel generous towards a poor, blind beggar.

But although Bartimaeus could not see, his hearing was sharp. He soon caught the name of Jesus on everyone's lips. And he had heard all about him. Jesus must be in the crowd that was on its way.

The pilgrims came nearer but there was very little chatter now. Everyone was listening hard to what Jesus was saying.

Bartimaeus was certain that Jesus must be God's promised Messiah, the true heir to King David. He was determined to take the golden opportunity and ask Jesus to help him.

Mustering all his strength, he shouted at the top of his voice, 'Jesus, Son of David! Have pity on me!'

'Stop that noise!' the people shouted back, 'we're trying to listen to Jesus!'

But Bartimaeus only shouted louder.

Jesus stopped.

'Call him here,' he said.

The message was passed back and

Friends of Jesus

What Matters Most

LUKE 10

Martha, Mary and their brother, Lazarus, were good friends of Jesus. They lived in Bethany, a small town on the slopes of the Mount of Olives, only half an hour's walk from Jerusalem. So whenever Jesus and his friends visited Jerusalem, they called on their friends at Bethany.

One day Martha caught sight of the disciples, coming up the road with Jesus, looking dusty and tired. She flew to put more sticks under the oven, so that she could cook them a meal.

Mary went to meet the visitors. She made sure that Jesus had a cool drink and water for washing. Then she sat beside him, listening to every word he had to say.

Martha grew hot and flustered as she cooked one dish after another. She began to feel very angry with Mary for leaving her to do all the work.

At last she could bear it no longer. She bustled across to Jesus, interrupting his words.

'Can't you tell Mary to give me a hand?' she asked. 'I don't see why I should get the meal single-handed.'

'Martha, dear,' Jesus said kindly. 'Don't be worried and bothered. All we need is something simple. Then you would have time to be with us and hear what I have to teach you all while you have the opportunity. A woman's place is not with the dishes all the time. Mary has chosen to do something far more important, and I'm not going to stop her.'

eager hands soon helped Bartimaeus to his feet and tried to push him forward. But Bartimaeus needed no prodding. Throwing off his cloak, he stumbled quickly forward in the direction of Jesus' voice.

'What do you want me to do for you?' Jesus asked.

'Lord, I want to be able to see,' Bartimaeus answered at once.

'You shall have what you ask for,' Jesus told him. 'Because you put your trust in me, I have healed you. You can go home now.'

But Bartimaeus took one look at Jesus' face and knew that he did not want to go home. Happily he joined the jostling crowd. He was ready to follow his King to the end of the world.

315
'Your Friend is Ill'

JOHN 11

One day, Lazarus became ill. As he grew worse and worse, Martha and Mary, his sisters, were beside themselves with worry. The doctor could do nothing to help and shook his head sadly.

'Jesus could make him better,' Mary said.

'Yes, let's send a message for him to come and help,' Martha suggested.

Jesus was in the north of the country once more, out of the way of the rulers in Judea, who had tried to stone him. But someone in the village would go for him.

'Tell Jesus that his dear friend is ill,' the sisters instructed the messenger.

Jesus was very fond of Lazarus and of Martha and Mary, too. The disciples could see the concern on his face when he heard the bad news. But he told them, 'Death will not be the end for Lazarus. This illness is going to bring glory to God and to his Son.'

Then, to their surprise, he went on with his work of healing and teaching, just where they were.

It was two whole days later that Jesus said, 'We're going to Bethany now.'

'It will be dangerous,' one of them reminded him. 'Remember what happened last time we were in Judea.'

'If the Master is prepared to risk death, then we'll stick by him and die too, if need be,' Thomas said bravely.

On the way, Jesus said, 'Lazarus has fallen asleep.'

'That's a good sign,' they replied. 'It must mean he's going to get better.'

But Jesus explained, 'When I said that he's asleep, I mean that he has died. Death is like a sleep, and I am going to wake him up. I'm glad about the delay for your sakes. What I am going to do will help you all to believe in me.'

None of them quite understood what Jesus meant, or what he would do when they arrived in Bethany. They would have to wait a little longer to find out.

Alive Again!

JOHN 11

By the time that Jesus and his disciples arrived on the outskirts of Bethany, Lazarus had been dead and buried four whole days. The house was still full of friends who had come to comfort Martha and Mary and mourn with them.

When news arrived that Jesus was near, Martha rushed out to meet him.

'I'm sure Lazarus would not have died, if you had been here!' she told Jesus.

'Listen, Martha,' Jesus said, 'I am resurrection and life. The person who believes in me will live again, even though he has died. Do you believe that?'

'I believe that you are God's Son, the promised Messiah,' Martha replied fervently.

When Martha left Jesus, she ran to tell Mary that he wanted to see her, too.

Mary set out from the house and a whole crowd of Jews followed her, thinking that she was going to her brother's grave to weep.

When Jesus saw Mary in tears and all the other Jews weeping, he cried too. Although he was going to bring Lazarus back to life, he was deeply grieved at the sadness that death brings to everyone.

'Show me his grave,' Jesus said and they made their way to the rock tomb together.

'Take away the stone that blocks the entrance,' Jesus ordered. When that was done, Jesus prayed aloud. 'Thank you, Father, for always hearing my prayers,' he said. 'May everyone see now that you have sent me to give life.'

Then Jesus called out loudly, 'Lazarus! Come out!'

A tense silence followed. Everyone held their breath.

Then there was the soft sound of shuffling feet and Lazarus, muffled and bound from head to foot in white grave-wrappings, stumbled across the threshold of the cave into the warm sunshine.

'Take off those grave clothes!' Jesus said.

Willing hands quickly unwound the long strips of linen, so that his face was uncovered and his hands and feet free.

Lazarus stretched his limbs, then strode across to his sisters, his face glowing with life and health. They all began to laugh and cry at once and to hug and kiss each other.

'Jesus *must* be the Messiah,' some of the bystanders began to say. But others, who did not want to believe in Jesus, set off for Jerusalem to tell Jesus' enemies the whole story.

'We must stop Jesus working such wonders,' the religious leaders agreed. 'If we don't, everyone will follow him.'

From that day they began to make plans to have Jesus arrested and killed as soon as possible.

A Present for Jesus

JOHN 12

When Jesus and his disciples arrived at Bethany, near Passover time, Martha planned a special celebration meal. It was wonderful to have Lazarus back—and it was all because of Jesus, their dear master and friend.

Everyone was happy that evening. They still did not realize what lay ahead for Jesus. Within a few days he would be arrested and cruelly put to death.

It was only Mary who realized that Jesus was heavy-hearted, even though he joined in the happiness of the supper party. She slipped quietly from the room and came back, carefully holding her most treasured possession. It was a large and beautiful flask, full of very expensive perfume. A man would have to work for half a year before he could afford to buy such a gift.

Mary went across to the place where Jesus was reclining on the couch beside the table and poured every drop of perfume the bottle contained over his bare feet. Then she gently wiped the trickles of perfume with her long hair.

Jesus was glad; it comforted him that someone had understood and given him such love and care. The scent began to fill the air all around.

But the harsh voice of Judas Iscariot broke the silence that had fallen.

'What a waste!' he exclaimed. 'Think of the price of that perfume. We could have sold it and given the money to the poor.' (Judas did not really care much about poor people, but he looked after all the money and sometimes helped himself to the funds.)

Jesus saw the shadow that passed over Mary's face. Her happiness was clouded and she looked near to tears.

'Leave Mary alone,' he told Judas sharply. 'She has done something beautiful for me. My death is near. I shall not be with you much longer, but the poor are always with you. You can give to them any time you want. In years to come, whenever the good news about me is told, the story of Mary's love and generosity will be told, too.'

Palm Sunday

318
The Big Procession
MARK 11; JOHN 12

The city of Jerusalem was seething with people. Jews from near and far were arriving for the week-long Passover festival. Just when it seemed that the narrow streets could hold no more, fresh batches of pilgrims surged in.

The city was buzzing with the latest story about Jesus. He had actually brought back to life a man who had been dead and buried for four days! As soon as news arrived that Jesus was on his way, an excited crowd set off to meet him.

Jesus and his disciples had come as far as Bethany.

'Go into the village,' Jesus told two of his disciples. 'Bring me the young donkey you'll find tied up near his mother. If anyone asks what you are up to, tell them that the Master needs him and will soon send him back.'

The disciples did as Jesus said. When the bystanders heard that it was Jesus who wanted the donkey, they gladly let him go.

When they had brought him to Jesus the disciples spread their coats on the donkey's back, to make a saddle.

The donkey was not frightened when Jesus climbed onto his back, even though no one had ever ridden him before. He stepped proudly forward and the pilgrims who had journeyed with Jesus began to jostle and cheer as they all began the steep climb into the city.

Long ago, the prophet Zechariah had foretold that one day the true King would come, not galloping on a war-horse, but riding a peaceful donkey. Jesus was showing all who had eyes to see that he was that King, entering his capital in peace.

The crowd from Jerusalem hurried down to join the new arrivals, and the whole huge procession moved forward again with cheers and shouts. Some went ahead and threw down their cloaks to make a royal road for Jesus. Others stripped branches from the trees to strew on the path.

'Hosanna!' they shouted. 'Save us now, God! The long-promised King has come! God bless the one who comes in the name of the Lord!

'At last the little donkey, with the King on his back, entered the streets of Jerusalem.

Jesus' Enemies Grow Stronger

📖 **319**
Jesus in the Temple
MARK 11

Jesus arrived in triumph at the very walls of the huge temple area. He had a good look around, but as it was evening and Jerusalem was packed to overflowing, they all went back to their Bethany friends for the night.

Next morning, Jesus returned to the temple. The first big area, or court, was open to all. But this was the only part where non-Jews, called Gentiles, were allowed to go. A big notice warned them to go no further on pain of death.

This court should have been a quiet place, where people could come to pray and learn about the true God.

Jesus was horrified at the scene that met his eyes and ears. There was a deafening hubbub of noise. Sheep bleated, cows lowed and birds twittered, while traders shouted hoarsely. People with big packs threaded their way through the stalls, using the temple as a short cut. Jesus knew that the traders, selling the animals as offerings for the pilgrims to give to God, were charging more than twenty times too much for them. The money-changers were cheating, too. Every Jew had to pay a temple tax at Passover time, but those who changed the pilgrims' coins into the temple shekel used for payment, were making a fat profit. The priests themselves were behind much of the trading.

Jesus was very angry that the poor should be cheated and that God's house should be turned into a dishonest market. He strode forward, unafraid of his enemies, the priests, and with a strong arm overturned the stalls.

Tables and stools were soon upside down and coins rolled everywhere. Then Jesus shooed out the animals and turned away the people with their baggage.

The pilgrims looked on in amazement. How brave Jesus was, to defy the most powerful people in the land!

Jesus explained to them: 'God said that this temple should be a place where everyone, from every nation, could come to pray and worship him. It shall not be turned into a thieves' den.'

The people understood and were glad.

Enemies Outside

MATTHEW 26; MARK 12

Passover celebrations lasted a full week. Every night Jesus went back to Bethany, but by day he taught in the temple courts.

The religious leaders were growing more and more determined to silence Jesus, once and for all. Two days before Passover supper they called a meeting of their seventy-strong Council. The chairman was the high priest, Caiaphas, and the meeting was held in his house.

'We *must* arrest Jesus,' he told them. 'But he is so popular that we shall have to do it secretly, or risk a riot.'

'That means waiting until after Passover, when the crowds have gone,' another said.

But Jesus knew more than his enemies about what was going to happen.

'This Passover, I am going to be handed over to the Romans to be crucified,' he told his disciples.

As Jesus was teaching the people, the religious leaders joined the crowd, and began to ask questions. They hoped to trap Jesus into saying something that would get him into trouble.

'Do you think we should pay taxes to the Romans, or not?' they asked him one day. They knew that if Jesus said 'yes', he would not be popular with the people, but if he said 'no', they could report him to the Roman rulers. They were sure that they had caught him out this time.

'Hand me a coin,' Jesus said. When someone passed a coin to him, Jesus held it up.

'Whose head is that on the coin?' he asked.

'Caesar's,' they replied.

'Then give Caesar what you owe to him and give God what you owe to *him*.'

Jesus had escaped their trap but he had not given a trick answer. He had told them what was right and true. The Jews owed much to their Roman rulers. They provided them with roads and water and kept peace between nations. But they owed far more to God.

321
The Wicked Tenants
MARK 12

One day Jesus told a story meant for the religious leaders and priests in the crowd.

'There was once a man who planted vines and prepared everything needed to grow good grapes and turn them into wine. Then he had to go abroad, so he put tenants in charge of his vineyard.

'When the grape harvest was due, he sent a servant to collect his share of the grapes as rent. But instead of handing over what they owed, the tenants beat up the servant and sent him off empty-handed.

'The owner sent another servant, and then another, but every time the tenants ill-treated and sometimes killed them. The owner decided to have one more try.

' "I'll send my son to them," he said. "They are sure to show *him* respect."

'But those wicked tenants seized the owner's son, killed him, and threw out the body. They thought that once they had got rid of him, they would become the owners.

'What do you think the owner will do next?' Jesus asked his listeners.

'He will come himself and take the vineyard away from those tenants,' they mumbled in reply.

Silence followed.

Jesus' hearers knew very well what his story meant. The nation was often pictured as a vineyard. They, the leaders, were the tenants, put in charge by God. Many kings and leaders of the nation had refused, down the centuries, to take notice of God's servants, the prophets. *They* were refusing to listen to God's last and most important messenger, his own Son. Even now they were plotting to kill him.

But instead of heeding the warning, the priests and leaders grew even more determined to get rid of Jesus. They would have seized him then and there, if they had dared. But the ordinary people loved Jesus. So his enemies slunk away, burning with hatred and planning to kill him at the first opportunity.

The Enemy Inside

MATTHEW 26

When Jesus rode into Jerusalem at the beginning of the Passover celebrations, his disciples were even more excited than the crowds. They had longed for the day when Jesus would be openly owned as king. Perhaps at last that day was near.

But Jesus kept patiently warning them that he was not going to be that kind of earthly king. At first he would rule only in the hearts of his followers. Soon he would be arrested and killed. After that, he would come alive again for ever and his kingdom would spead through the whole world.

Most of the disciples still did not grasp what Jesus meant. But Judas Iscariot began to understand only too well. He was an ambitious man and he loved money. He, more than any of them, had looked forward to the day when, as one of King Jesus' chief advisers, he would have power and wealth.

But Jesus' words at the Bethany dinner party, when Mary poured out her precious perfume, made Judas realize that Jesus was preparing for a very different future. He did not intend to become an earthly king and throw off Roman rule.

Now Judas' dreams of wealth and power would never come true. He had been wasting the best years of his life. He was bitterly disappointed and sick at heart.

He knew that the priests and leaders of the nation needed someone on the inside to help them, if they were to succeed in arresting Jesus— someone who could tell them where to find Jesus when no crowds were present.

Judas made his way to the temple, where he knew he would find the Council members and priests.

'How much money will you give me, if I tell you where and when you can catch the man you want?' he asked. The conspirators' faces brightened. This was too good to be true. They had scarcely expected help from one of the man's own followers.

Someone pulled out a bag of money and carefully counted out the silver coins.

'There you are, Judas,' he said, 'Thirty of them—and you can have them now. Let us know as soon as possible where to find your master.'

Judas walked off, his thoughts in a whirl. From now on he must watch carefully for the best way to keep his side of the bargain with his new masters.

The Last Supper

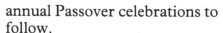

📖 **323**
Preparing the Passover Meal

MARK 14

Passover week was slipping away. It was time now to begin preparing the Passover meal.

Long ago, God had rescued the people of Israel from death and led them out from Egypt into a land of their own. They had kept the first Passover then, and Moses had given clear instructions about what they should eat and how they should cook it, both for that day and for the many annual Passover celebrations to follow.

Families met together to eat roast lamb with bitter-tasting herbs and bread made without yeast. Every part of the meal had special meaning and the children in the family would be told about God's wonderful goodness to his own people when they had been slaves in Egypt.

Jesus planned to share his last Passover meal with his own close disciples.

'Go and get the Passover meal ready,' he told Peter and John.

'Where shall we prepare it?' they asked.

Jerusalem was packed and none of them had a house of their own in the city. But many friends of Jesus were glad to lend him whatever they possessed—just as the owner of the donkey had done. Jesus had already made arrangements with one of these friends.

'Go into the city,' he told Peter and John. 'Follow a man carrying a water-pot.' (That would make anyone look twice. In those days men usually left the water-carrying to women.)

'When he goes into a house, go after him,' Jesus went on. 'Ask the owner of the house to show you the room that he has promised to lend us. It will be a big, upstairs room. Get our meal ready there.'

Jesus knew that his enemies were looking for him. It was important that he should have a safe, private place where he could enjoy this last supper with his friends.

He still had many things to tell them before he was taken away from them.

324
Looking After Others

JOHN 13

The day for the Passover supper had come. Jesus arrived with his disciples at the upstairs room in the Jerusalem house. Everyone was hot and dusty, after trudging through the busy streets.

As the twelve argued and grumbled and laughed among themselves, Jesus looked at them with great affection. He knew them through and through, with all their faults, and he loved them dearly. He knew that even now Judas was looking for an opportunity to betray him to his enemies, but Jesus loved him still.

The disciples were looking around, anxious because there was no servant to wash their feet. The least important servant in a household had the job of washing the dust and sweat from the feet of guests who had walked dusty roads in open sandals. The pitcher of water and a towel lay ready, but not one of them was willing to do such a despised job.

An obstinate silence fell.

Then Jesus stood up, poured some water into a basin and picked up the towel himself. He went from one disciple to the next, washing their feet in turn. They felt very ashamed.

When at last Jesus sat down, he said, 'Do you understand what I have been trying to tell you? You call me your master and Lord—and you are right. That is what I am. Yet I am willing to do anything for you, even to wash your feet, because I love you. I want you to follow my example. Care for each other and love one another as I love and care for you. Don't always be thinking of yourselves and your own importance.'

325
The Passover Meal
JOHN 13; MARK 14

The disciples had been excited about celebrating the Passover supper, but now they began to feel more serious. They could see that Jesus was very sad.

'One of you is going to betray me to my enemies,' he told them at last. They were horrified.

'You don't mean me, Lord, do you?' each one asked in turn.

Judas Iscariot realized that Jesus knew about his treachery. But Jesus did not openly accuse him. Instead he tried to offer him friendship and forgiveness.

He handed Judas the best and tastiest helping of food. But Judas' face remained hard and set. He would not go back on his bargain with the Council. Besides, he now had the information that they wanted.

Jesus looked at him with great sadness. Then he said, 'Be quick and get on with what you are going to do.'

The rest of the disciples did not understand what Jesus meant. They thought he was giving Judas instructions to take some money to the poor.

Without a word Judas slipped from the room and went out into the darkness of the night.

As they went on eating the meal, Jesus did something new and wonderful. He changed the old Jewish Passover into a supper with special meaning, that Christians have kept from that day to this. First he took the loaf of bread on the table and shared it among the disciples.

'All of you, eat it,' he told them. 'This bread is my body, which is going to be given for you all.'

Thoughtfully and a little mystified, the disciples ate. Then Jesus took a cup of wine and handed it to them.

'Drink this,' he said. 'This wine is my life-blood, which is going to be given for many. My blood will be the seal of God's new covenant, which he is going to make with people of every nation.'

The disciples drank as Jesus told them.

Soon, not many days later, they would understand better what he meant. Jesus was not going to be a murder victim, put to death because a friend betrayed him and his enemies hated him. His death would be part of God's great plan to save mankind. Jesus was willingly giving his own life, so that people everywhere could have God's forgiveness and receive new life through trust in him.

326
Preparing the Disciples
MARK 14; JOHN 13, 14, 16

After supper was over, Jesus talked to his disciples for a long time. He wanted to prepare them for what was going to happen that very night, but they were slow to understand what he said.

'You are all going to run away and leave me,' he told them.

'Never!' Peter exclaimed. 'I don't know about the others, but I'll never do such a thing. I'm willing to die with you, if need be.'

'So are we,' the others all agreed.

Jesus shook his head. 'Peter,' he said, 'before cock-crow tomorrow's dawn, you will have said three times over that you don't know me.'

'I'd never do such a thing!' Peter insisted.

'None of you must be worried or upset, when it looks as though everything has gone wrong,' Jesus went on. 'You must trust me and believe in me, just as you do in God. I am going to leave you, but after I have risen from death, we shall meet and talk together once again in the fields of Galilee we know so well. I shall be there waiting for you.

'And when at last I go back to my Father, I promise that I won't leave you on your own. I am going to send my Holy Spirit to be your friend and helper. You will not be able to see him, because he doesn't have a human body as I have, but he will stay close to you and give you strength and encouragement. He will help you to remember all the things that I have taught you, and he will give you courage to be loyal to me.

'I am going back to my Father to make a home ready for you there. One

day I shall come for you, too. You know where that home is and how to get there.'

'Lord, we haven't any idea where you are going, so how *can* we know the way?' Thomas exclaimed.

'I am the way to God,' Jesus answered. 'I am the only bridge between God and mankind. No one can come to God except across that bridge.

'Before I leave you, I want to give you a parting present—it's the gift of my peace. It's not the kind of peace that you will find in this world. My peace will keep you strong and joyful, however hard life may be.'

When Jesus had finished talking to them, they all sang the special Passover hymn. Then, together, they left the safety of the quiet, friendly room.

Jesus' Arrest and Trial

📖 **327**

Arrest in the Garden

MATTHEW 26; JOHN 18

Judas knew where Jesus and the rest of the disciples would go when supper was over. Near to the city, on the slopes of the Mount of Olives, lay a quiet garden of silver-grey olive trees, called Gethsemane. Jesus often escaped from the busy streets and went to Gethsemane to think and pray.

That night they crossed the brook and went into the garden. Peter, James and John walked close to Jesus.

'Don't go,' he whispered to them. 'Stay close and keep me company. My heart is nearly breaking with sorrow and sadness.'

Soon Jesus went a little way from them to pray. His friends could see that he was shaken with distress and grief.

'Please, Father,' he prayed with deep earnestness, 'don't let me go through the terrible suffering that lies ahead! Rescue me from it, if that is possible. But above all I want to do what pleases you—not what I want.'

In spite of Jesus' need of them, the three friends were so tired that they fell asleep. Twice Jesus gently woke them, but when he began to pray again, they dozed off once more.

'Couldn't you stay awake with me, even for an hour?' Jesus asked them sadly. 'But now you must wake up. I am going to be taken prisoner. Look! Here comes the one who has betrayed me to my enemies!'

The startled disciples rubbed their bleary eyes. Now they could make out the dancing light of lanterns, weaving through the olive-trees. The dull gleam of metal told them that an armed guard was on its way.

As the procession advanced with certain steps towards them, they recognized with horror and disbelief the familiar figure of Judas Iscariot at its head.

'See that you take the right man,' Judas whispered to the guards. 'He's the one I'll greet with a kiss.'

Judas walked straight towards Jesus.

'Hello, Master!' he called out, and hugged him.

'Judas, my friend, why are you here?' Jesus asked sadly. 'Are you going to betray me with a kiss?'

But the armed guards, brandishing clubs and spears, rushed up and seized Jesus, as if he were a dangerous criminal.

Peter was furious. He pulled out a sword of his own and lashed out wildly, cutting off the ear of one of the high priest's servants.

'Put your sword away, Peter,' Jesus said firmly, 'If I wished to go free, I could call on armies of angels to fight for me. But I am ready to give up my life, according to God's plan.'

Then Jesus gently touched the wounded ear and made it whole.

The bewildered and terrified disciples could bear no more. Their master and leader was going to allow himself to be taken prisoner. That was the end of all their hopes. In panic and despair, they took to their heels and ran.

The armed band led their unresisting prisoner away.

328
'I Don't Know the Man!'

LUKE 22; JOHN 18

Jesus was led by his captors to the house of Caiaphas, the high priest. Although it was night time, the Council decided to meet at once and put Jesus on trial. They must not risk trouble from the excitable Passover crowds.

Meanwhile Peter and John had come to their senses. They must follow and see where Jesus was being taken. They kept a safe distance but when they arrived at Caiaphas' house, John, who knew some of the members of the household, walked straight into the courtyard. Peter waited outside.

'May my friend come in, too?' John asked the servant girl at the gate.

'Yes,' she agreed, but she stared hard at Peter as he came closer.

'Aren't you a disciple of that man?' she inquired, jerking her thumb towards the room leading off the courtyard, where Jesus stood facing his accusers.

'No, I am not!' Peter said indignantly. He thought of his rash attack on the high priest's servant and wondered if the story had got around already. He felt suddenly cold and made his way to warm his hands at the brazier of glowing charcoal that stood in the middle of the courtyard.

A man nearby peered at him. 'You're one of that lot!' he declared.

'I don't even know the man!' Peter insisted. All the while, a continuous low murmur of voices from the court-room reached their ears.

In one corner of the courtyard a group of the servants whispered together and stared at Peter.

One of them said out loud, 'Whatever he says, he is a follower of the prisoner. Anyone can tell he comes from Galilee—listen to his northern accent!'

Peter lost his temper and swore.

'I don't know what you're talking about!' he shouted. 'I tell you I don't know him!'

As he spoke, a cockerel crowed, welcoming the first pale streaks of dawn. With terrible clearness Peter remembered Jesus' words: 'Before cock-crow, you will say three times over that you don't know me.'

Peter looked across at the strong, quiet figure of Jesus, facing his interrogators alone. Jesus gazed back, with great understanding and love.

It was more than Peter could bear. He had failed the person he loved and trusted most. He rushed out of the courtyard, crying bitterly.

Judas' Story
MATTHEW 27

When Judas had led the armed guard to Gethsemane and shown them which was the man to be arrested, his part in the plot was over. He was free to go away and begin a new life. But now that the plan had been successfully carried out, the full horror of what he had done began to dawn on him.

Judas had lived close to Jesus for three years and he knew that Jesus had never done a wrong or unkind action. But he knew that those determined, ruthless men would not rest until they had brought about his death.

On a sudden impulse Judas set off—half-running—to the temple, to find the men he had bargained with.

'I have done wrong,' he told them. 'I have helped you to arrest a man who is completely innocent.'

'That's your affair,' they told him, a little amused at his earnestness. 'We really don't care how you feel about it.' And they went on with the conversation he had interrupted.

With a cry of despair, Judas hurled down the thirty silver coins that they had paid him and fled. Then he took a rope and hanged himself.

Jesus Stands Trial
MARK 15; LUKE 23

All night long Jesus stood before the Council, listening to the false charges they made. None of the witnesses they called told the same story. They could prove nothing against Jesus.

At last, in desperation, the high priest challenged Jesus directly.

'Tell me on oath,' he demanded, 'are you the Messiah, the Son of God?'

'I am!' Jesus replied.

'That settles the matter!' the high priest declared. 'The prisoner has claimed to be divine. He deserves by our law to die.'

But only Pilate, the Roman governor, could pass the death sentence. They must convince him that Jesus had committed crimes worthy of death by Roman reckoning.

They handed Jesus over to the guards, who tormented and ill-treated him, while they made their plans.

Early in the morning they took Jesus, in chains, to Pilate's palace. Pilate was in Jerusalem to keep order during the excitable days of Passover.

'This man has been stirring up trouble,' they told Pilate. 'He tells people not to pay taxes and says he's a king.'

If these charges were true, Jesus would be sentenced to death, but Pilate was certain that the religious leaders had trumped up the charges because they were jealous of him. He began to cross-question Jesus himself and could find nothing wrong that he had done.

All the while, a mob below in the street, mustered and led by the priests and leaders, were chanting over and over, 'Crucify! Crucify! Crucify!'

Pilate came out to speak to them. 'This man is completely innocent!' he announced. 'He doesn't deserve to die.'

The chant swelled to a deafening roar—'Crucify! Crucify!'

Pilate tried another way out. 'It's Passover time,' he said. 'I shall set a prisoner free as part of the celebrations. Let me set Jesus free.' But the leaders were ready with a new slogan: 'We want Barabbas! We want Barabbas!' And the crowd took up the cry. Barabbas was a mob leader, in prison for murder.

Pilate was at his wits' end. If the crowd rioted, he might lose his job. He dare not release Jesus, even though Roman justice declared him innocent. He decided to wash his hands of the whole matter and hand Jesus over, to be put to death by crucifixion, as the mob insisted.

Jesus' Crucifixion

331
The Road to Golgotha

MARK 15

Pilate gave in to the wishes of the mob and their leaders. He set Barabbas free and ordered his mercenaries to whip Jesus before taking him to be crucified. Roman whips were made from leather strips weighted with pieces of metal and prisoners sometimes died from the injuries they caused.

After they had whipped Jesus, the Roman soldiers teased him cruelly. He was supposed to be a king, was he? They dressed him up in a robe dyed royal purple. One of them quickly put together an imitation crown from sharp-speared thorn twigs and rammed it down on his head. Then they knelt to him, in mock homage, proclaiming 'Long live the king!' before spitting in his face.

Soon it was time to take the prisoner to the place of execution. By Jewish law, this had to be outside the city gates. The little procession set off down the hill towards Golgotha, which means Skull Place.

A mocking, shouting crowd followed and a few women went, too, crying to see the good, brave teacher being led off to die.

Prisoners were expected to carry the rough, wooden cross-bar on which they would be executed and the soldiers had already laid the heavy beam on Jesus' shoulders. But Jesus was weak from the long interrogations and the whipping. He could scarcely walk upright beneath its weight.

An African Jew, up for Passover, came striding up the hill towards them.

'Here, you!' the centurion called, laying a firm hand on his arm. 'Carry the cross for the prisoner. We'll never get there at the rate we're going.'

Simon was strong and broad-shouldered. He carefully lifted the cross from Jesus' torn shoulders and hoisted it onto his own. Together they walked the rest of the rough road to Golgotha.

Jesus on the Cross

MARK 15; LUKE 23; JOHN 19

The Romans crucified troublesome slaves and desperate criminals. Roman citizens were spared such a cruel death. Large nails were driven through the victim's feet and outstretched hands, in order to fix him to the cross-beams of wood. The cross was set in a socket in the ground and then lifted up, so that the criminal was suspended, left to die from heat and thirst.

There were three prisoners to be crucified that day and the execution squad set to work.

By nine o'clock the three crosses were lifted into position. Jesus was on the centre one.

Then the soldiers settled down to wait, gambling with dice to while away the time.

Jesus looked down at them with pity. 'Forgive them, Father,' he prayed. 'They don't know what they are doing.'

The religious leaders had arrived to gloat and jeer. 'You saved others,' they said mockingly, 'but you can't save yourself!'

One of the criminals hanging on the next cross muttered hoarsely, 'Aren't you supposed to be Messiah? Why don't you save us all?'

But the other criminal said, 'You be quiet! We deserve to die, but this man is innocent.' Then he begged Jesus, 'When you come as king, please remember me!'

'You don't have to wait until then,' Jesus replied. 'You will be with me in paradise this very day.'

Some of Jesus' disciples, mostly the women, were there too.

'Look after my mother,' Jesus whispered to his close friend, John. John nodded. 'He'll be a son to you now,' Jesus told his mother, who stood crying bitterly.

At noon, when the sun should have been brightest, thick darkness fell. For three hours Jesus suffered all alone, carrying the weight of the whole world's sin.

Then, at three o'clock, he called out in a clear, triumphant voice, 'Finished!' Then he gave up his life and died.

Joseph of Arimathea, a wealthy citizen, asked Pilate's permission to give Jesus proper burial. Nicodemus, who had visited Jesus at night, came to help him. The two men gently washed the body, wrapped it in clean grave-clothes and laid it on a stone ledge in the cave tomb in Joseph's garden.

Some of the women who had been at Golgotha followed to see where Jesus was buried. Then, worn out with sadness and crying, they went away.

Jesus' Resurrection

333
He is Alive!

JOHN 20

It was Friday evening when Jesus' body was laid in the garden tomb. The next day was the Sabbath, the Jewish day of rest. The long hours passed slowly for Jesus' heartbroken friends. They could not believe that the master they loved so much lay cold in the tomb.

'Once the Sabbath is over, we'll take sweet-smelling spices to put on his body,' the women agreed.

But that night Mary Magdalene could not sleep. It was dark when she made her way, with several of the other women, to the garden.

As they came close to the tomb, they saw, with horror, that the big round stone that closed the cave's mouth had been moved. Someone must have tampered with the grave and stolen Jesus' body.

The women ran back to find Peter and poured out the tale to him, then hurried on to tell John. Both men set off to see for themselves. John, who was younger, ran faster and arrived first.

By now there was enough light to peer inside. The linen wrappings lay tidily on the rock shelf, but the body had gone. As John looked, everything that Jesus had taught them clicked into place. Of course—Jesus was alive!

When Peter's heavy steps were heard, John stood aside and Peter went right in. He, too, saw the grave-clothes and the head-cloth lying on its own. But he shook his head, bewildered, and they left the garden.

But Mary stayed alone, silent tears coursing down her cheeks as she too gazed into the tomb.

Two shining angels were sitting where Jesus' body had been.

'Why are you crying?' they asked.

But Mary sensed that someone was behind her and she half-turned, to see a man she thought must be the gardener. Perhaps he could help her.

'Why are you crying?' the newcomer asked.

'Because my Lord's body has gone. Have *you* moved it, sir?' she asked.

'Mary!' the stranger said.

Mary wheeled around to face the one whose voice she knew and loved so well.

It was Jesus!

'Tell my disciples that I have risen and that I am on my way to the one who is my Father and their Father too.'

Mary ran back through the morning sunshine, all fear and sadness gone. She burst in on the huddled group of disciples.

'He is alive! He is really alive!' she announced with joy.

334
Walk to Emmaus
LUKE 24

That same Sunday, two other friends of Jesus left Jerusalem to walk home to Emmaus. As Cleopas and his wife trudged along, they kept going over the sad events of the past few days. They scarcely noticed when a stranger drew level with them. Instead of overtaking them, he matched his pace to theirs and began to talk.

'You're looking miserable,' he remarked. 'What's the matter?'

'You mean you haven't heard?' Cleopas answered. 'You must be the only person around here who doesn't know what's been happening. Jesus, our master, has been put to death. We were certain that he was God's Messiah and now our hopes have gone!'

The stranger laughed gently. 'You've made a big mistake,' he said. 'Think what the prophets had to say about the Messiah. Isaiah compared him to an innocent lamb, being led to the slaughter-house. The Messiah had to die—not for a crime he had committed but for the sins of other people, in order to bring them peace and forgiveness from God.'

The journey flew by as the stranger went from one Old Testament writing to another, explaining that it was God's plan that the Messiah should first die and then rise from death, because he had conquered evil.

It seemed no time before they were at their own door. The stranger looked as if he was going on up the street.

'Do come in!' Cleopas' wife begged. 'It's getting late. Have supper with us.'

The stranger accepted and, when supper was ready, he took the bread, thanked God for it and shared it between them.

They recognized the familiar way he did it all.

The stranger was Jesus—alive! They turned to him, but he had gone.

'No wonder our hearts grew warm when he talked to us!' Cleopas said. 'We must go straight back to Jerusalem and tell the others.'

But when they arrived the eleven greeted them with the news, 'Jesus has risen!'

As they all talked excitedly together, Jesus himself joined them. He shared their meal and explained to them all the wonderful things he had told the two on the Emmaus road.

335
Thomas' Story

JOHN 20

Thomas had missed it all. He was not there that first resurrection Sunday, when Jesus came to the disciples.

As soon as he arrived back, they all began to tell him at once, 'Jesus is alive!' 'We have seen the Lord!'

'I don't believe it!' Thomas answered bluntly. He had seen Jesus' dead body. No one could persuade him that a man could be alive again after a death like that.

'I'd have to see the marks the nails made in his hands and feel the gash in his side, where the Roman soldier thrust his spear, before I'd believe!' he told them.

A whole week passed.

The next Sunday the disciples were together again and Thomas was with them. The door was locked because they were still afraid of the religious leaders.

All at once, Jesus was with them in the room.

'Peace to all of you,' he said. Then he turned to Thomas and looked straight at him. 'You may touch the nail-marks in my hands and feel the place where the spear pierced my side,' Jesus said. 'But stop doubting, Thomas. Believe that I am alive.'

Thomas was overcome with happiness but he was also very ashamed. 'You are my Lord and my God!' he exclaimed in wonder.

'*You* believe because you have seen me,' Jesus said. 'There is a special blessing for those who put their trust in me although they have never seen me with their own eyes.'

'Do You Love Me?'

JOHN 21

The disciples went home to Galilee. Peter felt restless. It was wonderful that Jesus was alive, but he missed the old days when the twelve of them had tramped the countryside with Jesus and worked alongside him when he healed the crowds. He felt aimless now.

'I'm going fishing,' he announced one evening, and some of the others, including James and John and Thomas, said, 'We'll come too.'

They set off cheerfully, but as the night wore on they grew more and more disheartened. They hadn't caught a single fish!

At dawn they made their way back. They would not catch anything now. They could see a man standing on the shore. He had spotted them, too. Cupping his hands, he called to them and his voice carried over the still water of the lake.

'Have you caught anything?'

'Not a thing!' they shouted back.

'Throw your net over the right side of the boat and you will,' the stranger instructed.

Something about him made them obey. No sooner had they tossed the net over the side than it was bulging with fish. They could scarcely haul it back on board.

'It's the Lord!' John exclaimed.

At once Peter jumped over the side of the boat and made for the shore, leaving the others to follow more slowly in the boat.

Jesus was cooking breakfast by a charcoal fire and there was a delicious smell of grilled fish.

'Bring me some more fish,' Jesus said. He knew that the disciples would be hungry enough for second helpings.

Peter dashed back to help pull the heavy net up the beach. One of the others began to count the fish as they slithered, wet and shining, onto the shingle. There were one hundred and fifty three!

Soon they were warm and happy again, eagerly eating the bread and fish that Jesus had cooked for them.

After breakfast, Jesus walked a little way along the shore with Peter. 'Do you love me, Peter?' he asked quietly.

Peter felt a stab of shame. He could not forget how he had denied knowing Jesus.

'You know I love you, Lord,' he replied in a low voice.

Peter had disowned Jesus three times and now three times over, Jesus asked, 'Do you love me?'

'You know everything, Lord,' Peter said at last. 'You know that I love you.'

'Then I have work for you to do,' Jesus told him. 'When I have gone, I want you to take care of my sheep— the ones who will follow me.'

Peter knew now that Jesus had forgiven him completely. He was going to trust him to work for him once more. Peter did not think that he would go fishing again.

Jesus' Ascension

📖 **337**
Home to Heaven
ACTS 1

For a month or more after he had risen, Jesus appeared to his friends at many different times. Jesus showed himself only to his followers, although there were more than five hundred of them together on one occasion. There could be no doubt that Jesus was alive.

He was certainly not a ghost. His friends could touch him and he shared meals with them. But his body was different now. He could pass through closed doors and appear and disappear at will.

During those weeks Jesus helped his disciples to understand many things that they had not been able to take in before he died. He showed how the Old Testament scriptures pointed to a Messiah who would suffer and die for his people and then rise again. The religious leaders had studied the scriptures too, but they picked out those verses that described a Messiah that everyone would crown as king.

One day Jesus was talking to the disciples on the slopes of the Mount of Olives.

'Has the day come now for you to be crowned as king?' they asked hopefully.

'God will decide when that day shall be,' Jesus told them. 'I have work for you to do now. I am going back to my Father and you won't see me. But you are to be my witnesses, here in Jerusalem first, then to the whole world. Teach others to follow me and baptize them. I will be with you through my Holy Spirit. Wait in Jerusalem for him to come to you.'

Jesus held up his hands to bless them and in that instant he was taken away from them. They watched him go up until a shining cloud hid him from their view. For a while they went on staring.

Suddenly they realized that two men in white were standing by them. 'Why are you looking up at the sky?' they asked. 'One day Jesus will come back in just the same way that you saw him go.'

The disciples made their way back to Jerusalem and did as Jesus told them. They waited together for his Holy Spirit to come to them.

The Coming of the Holy Spirit

338
God's Spirit Comes
ACTS 1-2

The disciples met to talk and pray together while they waited for the Holy Spirit to come. They knew that Jesus would no longer appear suddenly, to talk to them. But once his Spirit came, he would be with them in a new and closer way.

Seven weeks after Passover, the Jewish people celebrate the festival of Pentecost. It is a harvest thanksgiving for the first ripe crops. Soon Jerusalem was packed with pilgrims once again, as Jews from all over the world returned for the happy celebration.

Early that Sunday morning, on the day of Pentecost, Jesus' disciples were all together, when something extraordinary happened.

They described it afterwards as a great rushing wind that swept down from heaven and filled the whole house with the noise it made. Then separate little tongues of flame settled for an instant on every person there.

But what they could see and hear was nothing compared to how they felt inside themselves. The warmth and life that Jesus always brought with him surged into them again, and they knew that his promised Holy Spirit had come to live inside them for ever, close and real.

They were bursting with joy and began to pour out aloud their thanks and praise to God.

Meanwhile, a huge crowd had collected outside the house. They had seen and heard some of the strange happenings and were curious to know what was going on. But when the disciples came out of the house and onto the street, they were even more amazed.

Everyone there, whatever country he came from, understood perfectly what the disciples were saying, as they praised and thanked God for his wonderful gift to them.

'Whatever can have happened to them?' the people asked one another. But some of the bystanders were not impressed. 'They've just been drinking too much wine!' they said.

Peter made up his mind to explain.

339
Jesus is Lord!
ACTS 2

The crowd surged forward as Peter stood up to speak to them. The rest of the apostles stood close to Peter, to show that they supported him.

'Listen, everyone!' Peter began, and the chatter died down as the crowd settled to hear Peter's explanation.

'We're not drunk!' Peter asserted. 'It's too early in the morning for that. We'll tell you what has changed us. Do you remember how the prophet Joel, centuries ago, said that one day God would pour out his Holy Spirit on every one of his children? This is what has happened today. God has given us his Spirit—and I'll tell you why.

'Only a few weeks ago, at Passover, *you* helped to hound Jesus to death. He was a wonderful teacher, who showed by his acts of power that he

came from God. But you and your
leaders wanted him to be crucified.
And you had your way.

'But Jesus' death was not really the
result of wicked men's plots. It was all
part of God's own wonderful plan
that Jesus should suffer death. He did
not die because he deserved to; he
died for *our* sins.

'And that was not the end of the
story. God did not leave Jesus to rot
in the grave. He made him alive again
and today we can tell you, beyond a
shadow of doubt, that God has made
Jesus Lord of all. He is God's
Messiah King!'

There was a great stir and sigh as
Peter stopped speaking. If he was
right, they had done a terrible thing.
They had shouted for the death of

God's chosen Messiah. They were
full of remorse and their consciences
were deeply pricked.

'Whatever can we do?' they asked.

'If you are truly sorry,' Peter
replied, 'turn back to God and put
your trust in Jesus. Be baptized to
show that you mean to leave your sins
behind and follow Jesus. God will
forgive you and will give you his Holy
Spirit, too.'

Many people rushed forward to do
as Peter said. That day the number of
believers in Jesus swelled to three
thousand.

They all began to meet regularly in
the days that followed. They had
meals together, prayed and learned
more from the apostles about what it
meant to follow Jesus.

The Young Church

340
A Healing—and Trouble
ACTS 3—4

One afternoon Peter and John were going to the temple to pray, when they heard a voice, whining, 'Give us a coin, sir!'

They looked down at the miserable man who crouched beside the Beautiful Gateway. He was a familiar sight. He had never been able to walk, but friends carried him to that spot every day, to beg from those going to the temple to pray.

When Peter and John stopped, the beggar looked hopeful.

'I haven't any money to give you,' Peter said. 'But I'll give you what I have. In the name of Jesus Christ, I order you to get up and walk!'

He put out a helping hand and the beggar felt his ankles and feet grow strong.

First he walked, then he began to run and jump, pulling Peter and John along with him into the temple court. People came rushing to see what had happened to the beggar they knew so well.

'Don't stare at us!' Peter told them. 'We haven't cured him! It's Jesus, our Lord, whose power has cured him. Faith in him has made this man well.'

Some of the religious leaders were listening too and, before long, some burly temple guards seized Peter and John and threw them into prison, by order of the Council.

Next morning they were questioned. 'Who gave you the right to act as you did?' the members of the Council asked them.

'It is Jesus' power that made this man fit and well,' Peter answered.

'He is the one you despised and put to death, but God has made him alive again. He is the only one sent to save and rescue us all.'

The Council members were amazed to hear uneducated fishermen talking like this. But they knew that they were friends of Jesus. They could not contradict what they said because the beggar himself was living proof of Jesus' power.

'Don't preach about Jesus any more,' they ordered. But Peter asked, 'Who do *you* think we ought to obey—you, or God? We can't possibly stop talking about Jesus. We have heard and seen for ourselves everything we say about him.'

Reluctantly, the Council let them go free.

341
The Couple who Told Lies to God

ACTS 5

More and more people believed the good news about Jesus. His followers became known as people of the Way. They loved one another and shared everything. No one wanted to keep anything he owned for himself. Many rich people, who owned land, sold it and gave the money to the apostles to be shared around.

Ananias and his wife, Sapphira, decided that they would do the same.

'But it seems a pity to give *all* the money away,' Ananias said regretfully. 'Peter need never know how much we got for our land. Let's keep some for ourselves.'

Sapphira agreed.

Ananias handed the money to Peter but Peter knew what had been going on.

'Ananias,' he said gravely, 'why did you think up this plan to deceive? You did not have to sell the land, or even give all the money away. But you wanted to *pretend* that you were being generous and giving all you had to God, when you were really keeping some back for yourselves. You have been telling lies to God!'

When Ananias heard Peter's stern words, he fell down dead. Some of the young men, who were standing by, carried his body away and buried it.

Three hours later Sapphira arrived, wondering where her husband was. Peter held up the money that Ananias had given to him.

'Tell me, Sapphira,' he asked, 'was this the full amount that you got for your land?'

'Yes,' Sapphira lied easily.

'How *could* you both agree to lie to God?' Peter exclaimed. 'Do you hear those footsteps? Here come the men who have been burying your husband. Now they will carry away your body, too.'

At once Sapphira collapsed, dead. The terrible news spread far and wide. Everyone began to realize that having God's Holy Spirit meant being obedient to him, as well as enjoying his peace and power.

By their lies and selfishness Ananias and Sapphira spoiled the full trust that there had been among the followers of Jesus. Things would never be quite the same again.

Stephen the Fearless
ACTS 6—7

As the apostles went on preaching in Jerusalem, many more became followers of the Jesus Way. Everyone was made welcome and any in need were looked after. But so much of the apostles' time was taken up with caring for everyone, that they hadn't time to preach and pray as Jesus had told them to do. So they picked seven good men, to be in charge of sharing out the funds fairly, among the widows and others in want.

Stephen was one of the seven. He was energetic and enthusiastic and argued with members of the Jewish synagogues very skilfully, to prove that Jesus was the Messiah. But he soon made enemies. These people invented false charges against him and brought him before the Council.

As the charges were read out, Stephen faced his accusers bravely, his face like an angel's—full of goodness and light.

Then it was Stephen's turn to speak.

'All down the ages, our nation has refused to listen to the leaders God has sent to them. Now you have rejected and murdered God's most important messenger—his Son, Jesus.'

The Council members were furious. They shook their fists and shouted angrily at Stephen.

His voice rang out again: 'I can see Jesus in heaven itself and he is standing at God's side!'

With a snarl of rage, his accusers rushed at him, seized hold of him and dragged him outside the city. They picked up rocks and boulders and began to hurl them at him.

As the stones came thick and fast, Stephen sank to his knees.

'Lord Jesus, receive my spirit!' he called out.

Just before he lost consciousness, he prayed, 'Lord, please forgive them for this crime.' Then he fell to the ground, dead.

A young man called Saul was looking after the cloaks that the Council members had hastily thrown down. He fully agreed with what they were doing.

Later, some of the believers took Stephen's body, so that they could give it proper burial.

343
The African Official
ACTS 8

The very day that Stephen was stoned to death, a big hunt began for all the followers of Jesus.

Saul was the ringleader. He thought that he was pleasing God by trying to get rid of this new teaching about Jesus. He battered on the doors of every house where the people of the Way used to meet and dragged them off to prison.

Many fled from Jerusalem and were scattered far and wide. But wherever they went they told everyone the good news about Jesus.

Philip, one of Stephen's fellow helpers, went to Samaria and preached to huge crowds in the town there.

But one day God told Philip to leave the busy towns and go to a lonely desert road. An Ethiopian official was going home that way in his chariot. He was a very important minister, in charge of all the finance at the queen's court.

Someone had taught him about the true God and he had visited Jerusalem to worship him. On the long journey home he was reading from the scripture scroll that he had bought there.

'Go and talk to him,' God told Philip.

Philip ran hard to catch up with the chariot and, as he came near, he could hear the official reading out loud in a puzzled voice.

'Do you understand what you are reading?' Philip asked, as he drew level with him.

'How can I, when there is no one to explain it to me?' the official answered. 'Please climb up here and help me.'

Philip scrambled up beside him.

The official was reading Isaiah's words about God's servant who was led off to die, like an innocent lamb that is slaughtered.

'Is the prophet writing about himself?' the official asked.

'No,' Philip replied. 'He is speaking about Jesus, God's perfect servant, who willingly died for our sins. Then Philip went on to explain the good news about Jesus.

The official's eyes brightened. 'May I be baptized?' he asked. 'I believe with all my heart that Jesus is God's Son and I want to trust and follow him.'

They had arrived at a place where there was a pool of water. He stopped the chariot and they both got down. Then Philip baptized him in the water.

After that, God's Spirit took Philip away. The official set off on his journey once more, full of joy and bursting to tell his fellow countrymen all about Jesus.

Paul's Conversion

📖 **344**
Journey to Damascus
ACTS 9

Saul was born into a Jewish family who lived in Tarsus, a university city in the Roman province of Cilicia.

He was a clever young man and had learned Greek and Latin. In his home town he was known as Paul, which is the Roman form of his name. His family had been granted the privilege of Roman citizenship.

But, more than this, Saul was proud to be a Pharisee. He had studied under a famous Jewish teacher in Jerusalem. Saul was convinced that he must use all his energies to wipe out the new teaching about Jesus.

Sometimes he was haunted by the look of goodness and truth on Stephen's face, as those murderous stones had rained down upon him. To banish such memories, he worked even harder to get rid of every follower of the Way. If they had fled from Jerusalem, he would go after them.

One day he set off for Damascus, with letters from the Jewish Council that would give him power to arrest followers of Jesus in the city and bring them to Jerusalem for trial. Armed guards went with him.

They journeyed for about six days before the gates of Damascus at last came into sight.

Suddenly, the brightness of the noon sun seemed to grow pale, as a startling flash of brilliance lit up the sky and shone all around.

Saul fell to the ground, stunned by the dazzling light.

Then a voice spoke to him: 'Saul, why are you persecuting me?'

Fearing—yet guessing—what the answer would be, Saul asked, 'Who are you, Lord?'

'I am Jesus,' came the reply. 'Every time you ill-treat one of my followers you are ill-treating me.'

'What do you want me to do, Lord?' Saul asked, all pride and hatred gone.

'Go into the city and you will be told what to do next,' Jesus said.

Saul struggled to his feet. But he could see nothing. He had been blinded by the light from heaven.

📖 345
A Changed Man
ACTS 9

The armed guards had seen the light that shone from heaven but they did not see the one who spoke to Saul, or understand what was said. When they saw Saul blunder to his feet, and realized that he was blind, they took

his hand and led him to a house in Damascus, in Straight Street.

Saul stayed there three days, praying and thinking about his vision. He did not eat or drink.

Meanwhile Jesus spoke to Ananias, one of his followers in Damascus.

'Go to Straight Street,' he told him. 'Knock on the door of Judas' house and ask to see Saul of Tarsus. He is expecting you.'

Ananias was horrified. He had heard all about Saul. 'But Lord,' he protested, 'Saul is our enemy. He has come on purpose to arrest us.'

'He has become my servant,' Jesus reassured him. 'I have chosen him to take the good news far and wide.'

Ananias set off obediently. As soon as he saw Saul, he went quickly across to him and put his hands gently on his shoulders.

'Brother Saul,' he said kindly, 'Jesus himself, who spoke to you, has sent me here, so that you may see once more and may receive his Holy Spirit.'

At once, something like fish-scales fell from Saul's eyes and he could see again. Then Ananias baptized him and he ate a good meal.

Saul stayed on in Damascus, not to arrest believers but to preach about Jesus to all in the synagogues there. They were amazed at the change that had come over him.

But his own people, who would once have been his friends and allies, became Saul's bitter enemies. They made up their minds to stop his preaching and made a plot to kill him.

Day and night they watched the city gates to catch him as he went out. So Saul's friends lowered him over the city walls in a basket, under cover of darkness and he escaped from his enemies.

Peter the Leader

📖 346
Tears for Tabitha

ACTS 9

Now that Saul had been converted, the church was left in peace for a while. It grew bigger and stronger. Peter had remained in Jerusalem but he moved around a great deal, preaching and helping new Christians. He was 'feeding the flock', just as Jesus had told him to.

While he was visiting Lydda, two men arrived from a nearby seaside town called Joppa.

'Please come quickly!' they begged. Peter lost no time, and listened to their story as they went on their way.

Everyone was very sad because Tabitha, one of the believers, had died. As soon as Peter arrived at Tabitha's house, he could hear the sound of crying and wailing.

He climbed the stairs to the room where her body lay, and was met by a swarm of weeping, chattering widows. They clustered around Peter, full of stories about Tabitha's kindness to them.

'Look!' one of them said, 'Tabitha made this for me.' She fingered the well-sewn gown that she was wearing. Others pointed to their own beautifully-made coats and dresses.

Tabitha was skilled at dressmaking and needlework and had used her gift for God. She had made clothes for all who were too poor, or too ill, to buy and make for themselves.

Peter looked past the women to the still, white body lying on the sleeping-mat. He listened kindly for a while, then said, 'You must all be quiet now and go out of this room so that I can pray alone.'

The widows tiptoed obediently out and Peter closed the door. First he knelt and prayed, then he turned to the body.

'Tabitha, get up!' he said.

At once Tabitha opened her eyes. When she saw Peter, she sat up. Peter helped her to her feet and then called the widows and other believers. They ran up to Tabitha with cries of happiness and excitement.

Before long the news had spread all over Joppa and many people believed in Jesus because of what Peter had done in his name.

347
A Sheet Full of Animals
ACTS 10

Peter stayed on in Joppa, at the house by the seaside that belonged to Simon, a tanner. That was a brave thing to do, for most Jews treated tanners as 'unclean' because they handled the skins of dead animals.

Peter remembered what Jesus had taught. He had said that God did not treat someone as unclean because of what they touched or ate. He looked inside, to see if their thoughts and concerns were clean and right.

But Peter and all the apostles still believed that Jesus had come to be the Messiah of Jews only. *They* were God's chosen people.

One day, Peter was feeling hungry but dinner was not ready, so he climbed up to the flat roof to pray while he waited. Below him lay the sparkling blue sea, with a few little boats bobbing about. In spite of the leather awning that kept off the fierceness of the sun's rays, the air was shimmering in the midday heat. Soon Peter was fast asleep.

While he slept, God spoke to him in a vision. He saw in front of him a huge sheet, like the leather awning above him, being lowered by its four corners. Inside were animals, snakes and birds of all kinds. Every one, Peter noticed, was a creature that Jews were forbidden by law to eat.

Then God's voice said, 'Get up, Peter; Kill one of those animals and eat it.'

'Certainly not, Lord!' Peter exclaimed. 'I've never in my life eaten an unclean animal.'

'Don't call anything unclean when God has said that it is clean,' the voice commanded.

Three times over the same thing happened. Then the sheet was lifted up again and Peter awoke. He sat pondering what his vision meant. He was sure that God was trying to teach him something important.

Just then he heard visitors arriving at the front gate. 'Is there someone staying here called Peter?' they called out.

God's Spirit whispered to Peter, 'Three men are looking for you. Don't be afraid to go with them because I have sent them.'

Peter bounded down the steps, two at a time. 'I'm the person you are looking for,' he said.

Then he saw that the new arrivals were all Gentiles and one of them was a Roman soldier.

348
The Roman Soldier
ACTS 10—11

Cornelius was a Roman centurion, stationed at the army headquarters in Caesarea. He had learned about the true God in the land his troops had come to occupy. He and his family prayed to God and cared for any Jewish people in need.

The very day before Peter had his vision, an angel appeared to Cornelius. 'God has heard your prayers and seen your kindness,' the angel said. 'Send for a man called Peter, who is staying in Joppa with Simon the tanner. He will teach you more.'

Cornelius sent off a trusted soldier and two servants right away. They were the three who arrived at Simon's front gate.

Jews never invited Gentiles inside their homes because they thought they were 'unclean' in God's sight. But Peter asked these three to stay the night. Next day they all set off. Now he understood what his vision meant. God did not think of Gentiles as 'unclean'. He was ready to accept them, as well as Jews.

There was a room full of people waiting to listen to Peter and they drank in every word he said. They gladly believed the good news about Jesus with all their hearts and, while Peter was still talking, God's Holy Spirit came down on them.

They were filled with joy and excited praise to God, just as the disciples had been on the day of Pentecost. So Peter gladly baptized them. When he went back to Jerusalem, he told the Jewish believers all about his vision and what had happened at Cornelius' house.

'Praise God!' they said. 'He is willing to save Gentiles, too!'

Some of the believers who had left Jerusalem had arrived in the big city of Antioch, in Syria. They began to preach the gospel to Gentiles, too, and many of them believed. The local people nicknamed them all Christians—those who followed Christ.

Barnabas left Jerusalem to care for the new church. When he saw how much help they needed he sent for Saul, and together they taught them more about the new way of life.

349
Prison Gates Open
ACTS 12

The Jewish believers were not left in peace for long. The Romans had made Herod Agrippa king in Judea. He was grandson of Herod the Great, who had murdered the Bethlehem babies when Jesus was born.

Herod Agrippa found that ill-treating the believers made him popular with some of the Jewish leaders. So he put to death James, one of Jesus' twelve disciples, and threw Peter into prison. He planned to behead him once the Passover festival was over.

A squad of four soldiers guarded Peter, day and night. He was handcuffed either side to two, while the others guarded the door of his cell.

The night before he was due to be executed, the Christians in Jerusalem met to pray at the home of Mary, a wealthy believer.

Peter slept peacefully, in spite of his chains.

Suddenly, in the middle of the

night, an angel appeared in his cell. He shook Peter hard to wake him, then whispered, 'Hurry! Get up! Put on your sandals and wrap your cloak around you and follow me.'

Peter's chains fell from his wrists. He obeyed the angel like one in a dream. As they passed the two guard posts unchallenged, and the heavy iron door to the outside world swung open of its own accord, he thought he *was* still dreaming. He began to walk down the street, a free man, and his visitor disappeared as mysteriously as he had come.

Peter took a deep breath. He was awake—it was real, God had rescued him. Quickly and quietly he made his way to Mary's house and knocked on the door.

When Rhoda, the servant girl, came to answer, she was so excited to hear Peter that she dashed back inside to tell the others, leaving him still in the street.

'It's Peter!' she exclaimed, but no one believed her.

Peter went on knocking and at last someone opened the door. Peter put his finger to his lips, to warn them to be quiet. He told them the wonderful story of his escape and asked them to pass the good news on to all the other Christians. Then he slipped away, somewhere safe, until the hue and cry for him was over.

Paul the Preacher

350
'The Gods Have Come to Earth'

ACTS 13—14

The church at Antioch flourished. Saul and Barnabas stayed for a year, teaching the young Christians. Because he was living among Gentiles, Saul was known by his Roman name, Paul.

One day, as the Christians were fasting and praying together, God made it plain that he wanted Paul and Barnabas to leave Antioch and take the gospel to other lands.

Both men realized that there would be many hardships ahead. There would be danger on the high seas, and danger on land. They would have to cross mountains and marshes, face angry mobs in the towns and brigands in the desolate countryside. But God, who was telling them to go, would be with them all the way.

The Christians at Antioch prayed that God would bless them, and then saw them off on the first stage of their journey.

First they crossed the sea and preached on the beautiful island of Cyprus, which was Barnabas' home country. Then they sailed to the mainland that we now call Turkey.

Whenever they arrived in a city, Paul looked for a Jewish synagogue and first preached there. His hearers would know the Old Testament and understood when Paul announced the good news that Jesus was Messiah.

But many refused to listen and angrily turned the two out. So they preached instead to Gentiles, which made their own countrymen even more angry.

Often Paul and Barnabas were threatened and beaten up.

One day they arrived in Lystra, where few people had heard about the true God. Paul explained the good news in a way that they would understand. But when he healed a man who had been lame all his life, the crowd grew very excited. They began to jabber together in their own dialect, which the two visitors could not understand.

Then, to their horror, they saw priests of Zeus, the father of the Greek gods, leading a procession and bringing them garlands and a bull to be sacrificed.

'The gods have come down to us,' they were saying. They had decided that Barnabas was Zeus, and Paul, who did all the talking, was Hermes, the messenger of the gods.

'Stop!' Paul called out. 'We are ordinary people, like you! We want to tell you about the true God!'

At last he persuaded them to stop their ceremony.

After many exciting adventures, the two men retraced their steps, encouraging and helping the young Christians in every city. They chose leaders for the new churches. It did not matter that they had no fine church buildings. A church is made of people, who are joined together by their love for Jesus and for one another.

Mission Europe
ACTS 15—16

Three years passed before Paul and Barnabas arrived back in Antioch, full of what God had done. But after a while Paul began to worry about the young Christians they had left behind. He wanted to go back to see them and to travel further afield. He planned to preach in every city that was on a trading route, so that the good news would travel further than he could take it and people passing through would hear the gospel, too.

Paul set off on a second expedition with Silas. First they went back to every new church, then they journeyed on, not sure where God wanted them to go next.

When they were at Troas, near to the ancient city of Troy, Paul dreamed that he saw a man beckon to him, pleading, 'Come to Macedonia and help us!'

Next morning, the friends agreed that God had sent the vision, so they crossed the strip of water into Macedonia, which is in modern Europe.

A doctor called Luke joined them there. Later he wrote the book of Acts and one of the four Gospels, too.

There was no synagogue in Philippi, the city they visited first. But they found a little group of people praying by the riverside on the Sabbath and sat down with them.

Paul began to tell them about Jesus and one of his listeners believed. Her name was Lydia and she sold purple cloth. She begged the friends to come and stay at her home, all the time they were in Philippi.

Every day, as Paul and his friends crossed the city from Lydia's house, they were followed by a slave girl. She made a lot of money for her owners by telling fortunes.

She kept shouting wildly, 'These men are followers of the Most High God! They will tell you how to be saved!'

At last Paul could bear it no longer. He turned and said, 'Evil spirit, I order you to come out of this girl, in the name of Jesus!'

At once her wild rantings stopped. But her power to tell fortunes had vanished, too. Her owners were furious. They went straight to the Roman officials.

'These men are trying to overthrow Roman laws,' they claimed. The officials did not wait to hear Paul's side of the story. They seized Paul and Silas, tore the clothes from their backs and gave orders for them to be whipped, then thrown into prison.

'Lock them up safely,' they told the prison officer.

352
Singing in Prison
ACTS 16

The Roman prison officer chained Paul and Silas to the walls in the innermost cell of that black, foul-smelling jail.

In spite of the wounds on their backs and the chains on their feet, Paul and Silas were full of thankfulness to God. At midnight they burst out singing God's praises.

The other prisoners listened, amazed. They had never before heard anything but yells and curses and angry threats in that horrible place.

Suddenly, a violent earthquake shook the prison to its foundations. The doors were lifted free of their hinges and the chains broke loose from the walls.

The terrified prison officer rushed over from his own quarters. When he saw the prison wide open, he was certain that his charges must have all escaped. He pulled out a sword to kill himself.

But Paul called out urgently, 'Don't hurt yourself! We are still here!'

The officer called for a light and went straight to the inmost cell. He knelt in front of Paul and Silas.

'Please sirs, tell me what I must do to be saved!' he begged.

'Put your trust in Jesus Christ and you will be saved—and your whole family, too,' Paul told him.

The prison officer gladly believed what Paul had to tell him about Jesus. He took them both to his own rooms and gently bathed their bleeding backs. His wife gave them supper. Then Paul baptized the whole family.

Next morning the Roman officials sent police to the prison with the message, 'Let those men go.'

But Paul replied, 'We are Roman citizens, yet we have been publicly

whipped *and* imprisoned without trial. Tell them to come themselves to free us.'

When the officials heard that Paul and Silas were Roman citizens they were very frightened. They had broken the law by treating them as they had. They hurried to the prison to apologize and beg them to leave Philippi.

So Paul and Silas visited Lydia and the other Christians once again, then went on their way.

353
Riot at Ephesus
ACTS 19

On his third and last expedition from Antioch, Paul settled in Ephesus for three years. Tourists flocked to Ephesus to visit the beautiful temple of the Greek goddess Artemis, which was the pride of the city. They used to buy little silver souvenirs of the goddess and magic charms, for which Ephesus was famous.

Paul set up his headquarters in a lecture-hall belonging to a philosopher. He used it during the hottest hours, in the middle of the day, when the philosopher and his followers were having a sleep.

But, in spite of the heat, crowds flocked to listen to Paul and many believed the good news. When they became Christians they burned their books of magic and threw out their idol figures.

At last Demetrius, who was a silversmith, called a meeting of his fellow craftsmen.

'We make our living by selling silver models of Artemis,' he said. 'But at the rate Paul is carrying on, we shall all soon be bankrupt. No one wants images of the gods once they've believed what Paul preaches. So what are we going to do?'

Everyone grew noisy and excited and at last they began marching down the street, chanting, 'Great is Artemis of Ephesus!'

More and more bystanders joined them on their way to the public meeting-place. When they arrived, there was an uproar. Half the people did not know why they were there and everyone was shouting something different.

When Paul heard what was happening, he wanted to go and speak to the crowd, but his friends and some of the Roman leaders would not let him. They knew he might be murdered on the spot.

Some of the people in the crowd thought that the Jews were at the bottom of the trouble and a leading Jew, called Alexander, went to the front to try to speak to them.

But the ringleaders began to chant, 'Great is Artemis of Ephesus!' over and over again. Everyone joined in and they kept it up for two hours. At last the town clerk restored order and sent them all home.

Paul realized that he would make life harder for the Christians by staying longer, so, sadly, he said goodbye to Ephesus.

The Long Sermon

ACTS 20

Although Paul had spent most of his time with Gentile Christians, he was anxious to help the Jewish Christians in Jerusalem, who were very poor. So when he left Ephesus, he visited many of the churches who had promised to contribute to his collection for the Jerusalem church.

Then Paul and his friends started out to take the gift to Jerusalem. On the way they stopped at Troas, one Saturday night.

The Christians were delighted to see Paul and packed into an upstairs room to listen to him. The room grew hot and stuffy and the air was thick with fumes from many oil-lamps.

As Paul went on talking, one of his listeners grew sleepy. Eutychus was a young man, but he had been hard at work since daybreak. As he sat on the window-sill, his head began to nod. In another moment he dropped off to sleep and fell crashing from the third floor to the ground beneath.

There were cries of horror. Some rushed to the window to look down, while others, Paul among them, ran down the stairs.

The first arrivals picked Eutychus up. He was dead. But Paul arrived, took him into his arms and hugged him tight.

'Don't worry,' he told them, 'he's still alive!' How happy and thankful they were, as they helped the bewildered young man upstairs! Then they all had a meal before Paul began talking to them again.

It was day-break when he left them at last, to continue his journey to Jerusalem.

Paul the Prisoner

📖 355
Arrested!

ACTS 21—22

When Paul and his friends had crossed the sea, they stayed at Caesarea for a few days with Philip, the man who had met the Ethiopian official on the desert road.

While they were there, a prophet called Agabus arrived. He took Paul's belt and used it to tie up his own hands and feet. Then, as everyone watched, puzzled, he said, 'Paul, this is what will happen to you if you go to Jerusalem. God has told me that you

will be arrested and handed over to the Romans.'

'Please don't go!' they all begged Paul. Some of the women began to cry.

But Paul said, 'Don't break my heart with your tears and pleas. I have made up my mind to go to Jerusalem, whatever happens. I am ready to die for Jesus, not just to be put in chains.'

So the little party set off. The Jewish Christians at Jerusalem welcomed them but warned Paul that all kinds of wild stories about him were flying around.

One day, when Paul was in the temple court, some of the Jews seized him.

'Help!' they shouted. 'We've got the man who teaches everyone to break God's laws and brings Gentiles into the temple!'

There was a mad stampede. Everyone rushed at Paul, drove him out of the temple and began to beat him, again and again.

An urgent message was sent to the Roman commander, who soon arrived with his soldiers to take charge. He arrested Paul.

'Put him in chains,' he ordered his men. Then he asked the crowd, 'What has he done wrong?'

But everyone said something different. Then they began to shout, 'Kill him! Kill him!'

In the end the soldiers had to carry Paul to the Roman fort to get him out of the reach of the frenzied mob.

The Secret Plot

ACTS 22—23

The soldiers half-dragged, half-carried Paul up the steps that led to the Roman fort, overlooking the temple.

'May I speak to the people?' Paul asked. The commander was surprised.

'You speak good Greek,' he said. 'I thought you were that Egyptian terrorist, who led a revolution a few years back.'

'I am a Jew,' Paul replied. 'I come from the well-known city of Tarsus.'

'You may talk to them if you want to,' the commander agreed. Paul looked at the sea of faces below and raised his hand for quiet. As he began to speak to them in Hebrew, the noise died down.

'I am a Jew,' Paul began. 'I was brought up to know the law and studied under the great teacher, Gamaliel. I, too, tried to get rid of the followers of Jesus, until I met Jesus for myself. I discovered that he is really alive! He was the one who told me to go and preach to Gentiles.'

When Paul said that, the mob began to shout, 'Kill him! He's not fit to live!'

'Take him inside the fort!' the commander ordered urgently. 'Give him a whipping,' he went on. 'Perhaps that will make him talk and we'll find out what he's really done wrong.'

As the soldiers tied him up Paul asked, 'Are you prepared to whip a Roman citizen?'

The commander was called. 'Are you really a Roman citizen?' he asked. 'I am one myself—but I had to pay a lot to buy the privilege.'

'I was born one,' Paul said.

The soldiers quickly untied Paul. They must treat a Roman citizen with respect.

For a few days Paul was kept safely at the fort. But a little group of Judeans took a solemn vow not to eat or drink until Paul was dead. They asked the Jewish Council to send for Paul.

'Tell the Roman commander you want to question him,' they said. 'We shall be waiting to kill him, as soon as he leaves the safety of the Roman fort.'

But Paul's nephew overheard them plotting together and went straight to his uncle with the whole story.

'Take this young man to your commander,' Paul told the soldier guarding him.

'The prisoner Paul sent this young man to speak to you,' the soldier said, as he ushered Paul's nephew in.

The commander took him on one side.

'What do you want to tell me?' he asked kindly.

When he heard about the plot, he decided to get Paul out of Jerusalem at once. He ordered an armed guard to be ready by nightfall. In the darkness, Paul was smuggled out of the fort and sent on the way to the Roman headquarters at Caesarea.

357
Shipwreck!
ACTS 24—27

Paul was kept in custody for several years. From time to time he was called to defend himself before the Roman governor, but his case was never settled.

At last he said, 'I appeal to Caesar.'

As a Roman citizen he had the right to have his case heard in Rome by the emperor himself.

'Very well,' the governor agreed, 'to Rome you shall go.'

He was handed over to Julius, the Roman centurion in charge of prisoners bound for Rome. Julius took a great liking to Paul. Some of Paul's friends, including Luke, went with him at their own expense.

At first the sea was calm, but when the wind changed the captain had difficulty getting their ship into port. It was autumn, and during the rough winter storms ships used to stay in a safe haven.

'Don't sail any further,' Paul advised. 'I know that we shall all face disaster if we go on with the voyage.'

But the owner of the ship wanted to get the cargo on its way and the captain was eager to sail on, too. Julius paid more attention to them than to Paul, the land-lubber. Besides, the wind was right for them to set off.

But they had not gone far when the fair wind changed to a fierce north-easter. It howled and shrieked in the rigging and bore down on the ship's timbers. Heavy seas lashed the decks.

The crew worked feverishly, roping down the loose fittings and securing the ship's boat. Then they threw cargo and equipment overboard to lighten the ship.

For days and nights on end they could see neither sun nor moon, but in any case it was impossible to steer the ship. They left it to drift, driven by the wind and battered by waves. The anxious crew and the frightened, seasick passengers were sure that they would never see dry land again.

Then Paul called everyone together.

'You should have taken my advice,' he reminded them. 'But don't give up hope. An angel of the God whom I serve appeared to me last night. God has promised me that every one of us will arrive safe on land. And I believe God!'

That very night the sailors found that the sea was shallower. They took soundings and were certain that land must be near. Once morning came they might be able to steer the ship ashore. But they planned instead to escape themselves, then and there.

Paul saw them trying to launch the ship's boat and told Julius. 'Stop them going—or we won't be able to get the ship to land.' So Julius ordered them back.

Then Paul said, 'We've had nothing to eat for a long time.' So he took food, thanked God for it, and set them an example by eating some himself. Everyone else ate, too, and felt better for it. Then they waited eagerly for morning to come.

Safe Ashore!

ACTS 28

By first light, the sailors could make out the coastline and see an inviting, sandy bay. They had no idea where they were, but they hoisted sail, hoping that the ship would be blown onto the shore. Instead it hit a sandbank and began to break up, smashed by the heavy waves.

'Shall we kill the prisoners, to stop them from escaping?' the soldiers asked their centurion. But Julius wanted to save Paul, so he gave orders instead that everyone should make for the shore as best they could.

Those who could not swim grabbed pieces of timber from the ship and floated in to land. One way and another, all two hundred and seventy-six people on board got safely ashore, just as God had promised. They were on the island of Malta.

Everyone was cold and wet through and it had begun to rain. But the friendly islanders lit a welcoming fire to warm them.

Paul helped collect sticks. But as he was throwing a pile of them on the fire, a snake glided out from the bundle and fastened on his hand.

'Look!' the islanders whispered to one another. 'That man must be a murderer! He's escaped death by drowning, but fate is going to get him just the same!' They kept staring at Paul, expecting him to drop dead from the snake bite. But he just shook off the snake and went on as if nothing had happened. So they changed their minds about him and decided instead that he must be a god!

Soon the Roman governor arrived to welcome them and took them to stay for a few days in his fine villa.

Paul was glad to be able to return the governor's kindness by healing his father, who was lying desperately ill. When the news spread, everyone on the island who was ill came to Paul to be healed. The whole party stayed for three months in Malta, until a ship arrived that was going the right way. Then they set sail once more, laden with presents and provisions from the kind people of Malta, who waved them goodbye.

359
Rome at Last
ACTS 28

At long last, Julius and his prisoners landed on the mainland of Italy. They began the weary journey overland to Rome. Paul was very tired after the experiences of the last months—and years. But God had been with him and now a lovely surprise was waiting for him.

The Christians at Rome had heard that he was on his way. Although they had never met Paul, they loved him dearly. He had written a letter to them and told them how much he longed to visit them. So a little group of them set out to meet Paul, when he was still some way from Rome. They gave him a warm welcome and kept him company on the last stage of his journey.

When he arrived at Rome, Paul was not put in prison but was allowed to live in a house that he rented, with a Roman soldier to guard him. Although he was not allowed to go out and about, anyone could visit him. He knew he might have a long time to wait before the emperor heard his case.

Paul invited the Jewish leaders who lived in Rome to visit him first. He told them about Jesus, their true Messiah. Some believed, but others were not ready to accept Jesus as Messiah. So Paul welcomed Gentiles to come and hear the gospel.

Luke does not tell us how Paul's story ended. He gives us a last glimpse of him preaching to everyone who came to his house, glad to be telling the good news about Jesus at the very heart of the great Roman Empire.

The Letter Writers

📖 360
Letters from Paul

PHILIPPIANS; TIMOTHY

Wherever Paul preached, those who heard and believed the good news came together to form a church in the city where they lived.

Paul chose leaders for these new churches and taught the Christians all he could, before he had to move on. After he left, he went on thinking about them and praying for them. Often he wrote letters to cheer them, to tell them when they were going wrong and to answer their questions.

When Paul was put in prison for preaching, he had time for letter-writing. A Christian friend would often write as Paul dictated.

One day, Epaphroditus arrived to visit Paul in prison, bringing a gift of money from the church at Philippi, where Lydia and the Roman prison officer belonged.

Paul was delighted to see him and later wrote a letter for him to take back.

'Thank you so much for your generous gift,' he wrote. 'It's not just the money, but the fact that you thought and cared about me that warms my heart—and brings joy to God, too.'

But Epaphroditus had brought bad news as well. Two women in the church had quarrelled and refused to be friends again.

'Please put things right,' Paul pleaded. 'Remember how Jesus, although he is God, was willing to be humble and kind and forgiving. You must copy him.'

A few of Paul's letters were sent to individual Christians. Timothy was a young helper who sometimes stayed to look after a new church for Paul. Paul wrote to advise him about how to lead a church.

Paul loved Timothy dearly and told him about his own feelings as he faced death for Jesus' sake. He looked back on his Christian life as if it had been a race.

'I have nearly finished the course,' he told Timothy. 'Now I am looking forward to the prize that will be presented to me—and to everyone who truly loves our Lord Jesus.

'Please try to come and see me soon—before winter, if possible. And please would you bring me my warm cloak? I left it at Troas. Could you bring my books, too? All the Christians here send love to you all.'

361
The Runaway Slave

PHILEMON

Onesimus was a runaway slave. He knew that if he was caught, he could be branded with a red-hot iron, or sent to work in chains. But he was far from his owner's home by now.

Then he met Paul, and through his preaching he became a Christian. He discovered that Jesus loved him, even though he was a slave, and that Jesus had died to set him free from all the wrongs he had done.

Paul was in prison and Onesimus stayed to look after him. But he knew that now he was a Christian he ought to return to his master.

Then they discovered that, by a wonderful chance, Paul knew his owner. He was Philemon, a Christian living in Colossae. The church there met in his house.

So Paul gave Onesimus a letter to take back with him.

'Dear Philemon,' Paul wrote. 'Warm greetings to you and your wife and the whole church in your home. I feel full of thankfulness to God, whenever I think of you. I hear so much about your kindness and love to others. It really cheers me up.

'Now I'm writing to you from prison to ask you to do me a special kindness. I'm sending you back someone you never expected to see again—your slave, Onesimus. You probably think of him as utterly useless—but he's a changed man! He's going to be as useful to you as he has been to me.

'You see, through me, Onesimus has become a Christian. That means that now he is your brother, as well as your slave. So I want you to welcome him as one of God's family. I only wish that I could keep him here with

me—he's been a great comfort and help. But that's for you to decide.

'Meanwhile, please give him a warm welcome—the kind of welcome you'd give to me! If he stole any money from you, please charge it to me. Here's a promise in my own handwriting—*I, Paul, will pay you back.*

'All the Christians here join in sending love to you all. And please get the spare bedroom ready for me. I hope that God will soon answer your prayers and that I shall be out of prison and on my way to you before long!'

362
Letter to Jewish Christians
HEBREWS

Many leading Jews refused to listen to the good news about Jesus. They would not believe that he was their Messiah. But some Pharisees, like Paul, did believe and so did some of the priests in Jerusalem.

These strict Jews often found it hard to give up their old rules. Some even ordered Gentile Christians to keep Jewish customs, too. Paul would not stand for that. It is faith alone that saves the person who puts his trust in Jesus.

There were other Jewish Christians who hankered after their old ways, when the Christian life grew hard. One letter in the New Testament was written especially for them.

The letter compares the old covenant that God made with the Jewish nation, with the new covenant made with all people, through Jesus. How much better the new is than the old! Moses was a wonderful leader, but Jesus is far more important. He is not just God's servant, but his Son!

For Jews, the gold covenant chest in God's temple was the sign of God's presence with them. But a thick curtain had blocked off the door into the holy place, where it stood. When Jesus died, that curtain was torn down. Through Jesus, the way to God had been thrown wide open.

In Old Testament days, the high priest went to God on behalf of the people and prayed for them and their needs. He offered animal sacrifices regularly, to try to make the people clean from the wrong things they had done.

But Jesus has become a far more wonderful high priest. He gave his own life, as the perfect sacrifice for all time. His death can make people completely clean in God's eyes. Jesus is not weak and full of failure, as the high priests used to be. Nor does he grow old and die. He is alive for ever, always ready to give help and strength to his people. And he knows what it is like to be human, so he is gentle and sympathetic.

The letter lists many of the heroes and heroines of the Old Testament. They all put their trust in God, however black things seemed. Many looked forward to the good things God had in store—which Christians now enjoy!

'They want to see you put your faith in God and persevere,' the letter-writer explains, 'however hard it may be. Just keep your eyes on Jesus! He has covered the course first and he will help you to finish it, too. So don't give up!'

Letter from James

JAMES

James grew up with Jesus in the family at Nazareth. He did not believe that Jesus was God's Son until he saw him alive after his resurrection. Then he was converted and later became leader of the church at Jerusalem.

James wrote his letter to Christians scattered everywhere. Like Jesus himself, James often used pictures to help his readers understand.

'Don't just listen to God's word without obeying it,' he warned. 'If you do that, you are like someone who looks in the mirror and then goes off and forgets to do something about his untidy hair, or dirty face. Always act on what God says.'

James stood up for poor people, who were often treated badly by their rich masters. He hated snobs.

'Suppose two visitors arrive at your church service one day. One is wearing expensive clothes and a gold ring but the other is in worn-out, old things. Don't say politely to the rich one, "Please come up to the front and sit here in this special seat," then turn to the poor one and say, "You can sit on the floor, there at my feet!" If you behave like that you are saying that rich people matter more than poor ones. God doesn't think like that. In fact God has a special place for the poor in his kingdom.'

James had a lot to say about speech. 'The tongue may be small but it is very powerful. The bit in a horse's mouth is tiny but the rider can use it to make the horse go where he wants. The sailor uses a little rudder to steer a huge ship. The tongue is small but it can make big boasts! Think—one tiny spark can set off a raging forest fire.

In the same way, one spiteful or gossiping word can spread to a big blaze of anger and cause all kinds of trouble. So be careful what you say!

'Be practical! It's no good telling a cold and hungry person, "Keep warm and eat well!" unless you give him clothes to wear and food to eat. Show that your faith in God is real by putting it into action and living to please him.

'Don't forget—whatever your circumstances—pray! Pray if you are in trouble, praise God if you are happy, pray if you are ill. God hears and answers prayer!'

Letters from Peter

1 PETER

Peter was a fisherman, not a scholar like Paul, but he wrote letters to the Christians living in many different Roman provinces. At the time, Peter was probably in Rome, where the emperor, Nero, was beginning to ill-treat Christians. Peter knew that the persecution would soon spread to Christians throughout the empire, so he wrote to prepare them for what was coming.

'Don't be surprised when you go through a fire of trial and suffering,' he told them. 'Jesus suffered, too. He never did a wrong deed, or told a lie, yet they put him to death.

'I watched him stand in front of the Jewish Council and the Roman governor. When they insulted him, he did not answer back. when they accused him of things he had not done, he did not threaten them. He could have called on armies of angels to fight for him but he quietly let them do what they wanted to him. He gave his life to take away our sins. He wants us to face up to suffering, too. We must follow his example.

'If any of you slaves have bad-tempered masters, don't scowl, or swear at them. Treat them with respect, whether they deserve it or not. You wives, whose husbands have not become Christians, don't try to win them over by wearing expensive clothes, or having fancy hair-styles. Just be loving and quiet and helpful to them. When they see the way you behave, they will want to be Christians too, because your character is beautiful.

'All of you in the church, love one another! Invite each other into your homes. If anyone is unkind to you, do them a kindness in return! Jesus will soon come back to earth. Be ready for him by living in a way that will please him. Your suffering won't go on for long!

'Give one another a big hug from all of us here! May you all know Christ's peace.'

New Heaven—New Earth

365
A Glimpse into Heaven
REVELATION

John, the much-loved disciple of Jesus, lived to a great age. Revelation, the last book of the Bible, records John's vision of the future. It is in picture language, a code that Jewish and Christian readers would understand. It was probably written at a time when the Roman emperor was persecuting the church.

Many Christians were asking: is God *really* in charge? Will Jesus come back?

John himself had been sent to a prison camp on the island of Patmos, when, one Sunday morning, Jesus appeared to him, shining with glory.

He gave John messages to the churches in seven different cities. Then John had a glimpse into heaven itself, where God, blazing with jewel-brightness, was sitting on a throne circled with rainbow light. In his hand he held the sealed scroll of the future.

Only one person among the multitudes in heaven was fit to undo the seal and set the events of the world in motion. That person was Jesus.

John gazed, expecting to see a strong, lion-like figure, but Jesus looked like a lamb ready for sacrifice. He is the Lamb of God, who died to take away the sin of the world.

When Jesus took the scroll, thousands upon thousands in heaven burst out singing, 'Worthy is the Lamb who was slain, to receive power and glory and blessing!'

As Jesus began to unroll the future, John knew for certain that God *is* in control. Satan, the old enemy of God,

has plunged the world into sin and suffering. But Jesus has won the victory against evil, by dying and rising to life for ever.

Then John saw the end of everything old and ugly and spoiled, and the beginning of a new world, fresh and lovely and good.

No one who might spoil that lovely world could be allowed in, but only those made clean by Jesus. Everyone who says 'No' to Jesus in his lifetime and refuses his forgiveness, will be sent far away from God.

'I saw a new heaven and a new earth,' John wrote. 'And I heard a loud voice saying, "Now God's home is with mankind. God himself will be with them. He will wipe away all tears. There will be no more death, no more grief or crying or pain. God's Holy City has no need of sun or moon, because the glory of God shines on it, and the Lamb is its light."'

How John longed for that day to come!

'I am coming very soon!' Jesus promised. And John gladly answered, 'Yes Lord Jesus—please come!'

All the people whose names appear in the 365 Bible stories are included, with the exception of Jesus.